SPY-TECH

SPY-TECH

GRAHAM YOST

Facts On File Publications
New York, New York • Oxford, England

SPY-TECH

Library of Congress Cataloging in Publication Data

Yost, Graham.
  Spy tech.

  1. Military intelligence—Equipment and supplies.
2. Espionage—Equipment and supplies.   I. Title.
UB250.Y67   1985   355.3′432′028   84-13769
ISBN 0-8160-1115-X

Printed in the United States of America
10 9 8 7 6 5 4 3 2 1

This book is dedicated to the people I saw my first James Bond movie with—my family, Elwy, Lila and Christopher Yost.

CONTENTS

ACKNOWLEDGMENTS

I would first like to express my gratitude to Mary Lee Grisanti for conceiving the idea for this book in the first place. I would further like to thank her for her agenting, editing and support throughout. I would also like to thank my editors at Facts On File: John Thornton, who acquired the book and got me started; and Jamie Warren who saw the project through the rest of the way. As well, I owe thanks to copy-editor John Berseth who asked the right questions and occasionally came up with better answers.

There were many without whose help researching and writing this book would have been impossible. I would like to thank Victor Marchetti for his insights into the operations of the intelligence community; Dino Brugioni for his invaluable help with understanding the sublime art of photo interpretation; Philip Klass for loaning me a copy of his excellent book on spy satellites; Raymond Lewis, a technical security consultant who explained many of the finer points of electronic surveillance; Mr. Peterson of Public Affairs at the CIA who put me in touch with Mr. Brugioni; Jack Pulwers at the Pentagon for DARPA documents; Dr. J.E. Thach at the Pentagon for pointing me in the right direction; Arnold Di Laura for his thoughts on how to tackle the subject; and Paul Dickson for his thoughts on how to tackle Washington.

I would like to extend my appreciation to the staffs at the New York Public Library, the Columbia University Butler and

Lehman Libraries, the Mid-Manhattan Library, the NASA Library at AIAA, and the Library of Congress.

For help in photo research I thank Frank Riddick, Tom Cross and Helen at the US Defense Audiovisual Agency; Phil Rosen at Law Enforcement Associates Inc.; Phil Wolvek at Privacy Protection Inc.; Alice Fribourg at CCS Communications Control; and Richard Heffernan at Information Security Associates.

Among friends and colleagues there were many who gave support and encouragement and who made helpful suggestions. In particular I would like to thank Marty Illingworth, Crystal Greene-Illingworth, Bill Alpert, Tom Barnard, Corinna Gardner-Barnard, Chris Newbound, Julie McGowan, Rob Howarth, Les Marton and Joel Sears, the famous underground poet.

Above all I must thank Doug and Elizabeth Kellner for allowing me entrance to their home and letting me use their computer to write this book. Their gracious hospitality knew no bounds, for even after I broke one of their disk drives, Doug arranged for me to use the computer at his office.

INTRODUCTION

In the 1960s a toy was introduced called "Secret Sam." It was just a plastic, spring-powered rifle that shot plastic bullets, but it had a few interesting features. It could be dissassembled, like an assassin's rifle, and stored in a small plastic briefcase that had an individually molded compartment for each part of the rifle. Better still, the firing section of the rifle, when set in the briefcase, was positioned with its muzzle up to an opening, and by pressing a button in the side of the briefcase, a child could fire the gun while it was concealed.

I was the proud owner of a Secret Sam, and for weeks (until it broke), clutching my briefcase, I would sneak up behind my unsuspecting parents or brother and plug them in the back with a plastic bullet.

My parents didn't think twice about buying such a toy then. No one ever imagined it would encourage a child to be an assassin, for to the public it was not the weapon of an assassin but of a spy, and in the 1960s, with the tensions of the Cold War and the success of James Bond books and films and "The Man From U.N.C.L.E.," "Mission: Impossible," and "Get Smart" television shows, the spy was the new heroic figure of adventure, replacing the cowboy and test pilot.

We loved the spy because, like heroes before and since, he was an individual who operated in situations fraught with danger and he fought alone against seemingly insurmountable odds, using only his wits and cleverness for survival. Some might also argue that we loved the spy because he was a war hero, albeit in a new kind of war, fighting for a noble cause—freedom. But if that's true, it's only part of the answer.

We didn't idolize James Bond in the same way we did a combat hero like Audie Murphy, for there was something else besides admiration for valor and courage in our love of the spy. There was, and still is, a fascination for the deviousness of spying. We may not be that interested in exactly how one soldier kills another on the battlefield, but when it comes to spy eliminating spy with a jab from a poison-tipped umbrella, we shake our heads and say "Wow!" We loved the spy because he did the shady, nasty things that intrigued us—burglary, surveillance, assassination—and he did them in tricky, ingenious ways. What made the spy so wonderful was that he did these things in the name of a cause that to many unambiguously justified such action. We could have our cake and eat it too. Of course, there were those who, cause or no cause, objected to the spy's methods, but even they had to admit one thing: The technology of espionage—spy satellites, bugs in martini olives, dart-gun pens, and all the rest—was amazing.

According to a perhaps apocryphal story, when a CIA representative goes before a congressional appropriations committee, he is sure to bring along the latest gadget that the CIA has come up with (camera in a watch, high-powered radio transmitter in a calculator, lapel pinhole camera, etc.). By passing the device around, the CIA man is not only showing the congressmen that taxpayers' money is being well spent, he is appealing to their natural boylike sense of wonder over such wizardry.

Of course the congressmen are not the only ones who are fascinated by spy technology—spies love it, too. In fact, they are probably the biggest fans of spy fiction. One of the reasons? The technology that their fictional counterparts use. Indeed, after watching episodes of the television show "Mission: Impossible" in the late 1960s and early '70s, CIA operatives started to ask their own Technical Services Division to come up with devices similar to the ones they had seen on the show. So, keep in mind while reading this book that some of the gadgets have sprung, not so much out of need as out of spies' own fantasies about what it is like to be a spy.

This book is concerned with the real and often complex

technology of espionage, from spy satellites to tiny "bugging" devices. It will show that while we have been repeatedly assured that the real world of espionage is actually quite mundane and that the equipment used is not at all like that handled by James Bond, in fact the technology used by real spies is as bizarre in its own way as the equipment used by the agents of fiction. Poison umbrellas may be used far less frequently than spy movies might have us believe, but there are other devices and gadgets in use that are many times more astounding.

The book is divided roughly in two parts. The first half, "Spying from Above," is concerned with the technology of spying that has global implications—the technology that costs billions of dollars to operate each year; the technology of spying on a national scale, involving airplanes and satellites. The second half, "The Secret Agent's Tools," deals with the less costly (but on occasion no less globally significant) equipment used by the individual spy.

"Spying from Above" chronicles the development of spy planes such as the U-2 and SR-71 and the origin of the spy-satellite programs (Discoverer and Samos in the United States, Cosmos in the Soviet Union). It covers the advances in technology over the years, culminating with a look at the spies in the sky today and some reasoned speculation as to what the future may hold. Included here is information not only on how this high technology works but also on how it is used, who uses it, for what purpose, and what the ramifications of its use are in the world today.

"The Secret Agent's Tools" examines the equipment used by the real-life James Bonds—cameras, bugs, wiretaps, cipher machines, lock-picking tools, weapons, explosives, and booby traps. We will see how these devices are used and, in some instances, even how they are made.

Although this book can be used as a reference work and flipped through for information on individual items of technology (if you wish to know how KH-11 spy satellites, secret inks, or silencers work, for example, you can look those subjects up in the index and find where in the book they are discussed), it can also be read, from beginning to end, as something of a tour through a world of startling technology; technology most of us will never in our lives come in contact with, but technology that nonetheless has had, and will continue to have, an impact upon our lives that is far greater than one would ever imagine.

PART I
SPYING FROM ABOVE

The spy is ever vigilant: day and night, every day of the year, the spy's eyes are open, watching. The spy is well traveled, in one day observing activities from the shipping out of Capetown to the rail traffic in Siberia; in just one two-week period the spy's prying eyes will have invaded every country on Earth. The spy is invisible and, thus far, invulnerable. This spy does not lurk around army bases or frequent the haunts of workers at an armaments factory—no, this spy keeps a safe distance, coming no closer to its target of interest than 100 miles. The spy is a machine, the CIA-built KH-11 reconnaissance satellite, operated by the top-secret National Reconnaissance Office of Air Force Intelligence.

The KH-11 is the world's finest spy satellite. Roughly the size of a boxcar (10 feet wide, 40-50 feet long, weighing in the neighborhood of 30,000 pounds), it contains three major remote-sensing systems that can, among other things, spot camouflage, see through clouds, and see in the dark. At its best in bright daylight, the KH-11 is able to discern objects on the ground the size of a bowling ball, perhaps even the size of an egg, from hundreds of miles out in space. The target of the satellite is, of course, neither a bowling ball nor an egg; rather, it floats silently over the Earth taking pictures of missile tests at the Tyuratam launching site in the

Soviet Union, troop deployments in Afghanistan, or the aftermath of the munitions explosion in Murmansk. The KH-11 is not alone in space. The Soviets and the Chinese each have their own spy satellites with their own respective targets (each other and the United States).

The KH-11 and its ancestors—Discoverer, Samos, and Big Bird—have played critical roles in world affairs, yet their existence has been officially revealed only recently. The first mention came in the 1972 SALT agreements between the United States and the Soviet Union, where there is notice of each country's right to use its own "national technical means" to verify the other side's compliance with the accords. On October 1, 1978, in a speech at the Kennedy Space Center at Cape Canaveral, Florida, President Jimmy Carter took this public disclosure a step further when he touted the astounding abilities of spy satellites to verify treaties as part of his last-ditch effort to gain ratification of the SALT II agreement. Still, the secrecy surrounding America's espionage in space has been breached very little, and the Department of Defense continues to decline comment when queried about its spies in orbit. Satellite surveillance is still one of the most sacred secrets in government.

While presidents from Kennedy to Reagan have routinely used photographs taken from spy planes such as the U-2 and the SR-71 to make a point (the arrival of missiles in Cuba, the building of an airstrip in Grenada, etc.), not one photograph taken from a spy satellite has ever been released. People who have seen one will only tell you so after a quick glance over their shoulder. Indeed, the very existence of the NRO (National Reconnaissance Office), established in 1960 to oversee spy satellite operation, was unknown even to many senators and congressmen until this decade. The relationship between the intelligence community in the United States and their satellites is like that between a magician and his tricks, involving stubborn refusal to divulge their secrets.

The necessity of such tight security is often debated. Some argue that it is just another example of the self-perpetuating "cult of intelligence"—a phrase coined by Victor Marchetti and John Marks in *The CIA and the Cult of Intelligence*—a cult that can only protect its position of power and influence by maintaining a wall of total secrecy around itself.

Others, however, say that such secrecy is necessary, for if information on the satellites leaks out and the Soviets discover the true capabilities and liabilities of U.S. satellites, they will find ways to thwart them. Senator Daniel Patrick Moynihan has said that Christopher Boyce and Andrew Daunton Lee's sale of intelligence satellite-related documents to the KGB in 1976 and 1977 was "as much as any one thing . . . responsible for the failure of the SALT [II] treaty. And if you think, as I do, that the breakdown of our arms negotiations with the Soviets is an ominous event, then nothing quite so awful has happened to our country as the escapade of these two young men."

While the question of secrecy surrounding satellite reconnaissance may be debated, the value of such intelligence gathering is rarely, if ever, questioned. The information that the satellites provide on missile testing, troop deployment, radar installations, crop yields, industrial activity (or lack thereof), and myriad other areas is of inestimable value. Since that time in human history when the first tribes were formed and the first wars waged, man has wanted to know what the enemy was up to. Today that knowledge is available, the result of the operation of dazzling machines, floating silently in space.

The first half of this book is about that technology. In order to understand the history of these spy machines and how they work, we must first put them in their context—the oft-mentioned "intelligence community."

The Intelligence Community

The Central Intelligence Agency is by far the most well known of the rather innocuously named intelligence community. Popularized and scandalized in fact and fiction, the CIA was born out of the remains of the OSS—the Office of Strategic Services—which was America's intelligence service during the Second World War. The CIA was originally designed to be the nation's intelligence clearinghouse, an agency that would gather, process, and analyze information from the government's operatives all around the world. This secret intelligence agency was established in the National Security Act of 1947. Two years later the CIA was institutionalized in the Central Intelligence Agency Act of 1949.

From the beginning there has been debate over what the CIA should and should not do. Should it just gather and analyze intelligence, or should it also engage in covert action and subversion? The early CIA was heavily staffed with OSS veterans, whose concept of an intelligence agency had been shaped by war, and for them covert and clandestine operations were all part of the intelligence game. Their influence can still be felt today. There was a provision in the 1947 act for the CIA'S performance of "such other functions and duties related to intelligence . . . as the National Security Council may from time to time direct." The ambiguity of "such other functions and duties" essentially opened the door for such CIA operations as the attempt to overthrow Sukarno in Indonesia in 1958; the coup in Guatemala in 1954; the invasion at the Bay of Pigs in 1961; the attempt to influence the Chilean elections in 1970; and their recent funding and training of the Contras in Nicaragua.

There are four directorates in the CIA: Intelligence; Science and Technology; Management and Services; Operations. The Directorate of Intelligence is the clearinghouse of intelligence that the entire CIA was once intended to be, gathering and analyzing intelligence according to the requests presented to it by other agencies and directorates. The National Photographic Interpretation Center (NPIC), which is responsible for analyzing photographs taken from spy planes and satellites, is an appendage of this directorate. The Directorate of Science and Technology was founded by DCI (Director of Central Intelligence) John McCone in the 1960s. It has two responsibilities: analyzing the level of sophistication of science and technology in other countries (especially in the areas of missile research and technical intelligence collection) and, most relevant here, continually upgrading U.S. technical intelligence-collection systems such as spy satellites and airplanes. The Directorate of Management and Services is responsible for personnel, training, finance, and security. The Directorate of Operations oversees clandestine operations—everything from planting rumors to planting bombs.

Above the directorates in the hierarchy is the Intelligence Resources Advisory Committee, which coordinates the various means of intelligence gathering according to the priorities assigned the information requests that come before it. (For example, a request for satellite pictures of the site of the munitions explosion in Murmansk would take priority over a request for an updating of information on the Soviet whaling fleet.) Also at this level in the CIA hierarchy are the national intelligence officers, who write the final National Intelligence Estimates—NIEs—which sum up a situation in the world (the successes or failures of the Contras in Nicaragua, the use of chemical weapons in the Iran-Iraq war, the state of tension in East Timor, etc.).

The NIEs go to the National Security Council and, in some cases, to the President, who often uses them as part of his foreign policy decision-making process.

The highest position in the CIA is director (DCI). As the word "central" implies, the CIA was at one time intended to coordinate all the activities of the entire intelligence community, and its director was to be the President's chief intelligence adviser. The DCI was also placed as head of the U.S. Intelligence Board, composed, for the most part, of the heads of the other intelligence organizations. The CIA is supposed to be "first among equals," and that is how it has been perceived by the public since the 1950s. This is a myth, however. The CIA is one member of a large community, but the other members keep themselves out of the public eye.

There are six large and four small agencies in the U.S. intelligence community. The four smallest—the State Department's Bureau of Intelligence and Research, the FBI's Internal Security Division, the Atomic Energy Commission's Division of Intelligence, and the Treasury Department's intelligence wing—have together something less than 2,000 employees and a budget of roughly $100 million, whereas the smallest of the six big agencies, the Defense Intelligence Agency, has roughly 5,000 employees and an annual budget of over $200 million.

The CIA's size has varied according to the level of support given the Agency by whatever administration is in power. Usually it has about 15,000 people working for it and a budget of over $1 billion per year. Certainly a sizable number of people and a large amount of money, yet both Army and Navy intelligence agencies are about the same size and the public almost never hears about them.

The two largest intelligence agencies maintain a low profile. The National Security Agency (NSA) was founded in 1952 by order of President Truman. For the next two decades its very existence was denied (to this day Truman's directive founding the agency remains secret), only coming to the surface in the 1970s. The NSA is responsible for monitoring communications around the world and for making and breaking codes. In 1978 it employed, either directly or indirectly, almost 70,000 people (50,000 alone at the NSA headquarters in Fort Meade, Maryland), and its 1985 budget was close to $2 billion. Air Force Intelligence contains the top-secret National Reconnaisance Office (NRO), which operates the nation's spy satellites. The NRO accounts for most of Air Force Intelligence's 50,000 employees and $3 billion annual budget.

In total, the U.S. intelligence community in the mid-1980s employs well over 150,000 people and spends approximately $10 billion each year. One comparison: In 1982 the State Department employed 24,000 and had a budget of $2 billion. A further comparison: The Soviet equivalent of the NSA (codemakers, codebreakers, and eavesdroppers) has something like 300,000 people working for it, and the KGB probably has even more. No budget figures are available.

Increasingly, the lifeblood of the intelligence community—information about what the enemy is up to—is being provided by technical means, especially spy satellites and spy planes. "Spying from Above" examines the history and development of spy planes and satellites, showing how they work and how they are used. We will see how the U-2 and the SR-71 spy planes fly; how the KH-11 can see in the dark; how the spy satellites of tomorrow will work. But we must begin at the beginning—over 200 years ago, when the first efforts to spy down from above began.

1 THE SPY PLANES
Early Reconnaissance

There are two types of intelligence gathering: tactical and strategic. The basic difference between the two is that tactical intelligence is primarily concerned with events on the battlefield or enemy activities directly preceding battle (where troops and weapons are, how they seem to be moving, etc.), whereas strategic intelligence deals with the long-term factors (crops, industrial output, weapons testing, etc.). Although the term "reconnaissance" can apply to both tactical and strategic intelligence gathering, it more aptly describes the tactical—winging out, taking a look at what the enemy is up to, then zipping back. When spying from above first began, it was used solely for tactical battlefield reconnaissance.

The precursor of the spy plane and the spy satellite was the hot air balloon, the 18th-century invention of the Montgolfier brothers of France. Although toyed with by Napoleon's army, aerial reconnaissance did not truly come into its own until the middle of the 19th century. One of the most strident advocates of the military uses of the balloon was Gaspard Felix Tourchon, also of France, who in 1858 was the first to take a photograph from a balloon. This was a monumental leap forward in the history of aerial spying. "The village belfry from which the officers of the General Staff can make

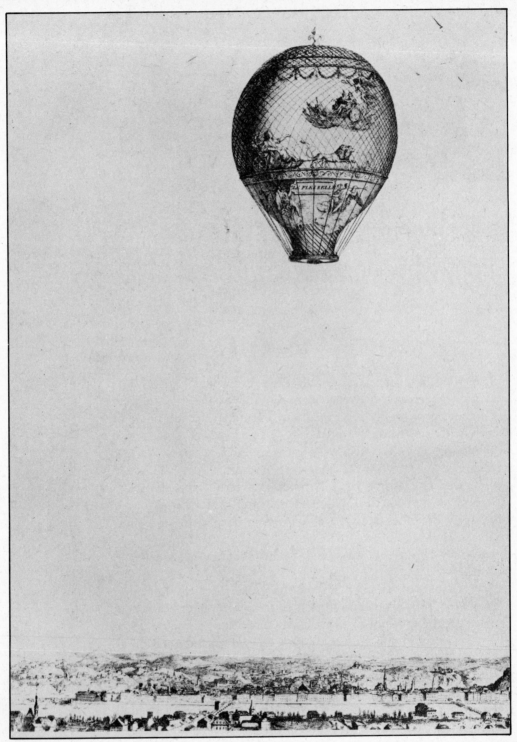

A hot-air balloon of the late 18th century.

observations is of great strategic value to the commanding general," wrote Tourchon. "I have such a belfry at any point, and thanks to my photographic apparatus I am in a position to send to the General Staff the most trustworthy intelligence every fifteen minutes in the form of a positive" (a claim equaled today by only the most advanced of the surveillance platforms).

The first full-fledged military exploitation of the balloon came during the American Civil War. The key figures—John C. Wise, John La Mountain, and Thaddeus S.C. Lowe—all served on the Union side. The first balloon of the war was a raw-silk creation that Wise built with his son. He designed it specifically for battlefield use, with metal plating across the bottom of the basket to ward off ground fire. Wise's balloon, like all others used in war at that time, was tethered: The balloon was allowed to rise, but was restrained from flying free by a rope connected to the ground. La Mountain, stirred by curiosity as to what was going on far behind enemy lines, took the bold step of cutting himself loose from the tether and floating free over enemy territory. His technique was to drift as far as he desired, then dump ballast and rise up into prevailing winds that, he hoped, would carry him back to safety. Although haphazard, his plan worked.

The greatest advances in military ballooning in the Civil War were made by Thaddeus S.C. Lowe, who gained the direct personal support of President Lincoln for his efforts. Lowe's innovations included a calcium light for night photography, a system of phosphorescent signal balloons, and a highly advanced photographic enlarger. Nevertheless, after the Civil War, the balloon was infrequently used for military reconnaissance—because of the unpredictability of winds, and because the balloons themselves were cumbersome and made excellent targets. Another reason for their obsolescence was that with the beginning of the 20th century came new technology and new methods for spying from the air that left balloons far behind.

In 1904 Alfred Maul, an engineer in Dresden, Germany, began to send cameras up in rockets, and by 1912 he had developed a reconnaissance system that could send a gyroscope-stabilized camera up to 2,000 feet, then return it gently to Earth with a parachute. Maul thought he had invented the ultimate means for aerial photography, but he was quickly overtaken by the infant airplane, which even by 1912 was capable of flying higher and undertaking more extensive reconnaissance missions than his rockets. Although Maul faded somewhat into obscurity, it is interesting to note how closely his work in photography combined with rocketry presaged the development of the surveillance satellite.

The very first military use of the airplane was for reconnaissance. Fighter planes only came into being in World War I, when the value of the aerial observation provided by reconnaissance planes grew so great that each side started to arm its reconnaissance pilots so that they could defend themselves and shoot down their opponents.

Aerial photographs were at first taken by a photographer—in the beginning, the pilot himself—who would lean out over the edge of the cockpit with a camera strapped to his chest and snap pictures of the scenes below. Later, cameras were mounted on brackets fixed to the side of the airplane, or over a hole cut in the airplane floor, using rubber cushions to absorb the vibration from the engine so that the pictures would not be blurred. Both vertical (straight-down) and oblique (off-to-the-sides) pictures were taken.

After the war, with the importance of aerial reconnaissance fully demonstrated, research and development continued. Prominent in this period was George W. Goddard. Since focal length (the distance from the lens to the point of focus inside the camera) determines how far and with what acuity a camera can see, Goddard developed huge, long-focal-length cameras that produced photographs with much higher ground resolution—the size of detail that can be picked up in the photograph. Other Goddard achievements included: a method for nighttime reconnaissance photography, in which the reconnaissance plane would tow a glider crammed with explosives and bright incendiaries that would be detonated to illuminate the ground below; the development of strip film that moves by the lens of the camera at the same speed as the ground moves by the plane below, so that the images are not blurred by the forward motion; and early infrared film.

There was another Goddard of this period whose work was key to the development of high-flying photography—Dr. Robert Goddard, the American rocketry pioneer, whose groundbreaking work with liquid-fueled rockets in the 1920s became part of the base for the U.S. space and missile programs of the 1940s and '50s. On July 17, 1929, Goddard sent up the first liquid-fueled rocket equipped with a camera. Thus, along with Maul, he should be considered one of the true pioneers of the spy satellite.

Developments in aerial photography in World War II and the Korean War centered on advances in the types of film used. Panchromatic film registers all light in the visible spectrum, and infrared film is designed to pick up light that is below red on the spectrum, light that is invisible to the unaided human eye. This period also saw increased use of the stereoscope. With a stereoscope, two pictures of the same feature—a town perhaps—are set down, slightly overlapping one another. By viewing the pictures through the stereoscope glasses, the brain can be tricked into thinking that each eye is seeing a slightly different angle of the feature, and so will suddenly see it in three dimensions. Thus, the details in the photograph—in this case, the buildings of a town—seem to pop off the photograph.

An intriguing, if slightly bizarre, technique for nighttime reconnaissance was discovered in Korea. A trained observer would spend five hours before the scheduled night flight in a darkened room, letting his eyes adjust to the low level of light. Then, shortly before takeoff, he would be blindfolded and escorted to the plane. Once in the air, he would lie down, remove the blindfold, and view the terrain below through a portal in the belly of the plane. With his dark-adjusted eyes he would be able to spot trains, truck convoys, and troop movements in the dead of night. With the invention of light-enhancement viewing technology, however, such time-consuming effort is no longer necessary.

The two big developments in aerial reconnaissance in World War II and the years following were not technological advancements but, rather, involved revolutionary rethinking of the purposes, targets, and abilities of reconnaissance. As mentioned earlier, in the beginning, spying from the air was used only for battlefield reconnaissance, or tactical intelligence. Early in World War II pilots were sent off on bombing runs using twenty-year-old maps, only to discover that a town didn't exist anymore or that a rail line had been moved. It became obvious that there was a need for intelligence that would be concerned with the whole of the enemy's activities and his long-term plans. This first big development—the birth of strategic reconnaissance—was followed by a second key development, the decision to keep on doing aerial reconnaissance after the war had ended.

With the memory of Pearl Harbor the U.S. government decided that a strategic reconnaissance effort was needed to hedge against the possibility of another surprise attack, which, with the introduction of atomic bombs into the world at Hiroshima in 1945, became an ever more frightening idea. Suddenly, aerial reconnaissance was thrust into a position of enormous responsibility—the watchdog against nuclear war—a long way from its status less than 100 years before, when it was little more than a curiosity performed by a handful of balloon enthusiasts.

The U-2

In the early 1950s the United States felt reasonably secure with its position in the world. While the Soviets had detonated their first atomic bomb in 1949 (earlier than expected, and, some felt, more the result of the Soviet's espionage than of their own technical expertise), by early 1954 they had tested only five such devices, while the United States had exploded 45. America had a strong superiority in bombers, too, both in number and range, and was

A Distant Early Warning station at Tatalina, Alaska.

building, with Canada, the DEW (Distant Early Warning) line of radar stations across the Arctic for further security. It was from such a position of confidence that on January 12, 1954, in a speech to the Council on Foreign Relations in New York City, Secretary of State John Foster Dulles revealed the Eisenhower administration's policy of massive retaliation. The United States said that it would use nuclear weapons to prevent conventional war, confident that the American armor of nuclear superiority would continue to be impenetrable for the foreseeable future. They were wrong. Within five months of Secretary Dulles's remarks the first chinks in the armor began to appear.

The first sign that the Soviets were not quite so far behind as everyone had thought was their detonation of a hydrogen bomb in 1953, less than a year after the United States had detonated its first. Then, in the 1954 May Day military parade in Moscow, startled foreign observers saw a new swept-wing, long-range bomber. The M-4, as it was designated in the United States, with its long range and its estimated speed of 600 m.p.h., effectively cut the advance warning of attack provided by the DEW line from four hours to two. Furthermore, the M-4 seemed closer to full-scale production than its American counterpart, the B-52. At that time there was only one B-52 off the production line. Analysts predicted that by 1955 the Soviets would have twice as many M-4s as the United States had B-52s. This was the so-called bomber gap, the first of several gaps to come.

The United States suddenly found itself in dire need of information on the true level of the Soviets' bomber strength and on the progress of their missile program. The U.S. intelligence community, however, found it very difficult to get reliable intelligence out of a closely regulated, totalitarian society like the Soviet Union, because the all-pervasiveness of its counterintelligence network made it next to impossible to penetrate with agents. While occasionally there were such windfalls as a defector or an agent-in-place (someone who defects but remains in the country, providing a continuing source of intelligence), they were few and far between. One of the solutions to this problem—though most dangerous, and most provocative, but also the most promising—was spying on Russia from the air.

The First Views of the Enemy

Some of the first attempts to spy on the USSR from overhead were reminiscent of John La Mountain's free-flying exploits in the Civil War. In the late 1940s and early '50s, almost with a sense of desperation, America turned to the crude methods of a century before. Huge, unmanned, camera-carrying balloons were launched into the sky with the hope that prevailing winds would carry them over the Soviet Union to the Sea of Japan, where they could be shot down by U.S. planes and recovered. But if the Americans could shoot one down, then so could the Soviets. And so they did, exploiting such instances for all the propaganda they were worth. This was not a long-lived program for the United States; not only were the balloons a propaganda risk, the intelligence they gathered was of marginal value, as there could be little or no control over where they would fly and what their cameras would photograph.

An RB-47 in flight.

154587 A.C

The prime source of U.S. high flying intelligence during this period was the RB-47, a medium range reconnaissance aircraft developed from the highly successful Boeing B-47 turbojet bomber. The RB-47 performed the dual tasks of gathering PHOTINT (PHOTographic INTelligence) and ELINT (ELectronic INTelligence). For PHOTINT there were seven precision cameras that continuously and automatically photographed the ground track; for ELINT, several crews on board the plane operated equipment that could intercept radio and radar signals. The problem with the RB-47 was that it was as big as a bomber and had a flight ceiling of 40,000 feet, making it an excellent target for antiaircraft missiles. An RB-47 was able to dart in and out of, say, Armenian airspace to trigger radio and radar alerts, but it had neither the speed, the altitude, nor the range to fly over more tantalizing targets, such as ICBM testing grounds that lay hidden far behind the borders of the Soviet Union.

What were the Soviets doing in there?

What President Eisenhower feared most was surprise attack. In 1954 he set up a Surprise Attack Panel, chaired by James Killian, president of M.I.T., to study the possibility of the Soviets mounting an attack without warning. The intelligence subcommittee of the panel was headed by two men: Dr. Edwin Land, inventor of the Polaroid Land Camera and head of the Polaroid Corporation, and Edward Purcell, professor at Harvard and winner of the Nobel Prize for physics in 1952. In the fall of 1954, after assessing what kind of intelligence would be necessary to eliminate the element of surprise, the subcommittee recommended that the United States begin reconnaissance overflights of the Soviet Union as soon as possible. One trouble: There was no airplane yet built that could fly such a mission.

A New Kind of Airplane Altogether

Across the country, in California, this problem had been very much on the mind of Lockheed Aircraft's preeminent aircraft designer, Clarence "Kelly" Johnson. During World War II, Johnson had designed and produced America's first jet fighter, the F-80, in 141 days. He was also responsible for the C-130 Hercules air transport (still a cargo workhorse for the Air Force) and the F-104 Starfighter. In 1954 he turned his thoughts to the problems of building an airplane that could fly at 70,000 feet for an extended duration.

Altitude was the central issue, for at 70,000 feet a jet engine produces only 6 percent of the thrust it has at sea level. This means that for the airplane to maintain speed, the engines have to work harder, therefore consuming more fuel. However, if the plane is to have a long range, then it must either carry extra fuel—which would weigh the plane down further, requiring that there be still more thrust to lift this added weight—or it must be incredibly fuel efficient. There are also problems of controlling an airplane at 70,000 feet, where the air is so much thinner, and the problems of fuel vaporizing at such an altitude because of the low atmospheric pressure, causing vapor locks, which can stop an engine.

Johnson's solution to these and other problems was to design what was essentially a completely new kind of aircraft, which would look and operate like some strange hybrid of a glider and a jet, with the lightness and lift of the former and with the speed (500 m.p.h. or more) of the latter. Full of enthusiasm, Johnson presented this revolutionary new design to the Air Force in 1954. To his chagrin, his design was turned down as too fantastic. Still confident in the integrity of his design, Johnson persisted.

In the fall of 1954, through Trevor Gardiner, a technical advisor to the Air Force's Research and Development division, Johnson managed to get his design before the secret Land-Purcell intelligence subcommittee of the Surprise Attack Panel. Impressed, Land and Purcell took Johnson's design proposal to CIA Director Allen Dulles, who was also won over. Suddenly, Johnson's plane was rapidly gathering support. Dulles's special assistant, Richard Bissell, a strong enthusiast for technical means of gathering intelligence as opposed to HUMINT (HUMan-gathered INTelligence), worked hard for Johnson's proposed plane, and it is he who is credited with finally swaying Secretary of the Air Force Harold Talbott in its favor.

Finally, there was only one more vote of support needed—the President's—and on the day before Thanksgiving in 1954, Land, Purcell, and Dulles went before Eisenhower with a proposal to build an airplane that would allow the United States to spy on the Soviet Union from the air with impunity.

Eisenhower had learned the value of aerial photo reconnaissance when planning operations during World War II. Like Bissell, he distrusted HUMINT and was excited at the prospect of reliable technical intelligence. He gave his approval for the plane on the spot, and Dulles immediately summoned Bissell to the White House for a briefing. As Bissell later noted, it was all well and good that they decided to build the plane, but no one had any idea how much it would cost, where the money was going to come from, where it was to be built and tested, or who would fly it. Answering those questions became Bissell's job.

Later that afternoon Bissell went to the Pentagon, where he informed Trevor Gardiner of the go-ahead. Gardiner in turn telephoned Kelly Johnson in California with the news. Within days Johnson had assembled a crew of 23 engineers and moved them into an empty Lockheed hangar in Burbank to start work on the plane. The project was given the name Aquatone and the plane itself was simply the Utility-2, or U-2. The engineers affectionately called the plane "The Angel," and in a joking reference to the absolute secrecy they worked under, they called the hangar where they toiled "Skunk Works," after the clandestine distillery in the cartoon strip Li'l Abner. (The name stuck, and now, thirty years later and no longer top secret, Lockheed proudly uses Skunk Works in its promotional material.)

If the United States was to spy on the Soviet Union from the sky, then there was more to do than just build an airplane that could fly the mission. In addition, whole new camera and film systems had to be developed. Ray Cline, one-time deputy director of the CIA, once called Richard Bissell, who oversaw the entire U-2 project (building the plane, making the cameras, finding the pilots, etc.), "one of the authentic heroes of the intelligence profession." Cline used similar words to describe Arthur C. Lundahl, the champion of photo interpretation.

One Picture Is Worth 1,000 Spies

Art Lundahl is sometimes credited with having prompted the whole idea of spying on the Soviet Union from above in the first place. During his appearance before the Land-Purcell intelligence subcommittee, long before they had heard of Johnson's plane, he greatly impressed them with the possibilities of aerial photographic reconnaissance and photo interpretation.

Lundahl had been a photo interpreter in World War II, stayed in that field and became a master of both photo interpretation and photogrammetry, which is the science of measuring the dimensions of objects on photographs. He was teaching these subjects at the

University of Chicago in 1953 when the CIA approached him to work for them. Eager to put his knowledge into practice, he left his teaching post and set up a small photo-interpretation unit for the CIA in Washington, D.C. Another reason for his taking the job was that he wanted to see photo interpretation get the attention it deserved in the intelligence community.

"I called Art the super salesman of photo interpretation," Ray Cline once said. That he was. Lundahl was well known for often quoting the Chinese proverb that a picture is worth 10,000 words—or, as he added, 1,000 spies. To advance his profession, Lundahl worked closely with those in the United States who were developing new cameras, lenses, and film, and he brought their talents to bear on the problems of high-altitude photography. These associations were important when it came time to work on the U-2 project.

Conveniently, Dr. Land of Polaroid was already on hand to aid in the development of the camera. It was made by Hycon Corporation of California. The big "B-camera," as it was known, weighed 450 pounds and was built specifically to fit in the fuselage of the U-2. It used new Mylar-based strip film, which had the thickness of Saran Wrap, thus, many more thousands of feet of film could be carried on a mission.

Perhaps the most revolutionary aspect of the camera was its lens, designed by Dr. James Baker, a Harvard astronomer. A key measurement of a lens is its resolving power—the number of white lines against a black background that it can distinguish per millimeter (a normal human eye can discern roughly ten lines per millimeter). The best World War II lenses had a resolving power of 12 to 15 lines per millimeter, but Baker developed a lens capable of resolving 50 to 60 lines per millimeter. The film used had a resolving power of approximately 100 lines per millimeter. The combination of high-resolution lens and film meant that the B-camera could pick out a tennis ball from 8 miles in the air and, at the U-2's proposed operational height of 13 miles, something the size of a newspaper page.

From that height the U-2 could photograph a strip of land 750 miles wide (the width of Texas) for general reconnaissance, or a strip 150 miles wide when higher resolution was required. Because of the thin Mylar film, over 12,000 feet could be shot on each trip—the entire United States could be photographed in 12 flights.

In December 1954 Art Lundahl was given the responsibility of handling and interpreting the enormous amount of film that the U-

2 would bring in. He set up shop above an auto repair garage in a rundown section of Southwest Washington.

While Lundahl and his men were ready to go before the plane was, "The Angel" was not long in coming. Living up to his reputation as a man who could do a job quickly and well, Johnson had a U-2 ready for testing in August 1955, only eight months after he had been given the go-ahead.

The Airplane

To those who first saw it, it was certainly a strange-looking machine. With an 80-foot wingspan it must have seemed to be all wing, and it must have seemed fragile, delicate, and with only one engine, set in the tail, not very safe or durable. There was even a rumor circulating that each plane could only be used once. But its appearance belied its abilities.

A modern version of the U-2 on the runway. Note the "pogos" under the wings.

The curious jet/glider cross-breed looked like no other plane that anyone had ever seen before, precisely because it was designed to do things that no other plane had ever done before. Johnson's primary concern had been weight, especially on the wings, and with the new lightweight alloys that were being developed, he was able to construct wings that had a loading of only three pounds per square foot—one third that of regular wings. For weight considerations, everything that wasn't absolutely necessary was omitted. In the early models there was no ejection seat, so that if a plane were about to crash, the pilot would have to bail out as if he were in a World-War-I biplane. Also to save on weight, there was no hydraulic system for the cockpit canopy, so it had to be lifted by hand; the tail section was held on by only three bolts. These planes were so light and so easy to take apart that they could be disassembled, put in the back of a truck, and driven to wherever they were needed.

The cockpit was designed like most Air Force fighter planes, with throttle, flap, and speed brake on the left, radio and navigation on the right. Because of the position of the cockpit, it was impossible for the pilot to see the ground he was flying over, so there was a floor mounted periscope to use for navigation, drift computation, and defensive surveillance. All the controls were nonhydraulic-pulley- and cable-operated, even the crucial gust control system that automatically adjusted flaps and ailerons to deflect wind and keep the light craft stable.

After its wingspan, the most startling feature of the U-2 was its landing gear. Also designed with weight in mind, the landing gear was like a bicycle—the wheels were arrayed single file under the fuselage, not parallel to one another as in most other planes. When the plane was standing still on the tarmac, it had no lateral stability whatsoever and would lean over on one wing unless both wings were propped up with "pogos"—basically, sticks with wheels on the end. Takeoff and landing were especially difficult with such gear.

On takeoff the pogos would keep the plane from tipping either way as it rolled down the runway. Two ground crewmen, one for each wing, would sit at the tips of the wings during takeoff. When the plane developed some speed and stabilizing lift, the crewmen would pull pins releasing the pogos, then jump off before the plane lifted off the runway. When the plane landed and slowed down, it would be sure to tip over onto one of the wings, so each had skids at the tips for protection.

This, then, was the airplane that Johnson had ready by August 1955. All they needed was someone to fly it.

The Pilots

Watertown Strip is in a desolate section of southern Nevada, a region of flat, dry, uninhabited land that stretches on for mile after mile. It is the perfect place to test a plane that no one is supposed to know about. According to Francis Gary Powers, who was among the first group of eight pilots to arrive at the Ranch, as the Watertown Strip became known, "It was a 'you can't get there from here' kind of place."

Powers and all the other pilots were officially civilians employed by the Lockheed Aircraft Corporation. So strict were Bissell and the others about this that the pilots who came from the military had to resign their commissions for the duration of the program. Eisenhower had insisted on civilian status, as he felt that the U-2 project should be an intelligence-gathering rather than a military mission (much to the chagrin of General Curtis Le May of the Strategic Air Command, who lobbied hard for control of the U-2 as part of the other reconnaissance squadrons operated by SAC). The pilots had been recruited by the CIA based on their excellent flying records, their endurance, their high sense of patriotism and devotion to country, and their top level security clearance. Patriotism certainly played a role in the pilots' accepting the CIA's offer, but so did the high $30,000 a year salary, about what a senior airline official made and about $100,000 in today's dollars.

Standing in the glaring Nevada sun, staring at a strange plane that looked as if it would just as easily break up as fly, the first group of pilots was faced with the problem that every plane of totally new design presents: No one really knew how to fly it. As the first eight pilots to sit in the U-2's cockpit, Powers and the others did not learn how to fly the U-2 as much as discover how to fly it.

Flying the U-2

The process of flying a U-2 began several hours before the pilot got into the cockpit. Because of the up to 12 hour duration of the flight, and because there were no toilet facilities on board, the pilot was given a high-protein, low-residue meal of steak and eggs. Because of the high altitude at which they would be flying, the pilots would have to wear full pressure suits and would have to breath pure oxygen at all times. Breathing oxygen is not as easy as it sounds. Normal breathing requires a small effort for inhalation—the expansion of the chest wall muscles and the movement of the diaphragm to draw the air in—and none for exhalation —we just let our muscles relax, and the air is pushed out. When breathing under pressure with an oxygen mask, however, the process is reversed. Jetting out of the tank, the oxygen forces its way into the lungs. Thus, no effort is required for inhalation, but exhalation requires the active contraction of the chest wall muscles to expel the oxygen. This is not an easy trick to master, especially when one also has to be concerned with flying an airplane. In the beginning of the U-2 program half of the trainees washed out because they couldn't master breathing oxygen under pressure. To accustom himself both to the oxygen and the reversed breathing process, the U-2 pilot would spend an hour or two breathing with the mask before flying. This would also serve to flush out all the nitrogen from the bloodstream, so that the pilot would not suffer from the bends during his rapid ascent.

The pressure suits, which took thirty minutes to get into, were not pleasant to wear. The helmet was tightly sealed with a cork-neck ring that would cause such chafing, just from the pilots turning their heads to look around the cockpit, that their necks would bleed. The pilots had other discomforts too—chief among them, dehydration. The planes had to have every bit of moisture removed from them so that they would not freeze up at high altitudes. With no moisture in the aircraft, and sealed up in their bone-dry pressure suits with nothing to drink, the word "dry" took on new meaning. Powers wrote in *Operation Overflight* that at the end of some long flights he would be thirstier than he had ever thought humanly possible. (The pilots who fly today's version of the U-2, the TR-1, are provided with squeeze bottles of fruit juice.)

Because of the enervating effect of breathing oxygen, pilots were kept as immobile and relaxed as possible until they were actually ready to take off. As a pilot sat in the cockpit, waiting for all systems to check out, he began to bake in the heat that built up in his flight suit. Relief would not come until he flew up to higher, cooler altitudes. Once everything was ready, the pilot taxied the airplane out onto the runway and began his roll, a crewman on each wing tip. When speed had been reached, the crewmen pulled the pogo pins and jumped clear. As the engine developed full thrust, the U-2 took off with a sudden acceleration that has been likened to a catapult launch off an aircraft carrier.

There were many dangers. One fatal accident occurred early in the U-2 program when a pogo failed to disengage. The pilot circled back over the airfield, waggling his wings to shake the pogo loose, and in the process lost control of the plane and crashed.

Once in the air, the first U-2 pilots had some interesting things to discover about the plane. For one thing, the long, slender wings flapped noticeably, which was understandably disconcerting. The plane was also prone to flameouts, which would stop the engine, so

A modern U-2 in flight

that the pilot had to glide down to a lower altitude to restart. But this points up one of the great advantages of the U-2—its ability to glide. Unlike most other planes of that era, it did not plummet like a stone the moment it lost thrust. Indeed, on U-2 spying missions the engine was not used all the time so as to conserve on fuel.

The aircraft was flown on autopilot most of the time, but on manual control it was found to be remarkably maneuverable. Turns were generally made slowly to keep the craft—and the cameras—stable, but they could be made quite sharply if the need arose.

The pilot had two pressing concerns—stability and velocity. The fuel tanks were in the wings, so the pilot always had to be aware of the fuel level in each tank in order to maintain stability. As for velocity, at the altitudes the U-2s flew there was a very narrow range between stall (a sudden loss of lift because of a drop in speed) and buffet (the loss of control as the plane goes too fast and no longer reacts aerodynamically with the air but merely buffets against it), occasionally as little as a few knots. On some turns, in fact, the outer wing, as it would be moving slightly faster than the inner wing, would go into buffet, while the inner wing, moving slower, would start to stall.

After discovering how to take off and fly the U-2, the pilots had the interesting prospect of landing it. The first problem was just getting it down onto the runway. With its 80-foot wingspan, the U-2 created so much ground effect—a buildup of air pressure between the wing and the ground, creating extra lift—between itself and the runway as it came in to land that it would not touch down. Therefore, when they were about a foot off the tarmac, the pilots would have to stall the engine intentionally so that the plane would drop the last 12 inches. While doing this they also had to be sure to keep the wings as steady and as level as possible because they were landing on only two wheels. The pilots used to wager with one another to see who, on landing, could keep the plane so steady that the crewmen could slip the pogos in place under the wings before the plane tipped over onto one of its wings.

Even with the flapping wings, the flameouts, the narrow stall-buffet range, and the difficult landings, Gary Powers said that he loved flying the U-2, and many of the other pilots agreed. But, as Powers wryly noted in *Operation Overflight,* "There was only one thing wrong with flying higher than any other man had ever flown—you couldn't brag about it."

The Skies Open

At the Geneva Summit Conference in July 1955, a few weeks before the testing of the U-2 was to begin, President Eisenhower made his "Open Skies" proposal for the prevention of nuclear war. He suggested that the United States and the Soviet Union exchange blueprints of their military facilities and allow one another to inspect the armaments of the other from the air. Some felt Open Skies was a remarkable step toward peace, while others suspected it was just an American ploy to get better targeting information. Khrushchev dismissed Open Skies out of hand, calling it "nothing more than a bald espionage plot." Whatever Eisenhower's motives for suggesting Open Skies really were, within a year the United States was able to embark on aerial inspections of the USSR unilaterally and with impunity.

Satisfied with the tests of the U-2, in August 1955 Richard Bissell ordered another 22 of the planes, each one essentially handmade and costing roughly $350,000 at the time. As the program expanded, there were increased public sightings of the plane, so a cover had to be devised. According to a 1956 press release from the National Advisory Committee for Aeronautics, NACA had contracted with Lockheed to build the plane for "upper atmosphere research."

Of course, the U-2 was designed to research the Soviet Union, not the upper atmosphere. In 1956 eight pilots, including Powers, were sent to Incirlik Air Force Base, just outside of Adana, Turkey. Incirlik was primarily used as a refueling stop for other military planes, so the busy activity of the base provided good cover for the U-

2 operations. So secretive was the U-2 project, in fact, that even people at Incirlik did not know what was going on. Powers and the other pilots constituted the 10-10 Detachment, commanded by Colonel Stanley Beerli. There were other U-2 detachments in Japan and West Germany.

The first spy flights just skirted the Soviet borders, allowing the cameras to photograph border installations and the "black boxes" aboard the plane to intercept radio and radar signals. On a few flights the pilots observed Soviet rocket tests, several of which, to their relief, were as spectacular failures as early American tests. However, these border skirting missions could have been done by almost any plane. The U-2 had been designed for something quite special.

In early June 1956 Allen Dulles and Bissell went to Eisenhower with the news that they were ready to exploit the U-2's abilities fully—to begin overflights of the Soviet Union. Eisenhower sent word of his answer the next day: They had an initial ten-day period to spy on Russia.

For the first four days of the period much of the Soviet Union was under cloud cover. On the fifth day, July 4, 1956, the skies cleared, and the U-2 took off on its first overflight of the Soviet Union. That day Dulles checked with Bissell to see if the U-2 had indeed gotten off the ground. "Yes," replied Bissell, "it's in the air now." When told that its flight plan took it over Moscow and Leningrad, Dulles gasped. "My God. Do you think that's wise, for the first time?" Bissell replied that it would be easier that first time than at any other time.

Unfortunately for the United States, the first real intelligence cache of that first flight was the discovery that Soviet radar technology was much more advanced than had been anticipated. It had been thought that the Soviets would be unable even to pick up the U-2's presence. Such was not the case. They had tracked it and they were furious, although they made no public statement, possibly fearing embarrassment when it was revealed that they could do nothing to stop the plane. However, in response to the fury that came through Soviet diplomatic channels, Eisenhower suspended U-2 flights for a month, from then on approving them one at a time.

The Overflights

The overflights began as looping patterns—the planes flew off over the Soviet Union and then circled back. Eventually the U-2s just made straight shots right across the country—say, from Pakistan to Norway—so that as much new territory as possible would be covered with each flight. These flights, even for seasoned reconnaissance pilots, were different from any they had ever flown before. Said one early pilot, "This wasn't like some reconnaissance missions that were flown in World War II or Korea where the pilot decided that it was too dangerous to try and take pictures over the assigned target so he made the excuse the weather was too bad and returned home. Once you got started over the Soviet Union in a U-2 you had no place to go but your destination."

These flights were not expected to be dangerous. The U-2 was designed to fly at 70,000 feet because of estimates that Soviet surface-to-air missiles (SAMs) could not reach higher than 60,000 feet. Originally, it was thought that the U-2 would have an operational life of only two years, until the Soviets developed a method for bringing it down. As it happened, the U-2 was able to fly over the Soviet Union for four years, much longer than had been initially anticipated and, as it turned out, perhaps a little longer than was safe.

Although rarely discussed, the prospect of a U-2 being shot down had been prepared for. Every ejection seat pack (finally added to later models when it was decided that, for the pilots' safety, the extra few pounds were permissible) contained a collapsible life raft, clothing, food, water, compass, flares, matches, chemicals for starting a fire with damp wood, and a first aid kit with morphine, bandages, dressings, and water-purification tablets. The survival kit also included a large silk American flag poster bearing the message, in 14 languages: "I am an American and do not speak your language. I need food, shelter, assistance. I will not harm you. I bear no malice toward your people. If you will help me you will be rewarded." For the reward the pilot was provided with 7,500 rubles, 24 gold Napoleon francs, and a small selection of wristwatches and rings, all worth something over $1,000. The seat pack also contained a knife and a .22 caliber pistol fitted with a silencer.

In *Operation Overflight,* Powers wrote that one of the frustrating aspects of the U-2 program was that the pilots were never given a clear indication of what they should do or say if indeed they were shot down. After the Korean War—a war in which not one American POW made a successful escape and in which a few American POWs were accused of collaborating with the enemy—there had been much debate as to how a POW should conduct himself. The Army drew a hard line—just name, rank, and serial number—but the Air Force was much more lenient—do whatever you have to do in order to stay alive. For the U-2 pilots the signals were mixed. Some pilots thought they might be expected to kill themselves, while one CIA official did say that if caught they might as well tell everything they knew, for if the Soviets had shot them down, they probably knew all they wanted to know anyway.

The pilots weren't really privy to that much anyhow. The day before his flight a pilot would be shown a color-coded map. A blue line indicated the general route, and red dots denoted the primary targets, beside each of which was listed the spy equipment to be activated at specified times. Brown lines indicated routes to alternate American bases if the pilot had to break off his course for some reason. The pilots were never informed of the exact purpose of their missions, and they were rarely shown any of the film they had taken. They could only guess at the importance of each mission. They knew, for example, that if the photo interpreters flew in to examine the film rather than wait for it to be sent to Washington, then it was obviously very important.

Two pieces of equipment that went along with every overflight mission were central to the issue of a plane's being shot down. The first was a 2 1/2-pound explosive unit that was set in the plane near the reconnaissance equipment in the fuselage. A pilot about to crash was supposed to activate the destruct unit, which was on a 70-second delay, then eject clear of the aircraft. The unit only carried enough explosive to destroy the cameras and other spy paraphernalia, not the entire plane.

The other piece of related equipment was a silver dollar good luck charm, within which was concealed an inch-long pin coated with curare, a poison that kills by relaxing all muscles—even heart and lung muscles. With the tales of the torture and brainwashing experienced by POWs in the Korean War, the curare-coated pin was provided not as a weapon but as a method for final escape. But this was an option, not an order. The pilots were never instructed that they had to kill themselves—indeed, before the curare pin was developed, the method provided for self-destruction was a cyanide capsule that they were given the option of carrying with them on the mission or not. (Powers never did, fearing the capsule might break.)

Both the destruct unit and the suicide pin were to figure prominently in the last U-2 flight over the Soviet Union.

The Last Overflight

Eisenhower maintained tight control over the U-2 flights. After a flight had been planned by a small group of Air Force and intelligence personnel, Bissell would take a map of the flight route to Eisenhower for approval. Occasionally, Eisenhower himself would be the one to instigate a flight, as during the Suez crisis in 1956 when he ordered a flight over the Middle East.

Toward 1960 the number and frequency of the flights began to taper off. This was in part because of the backlogs in photo interpretation that had built up because of the enormous amount of film that each flight brought back. Eisenhower thought it best to clear up the backlogs before proceeding with further flights and unnecessarily incurring additional Soviet wrath. The other reason for the reduction in the number of flights was the fears over improvements in Soviet air defenses. By 1958 the flight planners were already routing the U-2s away from the sites of the new generation of Soviet surface-to-air missiles, the SA-2 Guidelines. According to CIA estimates, these new SAMs could reach 60,000 feet. With the U-2 at 68,000 feet, a direct hit would be highly unlikely, but even the possibility of a near miss was disturbing. By the beginning of 1960, although the program had already gone far beyond its original life expectancy, there was a sense of urgency, a rush, to get in as many U-2 flights as possible before the Soviets would be fully able to knock one out of the sky.

In mid-April of 1960 Bissell went to Eisenhower with a request for another U-2 flight. Secretary of State Herter was present as Bissell showed Eisenhower a map of the route. Herter was worried about the flight. Considering the Paris Summit Conference scheduled for May, he felt it would not be a good time for a U-2 to be shot down. Eisenhower replied that no time would be a good time for a U-2 to be shot down and approved the flight. Bissell was given a two-week period during which to conduct the flight, but every day for those two weeks the USSR was covered with clouds. He received a one-week extension but was told on no account to send up the U-2 after May 2, as it would then be too close to the Paris Summit.

The pilot chosen for the flight was Francis Gary Powers. He had flown to Peshawar, Pakistan, in advance for the flight, which was scheduled to take him from Peshawar, right across 3,800 miles of the Soviet Union, to Bodo in northern Norway. Like Bissell, halfway around the world in Washington, Powers waited for the weather to clear. It finally did, just within the deadline. The flight was set for the morning of May 1—May Day, one of the biggest holidays in the Soviet year.

At 5:20 A.M., May 1, Powers climbed into the cockpit of a U-2 on the runway at Peshawar. It was his 28th mission. He was used to the rigors of breathing oxygen and to the irritation of wearing a pressure suit, but there was an added discomfort that day, as the takeoff was delayed. He baked in his suit for an extra 20 minutes, and by the time he took flight, he was soaked in sweat. He took off at 6:20 and only began to feel comfortable when he rose into the higher, cooler altitudes. Early in the flight he found that the autopilot was not functioning properly. This meant that he would have to fly most of the way manually—no great chore, but it did mean that he would be somewhat busier than usual.

About an hour after take-off, Powers crossed the Soviet border, alerting border radar posts, which in turn notified antiaircraft units along the U-2's projected route that a dark-blue plane had violated Soviet airspace. One of those notified was Major M. Voronov, commander of an anti-aircraft unit outside of Sverdlovsk. He put his gunners and SAM crews on alert.

Nearing Sverdlovsk, Powers was pleased. He was close to the halfway point, and so far his flight had been uneventful. In the middle of a 90-degree turn 30 miles from Sverdlovsk, Powers spotted an airfield that wasn't on his maps. Although the pilot's main duty was to turn the reconnaissance equipment on and off, he was also required to keep an eye out for anything that seemed interesting. Powers recorded the position of the airfield, made sure that all cameras and other spy equipment were operating as required, then checked his flight instrumentation dials.

Suddenly, without warning, the plane was hit. "I can remember feeling, hearing and just sensing an explosion. I immediately looked up from the instrument panel and everywhere I looked it was orange. I said, 'My God, I've had it now.'" The plane started to drop, nose up, very quickly. Powers had no reference—all he could see was spinning blue sky. He couldn't use his ejection seat because in the position he found himself after the explosion, firing the ejection seat would have cut his legs off. What could he do?

He realized that he would have to bail out manually. Time was of the essence—by that point he had already fallen 30,000 feet. He knew he had to arm the destruct unit, but he didn't know how long it would take to bail out and he didn't want to be in the plane when the charge went off. He decided to release the canopy, get set to jump free, and only then flip the ARM and DESTRUCT switches.

The moment he released the canopy, it whipped off out of sight. Powers still had not armed the destruct unit. He reached for his seatbelt release, and the moment he snapped it open, because of the way the plane was falling, he shot out of the cockpit. But he was not thrown free—his own oxygen hose restrained him, giving him one last chance to arm the destruct unit.

Powers was now sprawled over the nose of a U-2 falling out of the sky over the Soviet Union. Blinded by a faceplate that had frosted over the second he shot out of the plane, he tried to reach back to the destruct switches. They were just beyond his stretching fingers. Every second that passed brought him 300 feet closer to the ground. He then only had time to save himself.

He lunged against the oxygen hose again and again, until it finally snapped. He broke free and flew up and away from the plummeting airplane. Powers dropped several thousand feet before he remembered to pull his ripcord, but just as he reached for it, the automatic barometric control released the parachute itself. The canopy opened and billowed up above him in the air.

As he drifted down, he watched the U-2 crash some distance away. Then came his biggest decision. Powers took out the silver dollar with the curare coated needle inside. What was he supposed to do? He still harbored some faint hope that he was going to get out of it all somehow, so he threw the coin away.

Within moments of landing on Soviet soil, Powers was surrounded by a group of farmers who spoke a language he did not understand and who eyed him with a look of curious bemusement as they helped him gather in his parachute. Minutes later he was met by more official representatives—men who had been notified by Voronov's antiaircraft unit outside of Sverdlovsk that they had brought one of the prized planes down. Within hours Powers was in a cell in Lubyanka Prison.

The Soviets knew they had a powerful hand, and they played their cards judiciously. At first they did not announce to the world that the pilot had survived, just that a spy plane had been shot down over their soil. In response the United States, thinking Powers dead and the plane destroyed, denied that it was a spy plane, saying that it was a NACA atmospheric testing plane that had accidentally drifted over Soviet airspace and had been shot down without warning. It was then that Khrushchev played his trump: The pilot was alive. With Powers, the recovered plane wreckage, and the mangled but still identifiable espionage equipment, the Soviets had undeniable proof that the U-2 had been spying. Not only had they shot down a U-2, they had also caught the United States in a lie, a major victory in the international propaganda war between the two superpowers.

Tension was high at the Paris Summit. Many had expected that the conference would be canceled because of the U-2 incident, but the Soviets decided to use the Summit as a platform for further harangues against the United States. Khrushchev gave a long opening speech about the violation, ending with the exclamation, "I have been overflown!" French President Charles de Gaulle, host of the meeting, quietly remarked that he too had been overflown—by Soviet satellites. Khrushchev protested that they were innocent satellites. De Gaulle asked him then how they had gotten back pictures from the far side of the Moon. Khruschev replied begrudgingly, "In that satellite we had cameras."

"Ah," said de Gaulle, "in that one you had cameras! Pray, continue."

Such wit was short-lived. Soon after, Khrushchev and his entourage stormed out of the conference. In the aftermath Eisenhower promised that the United States would never again overfly the Soviet Union, and except for brief sorties over the border, that promise has remained unbroken.

In Washington there was little remorse over the U-2; rather, there was anger, and of the many people who were angry, many were angry at Powers. They wondered if he hadn't flown the plane too low; they were vexed that he hadn't set off the destruct unit; and some were even upset that he hadn't killed himself. Powers later maintained that he hadn't flown too low but that he'd been hit by a near miss, which was certainly within the capability of those SAMs. (Some believe that two SAMs were fired and that one took out a Soviet MIG trying to intercept Powers while the other exploded near enough the U-2 to cripple it.) In support of Powers, some have argued that the whole destruct unit was useless anyway, since it is nearly impossible to destroy a tightly wound roll of film, and the Soviets could find out all they needed to know from the film alone. Even though this means that Powers's suicide would have been futile, not everyone was soothed. Eisenhower's son John cried, "The CIA promised us that the Russians would never get a U-2 pilot alive. And then they gave the S.O.B. a parachute!"

There has been some suspicion over the years that there may not have been a 70-second delay on the destruct unit, that it was designed to go off the instant the pilot flipped the switches, taking him out along with the spy gear. It has been further theorized that

Powers knew about this, and that was why he didn't arm the device. Powers denied this, saying that as the destruct unit was the last piece of equipment installed before each mission, and as the pilot oversaw the installation, he would have been able to tell if it had been rigged in any way. Powers did think though that Eisenhower had been told that the pilots had been instructed to kill themselves. This has been denied by the government. What is more likely is that Eisenhower's surprise at Powers's survival was due to the fact that he, Bissell, the CIA, and everyone else involved in the U-2 project did not think that a pilot had one chance in a million of surviving a SAM strike and a crash from 70,000 feet.

The Soviets, of course, had struck gold. In the USSR wreckage of the U-2 was displayed in public, and Powers was tried on national television. Convicted of espionage, Powers was sentenced to ten years imprisonment. He was released not long after, however, as part of a Soviet-American spy trade in which the United States got Powers in exchange for Soviet agent Colonel Rudolph Abel, who had been captured in New York in 1957.

Many felt that the worst result of the U-2 crash was not so much the political mess as the loss of an invaluable intelligence source. In 1975 CIA Director Richard Helms said that, in its day, the U-2 had provided 90 percent of the intelligence required to produce the American estimate of Soviet strength. Among other things, the U-2 had discovered that there was in fact no "bomber gap" (the M-4 bombers that observers had seen fly by in great numbers at May Day celebrations were in fact just a small squadron that would circle around and fly by again, giving the illusion of an endless number of the planes), as well as uncovering a mother lode of missile-related information, including the discovery of the secret Soviet launch site at Tyuratam in Central Asia.

Allen Dulles once remarked that the U-2's intelligence product could only have been equaled ". . . by the acquisition of technical documents directly from Soviet offices and laboratories. . . . [It] marked a new high, in more ways than one, in the scientific collection of intelligence." When Secretary of State Herter—the man who had had misgivings about the last U-2 flight—was asked what lessons the United States had learned from the U-2 affair, he replied: "Not to have accidents."

There were understandably great fears that with the loss of the U-2s the United States would again be plunged into darkness regarding what went on beyond Soviet borders. This darkness lasted only until August 1960, however, when a capsule of film was ejected from the satellite Discoverer 14. Its recovery off Hawaii signaled a new era in the history of spying from above.

Even with the arrival of the spy satellite, though, the U-2 was by no means abandoned. Now larger and bearing the designation TR-1, it is still used today on spying missions. A satellite often takes weeks to get into position, while a plane can be up in hours. In recent times the U-2 and its successors have been used to monitor Soviet and Cuban activities in Central America and the Caribbean. Most recently these planes had a role in the planning of the U.S. invasion of Grenada in 1983. Perhaps the most notable mission of the U-2 after Powers was downed in 1960 was the discovery of Soviet medium-and intermediate-range missile bases in Cuba in the fall of 1962.

The Cuban Missile Crisis

It was in the summer of 1962 that the U.S. intelligence community first became aware that the Soviets were sending an inordinate amount of military equipment to Cuba. The United States has a worldwide network of shipwatchers who monitor the docks and "choke points" (such as the Bosphorus and the Suez and Panama canals) of shipping around the world. They take pictures of the ships and the crates loaded into them, and these pictures end up at NPIC (National Photographic Interpretation Center) in Washington. Art Lundahl and his PIs (photo interpreters) at NPIC had developed a new science of "cratology," which they used to determine, with remarkable accuracy, what was inside a crate.

From observations at Soviet May Day displays, the PIs knew the size of Soviet military equipment and roughly what size crate would be needed to ship each item. Photographs of crates on ships would then be studied. All the PIs needed was one known dimension in the photograph—say, a flag or a deckhand—and from that they could calculate the size of the crate and make a good guess at what was inside.

Other indications that something was amiss in Havana came from covert operatives on the Cuban docks, who watched the crates being off-loaded, but such HUMINT was not always trusted. The CIA routinely received so much HUMINT from Cuban emigres that they were swamped, and much of it was either plainly erroneous or had actually been planted by Castro's counterintelligence operatives. Hard intelligence was needed on the Russian hardware going to Havana, so a U-2 was sent up over Cuba on August 29. The photographs it brought back showed the familiar Star of David pattern of Soviet SAM sites spotted here and there over the island. Eight such sites were under construction. Why so many? What was there that was so important to protect? It was a disturbing question, for the only logical answer seemed to be that the SAMs were there to protect nuclear missiles.

President Kennedy expressed his grave concern to Khrushchev through diplomatic channels. On September 4 Khrushchev assured Kennedy that there would be no missiles in Cuba—he wouldn't give him any trouble during a congressional election year. As the two countries had been moving toward detente for years, Kennedy, among others, was inclined to believe the Soviet premier. The new head of the CIA, John McCone, was not so inclined. He felt that the Soviets might put missiles in Cuba, not necessarily to use them for war, but as a bargaining chip later on. Others argued: Why would the Soviets put missiles in Cuba and not the other Soviet-bloc countries? McCone replied that it was because the Soviets trusted no one. The intermediate-range ballistic missiles (IRBMs) given to Cuba would only be able to reach the United States or other targets in the Western Hemisphere, while such missiles in Poland or East Germany could be used to strike back at Moscow.

U-2s continued to fly over Cuba, but they were only used on "sheep-dipping" missions, zipping in and out as fast as possible. No startling new information came from these flights, and on September 19 the U.S. Intelligence Board declared that it was highly unlikely that the Soviets would place missiles on Cuban soil. McCone asked that his dissenting opinion be recorded.

It was then that the administration began to receive new reports from Cuba. American agents there spotted large Soviet open-hatched ships in port. They were the kind usually used to transport lumber, but they were seen to be riding higher in the water than they would if they were carrying lumber. Perhaps they were carrying something else. Then, on September 21, an agent reported spotting a shrouded long-range missile on a truck trailer. Further damning corroboration of the threat came from the Defense Intelligence Agency's Colonel John Wright, an expert on Soviet missile installations. When photographs taken from the U-2 finally landed on his desk, he noticed that the trapezoidal configuration of SAMs at the San Cristobal site in Cuba was very similar to the way they were arranged around medium-range missile sites in the Soviet Union.

The experts lacked hard intelligence, and on October 4 it was

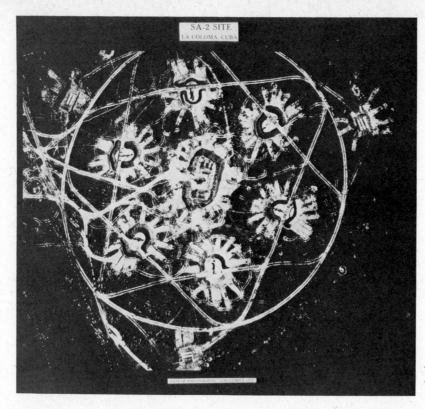

SA-2 SITE
LA COLOMA, CUBA

A photograph of a SAM site in Cuba, taken from a U-2, November 10, 1962.

decided that since overflights of the SAMs could reach the U-2, the flights were going to be dangerous. As such, the Air Force, rather than the CIA, took over these flights. If a CIA pilot were brought down, he would be shot as a spy, while an Air Force pilot would be treated as a POW. In addition, since the U-2 flights might possibly provoke armed conflict, the program should be a military responsibility.

Several days were lost because of cloud cover over Cuba. The first U-2 of this mission, piloted by Captain Richard Heyser, went up on October 14. He took 928 photos over Cuba and was luckily spared a SAM attack. The film was rushed to Art Lundahl's people in Washington, and on the afternoon of October 15 one of the PIs who had been examining the photos called Lundahl at home and asked him to come in. "We want you to look at something," he said.

When Lundahl walked in, no one said a word to him—standard procedure, so that nothing one PI says will influence the interpretation of the other. Lundahl got his stereoscopic glasses and went over to the light table. He bent over the photographs, adjusted his glasses, and was surprised to see, in startling 3-D, palm trees and

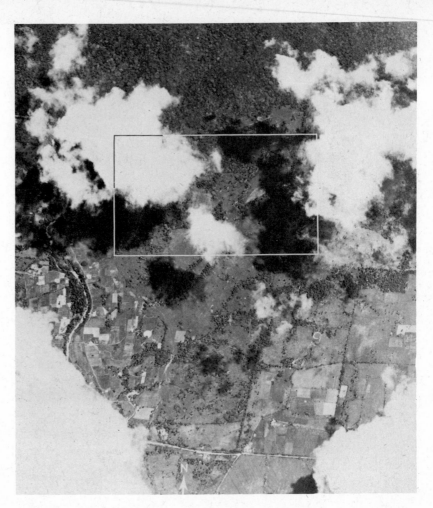

A high-altitude photograph of the San Cristobal site, taken from a U-2 on August 29, 1962. Note no sign of activity.

jungle slashed by the tracks of heavy equipment, empty missile transporters, blast deflectors, cherry picker cranes, long rectangular missile tents, and Soviet nuclear weapon transportation vans.

Lundahl looked up at the PIs in the room. "Okay, I know what you're thinking, and you're right. This is a medium-range-ballistic-missile site. I don't want anyone to leave this room. Call your wives, break up your car pools. Do it casually. But stay in this room."

Lundahl couldn't reach McCone, but he did get Deputy CIA Director Ray Cline. He informed Cline that they had discovered two MRBM sites with SS-4s ready for deployment. With their 1,020-mile range they could reach Washington, D.C.

Cline called presidential assistant McGeorge Bundy at home. There was no scrambler on the line, so Cline had to speak in broad, cryptic terms. "You know that island we were talking about the

A U-2 photograph of the same San Cristobal site on October 14, 1962, less than two months later. The MRBM's have been moved in.

7 MISSILE TRAILERS

TENT AREA

VEHICLES

ERECTORS

MISSILE TRAILER

A low level photograph of the San Cristobal site.

MISSILE ERECTOR

CABLE

MISSILE SHELTER TENT

TRACKED PRIME MOVERS

OXIDIZER TANK TRAILERS

FUEL TANK TRAILERS

other day? Well, they've got some big ones."

Bundy caught on and asked, "Are they ready to shoot?"

"No, but they are rapidly approaching it."

Bundy informed Kennedy, who was furious that Khrushchev had lied to him. Shortly, Cline and Lundahl arrived at the White House with the photographs. Kennedy examined them with a magnifying glass, but it is very difficult for someone who isn't a PI to look at such photographs and see all the things that a PI might. Kennedy looked up at them. "Are you sure?" he asked.

Lundahl answered, "It could be a papier-mache world out there. But I'm as sure of this as a photo interpreter can be."

Thus began the Cuban Missile Crisis, the closest this planet has yet come to nuclear war. Presented with few options, Kennedy decided against immediate military invasion of Cuba, opting instead for a blockade of the island in which all ships traveling either to or from the island were to be stopped and searched. Kennedy was firm. The Soviet Union must withdraw its missiles from Cuba. There was an implied "or else." Or else what? Miiitary invasion of Cuba and the risk of nuclear war.

During those two tense weeks in October U-2s continued to make passes over Cuba to make sure that the status of the sites was not changing. Then, on October 27, a U-2 was shot down over the island. No one could believe it. What were the Soviets doing? Was it a mistake? Were they preparing to launch and didn't want this discovered? Kennedy readied the American forces already massed in Florida, and the world slid closer to the brink. Everyone held their breath.

The next day Khrushchev announced that the missiles would be withdrawn and that the sites would be dismantled. Everyone could breathe again. The U-2s were used to monitor the Soviet withdrawal, making sure that they were living up to Khrushchev's promise. They were. The crisis had passed, and the U-2 had been instrumental in its resolution.

The SR-71

While the U-2's successor in spirit in spying from above was the spy satellite, its direct descendant was another airplane, the SR-71—also known as The Blackbird—perhaps the ultimate spy plane.

Although first flown over 20 years ago, the SR-71 still holds the world's record for highest and fastest horizontal flight—2,189 m.p.h. at 86,000 feet. It is a large plane for only two passengers (the pilot and reconnaissance systems operator or RSO)—107.4 feet long, 55.6 feet wide, 18.5 feet in height at its tallest point, and weighing over 100,000 pounds when fully fueled. Sleek, streamlined, and entirely black, it is a remarkable blend of utility and style. Like the U-2, this amazing spy plane was designed by Kelly Johnson and was built by Johnson and his crew at Lockheed's Skunk Works.

After Johnson designed the U-2 he was aware that at some time in the not-too-distant future Soviet radar and SAM systems would advance to the point where they could compromise the plane's safety. Well before Powers was shot down in 1960, Johnson went to work on a design for an airplane that would fly higher and faster than the U-2 while having a reduced radar cross section as well. The plane would have to fly at speeds over 2,000 m.p.h. at a height of 80,000 feet or more. The plane would also have to contain radar-jamming equipment and an advanced communications system.

When Johnson designed the U-2, his main problem was how to get a plane up to 70,000 feet and keep it there for 12 hours. Speed was not a key issue. However, it was the U-2's relatively slow flight speed—500 m.p.h.—that made it an easy target for Soviet radar to track. With his new plane Johnson was not concerned with flight time, for if it reached the speeds he wished, it would only have to stay aloft for three or four hours at most, as it would be traveling four times the speed of a U-2.

With new goals there came new problems. The most daunting of these was heat. At Mach 3 (near 2,000 m.p.h.) the air friction could create temperatures on the craft's hull of well over 800°F. This ruled out aluminum as a structural material, leaving only titanium and stainless steel. (Research into high-temperature plastics at this time was in a nascent stage.) The high temperatures also meant that new heat-resistant hydraulic fluids, greases, and electrical wiring would have to be developed, and the fuel used would have to have a wide stability range—from -90°F (for aerial refueling) to 600°F, the heat it could reach in the airplane before being fed into the engine's burner.

To reach the speeds that Johnson envisioned at the rarefied altitude of 80,000 feet, the plane would have to have a ram-type engine, an engine that was mostly theoretical in the late 1950s. A ram engine is almost ta perpetual-motion machine. It uses the velocity of air ramming into the front of the engine to provide the thrust out the back of the engine, requiring only a small amount of power to induce and augment the air's speed. The liabilities of ram engines are that they do not work at low altitudes, where the air is too thick, and they must operate at very high speeds for the ram effect to come into play. But these liabilities were perfectly compatible with Johnson's desire to build a plane that would fly high and fast.

Keeping the cockpit cool also posed a problem, as did keeping the rubber wheels on the landing gear from melting. Johnson realized that there also might be a problem for the reconnaissance systems, since photographs taken through a window of this plane might be distorted by the hot, turbulent airflow across the glass.

When Johnson had solved all of these problems on the drawing board, he took his design to his CIA and Air Force sponsors. As with the U-2 proposal, his plans for a new, improved spy plane were not immediately snapped up. From April 1958 to August 1959 he made repeated presentations for this Mach-3 craft to Richard Bissell at the CIA and others at the Air Force. One reason for the lack of a quick decision was that Johnson was not alone in designing such advanced aircraft.

The Navy had plans for an airplane that would be carried aloft by a balloon, then boosted by rocket to ram speeds. One problem with the Navy's design: To carry the airplane they designed to the height required would have taken a balloon one mile in diameter.

Another design came from the Convair division of General Dynamics. They designed a Mach-4 ramjet airplane that was to be carried up by a B-58 and launched when the B-58 reached supersonic speeds. However, a B-58 could not reach supersonic speeds with a plane attached, and the very survivability of a Mach-4 aircraft was questioned.

Bissell finally picked Johnson's design. He announced his decision on August 29, 1959, giving the go-ahead for production and testing of 12 planes on January 30, 1960. The first of the planes flew on April 26, 1962, and in December Lockheed was put under contract to produce the first six operational SR-71s.

The Blackbird Flies

On February 29, 1964, President Johnson announced that America had an airplane that could fly 2,000 miles per hour at over 70,000 feet. It was first thought by the press that the new plane must be a fighter interceptor or missile launcher, but the more observant of the military watchers, noting that it was another Kelly Johnson plane from the Skunk Works, correctly guessed that this was a reconnaissance plane—the successor to the U-2.

An SR-71, head on.

The CIA controlled the operations of the U-2 and was responsible for the design and development of the SR-71. In the ongoing fight between the Agency and the military, however, the Pentagon won a round, with the operation of the SR-71 going to SAC—the Strategic Air Command—which already had its own reconnaissance squadrons.

Like the U-2 pilots, the pilots and RSOs on SR-71s were and are all volunteers. It is a very prestigious plane to fly, and of the many who apply for duty aboard an SR-71, few make it. Pilots must be young, fit, and have at least 1,500 hours of jet flying time. The RSOs must also be in top physical condition and must have 2,500 hours of navigation experience on B-52s and B-58s.

For both the pilot and RSO the preparations for flying the Blackbird are similar to the flight preparations for U-2s—eating a big meal, donning the pressure suit, getting accustomed to breathing oxygen. The plane has two cockpits, one in front for the pilot, one behind it for the RSO. Although the plane itself may look like something out of a science-fiction movie, inside, neither cockpit is very exotic. The only special controls that the front cockpit has are a center-of-gravity indicator and several controls that are specific to the operation of ram engines.

The only flight-control device in the RSO cockpit is one that can affect the horizontal flight path. The RSO uses this in conjunction with the astro-inertial navigation system to line up the plane exactly over targets of photographic runs. In this cockpit there are also controls for the reconnaissance systems. For a typical operation 18 to 24 hours of lead time are required to install the reconnaissance equipment. There are five different nose configurations that can be fitted into the plane, each with a different reconnaissance package for a different type of mission. They all include a tape that controls both the inertial navigation system, which in turn governs the reconnaissance equipment and the autopilot that flies the SR-71 most of the time. The RSO's other responsibilities in addition to the operations of the cameras and receivers include monitoring fuel consumption and overseeing the in-air refueling procedure.

There are several striking features of the SR-71 that would be apparent just looking at one in a hangar. First, the craft is made almost entirely out of titanium—a metal so brittle and hard to work that the Skunk Works pioneers were forced by necessity to build their own titanium forge on the premises. In fact, building the plane advanced the field of titanium metallurgy several degrees. Second, the plane has no flaps to aid in either takeoff or landing. There is a narrow ledge, a continuous horizontal fin, that runs around the outside of the fuselage, and on takeoff this ledge provides just enough extra lift to get the airplane off the runway. On landing, the SR-71 relies on a powerful ground effect that builds up between the plane and the runway to cushion the drop and slow the plane.

Perhaps the most startling feature of an SR-71 in its hangar is the pools of jet fuel that would most likely surround it on the hangar floor. An incredible safety hazard? Not actually. The fuel used, JP-7, does not evaporate and has a very high flash point—so high, in fact, that if a lighted match were thrown into the fuel, the match would merely fizzle out. The puddles on the floor are not the result of carelessness but form because the seams in the fuel tanks have to be deliberately loose so that the tanks can expand without buckling when the plane heats up at supersonic speeds.

The Spy Plane Inventory

The SR-71 has evolved in several ways since it was first flown in 1961—it has been made easier to fly, and the reconnaissance systems and electronic countermeasure components are more sophisticated—but its duty has always remained the same: spying.

An SR-71, in flight.

While by all accounts the United States has remained true to Eisenhower's promise that America would never again overfly the Soviet Union, the SR-71 has been used on radar-triggering penetration sorties over the Russian borders. So far, SR-71s have survived close to 1,000 attempts by the Soviets to shoot them down! Their survival depends on their altitude and speed, for it may take a SAM a minute to reach 80,000 feet, and by the time it gets there, an SR-71 will be 30 miles away.

A good number of SR-71 missions are over the "hot spots" of the world—the Persian Gulf, Lebanon, Indochina, Chad, Libya, Namibia, and of course Central America and the Caribbean. Undoubtedly, the SR-71 played some role in the planning of the American invasion of Grenada in October 1983.

Because each SR-71 mission is very expensive and can involve days of preparation time, the Blackbird is not always the first choice for aerial intelligence gathering. The new, larger model of the U-2, the TR-1 (with a wingspan of 103 feet, compared to the U-2's 80 feet), can be put aloft quite quickly and is safe over all areas of the world that do not have advanced SAM systems. Both the SR-71 and the U-2/TR-1 are operated by SAC, and there exists a certain rivalry between the two squadrons. While the SR-71 is indeed the premier spy plane, the U-2/TR-1 is cheaper and more readily available for duty. It now seems that in the future the two types of spy plane will have their own specific areas of responsibility. The U-2/TR-1 will be used almost exclusively for tactical battlefield surveillance, making strategic intelligence-gathering the sole province of the SR-71.

SAC has other reconnaissance planes as well. There are four squadrons in the 55th Strategic Reconnaissance Wing at SAC headquarters, Offut Air Force Base in Nebraska. The squadrons operate the USAF/Boeing E-4A, the E-4B (National Emergency Airborne Command Post), the USAF/Boeing E-135, and the RC-135. In actuality, almost any airplane can be fitted with a camera to gather intelligence, and the Army, Navy, Air Force, and Marine Corps have probably used almost all of their aircraft on some sort of reconnaissance missions at one time or another.

While battlefield reconnaissance is often performed by jet, helicopter, or small spotting plane, one of the most effective means of gathering such tactical intelligence is the use of drones and remotely piloted vehicles (RPVs). A drone is any craft that operates completely on preprogrammed autopilot (a cruise missile is a drone), whereas an RPV, as its name suggests, is flown remotely by operators on the ground. Both drones and RPVs can be sent over enemy territory to take pictures, which are then either broadcast back to the base or brought back physically if the craft is designed to be retrieved. Other RPVs, based on helicopter principles, are connected to the ground by wires and sent up several thousand feet, with TV cameras at the ready to pick up images of what the enemy is doing on the other side of the hill—much the way balloons were used in the Civil War.

RPVs and drones round out the inventory of the basic methods of aerial photoreconnaissance. The altitudes at which the systems operate are indicative of both a sort of natural hierarchy—the spy satellites are at the top of the heap, while the RPVs and drones are at the bottom—and a form of evolution: from the spy balloon came the spy plane, and from the spy planes came the spy satellite.

As Ray Cline wrote in 1976, in his book *Secrets, Spies and Scholars*,

"It is ironic that the peace of the world now depends to a remarkable degree on the unilateral U.S. and Soviet technical means of monitoring arms agreements that evolved from the U-2 technology of 1955. In any case, the balance of strategic nuclear power that now protects U.S. security is guaranteed by U.S. intelligence efforts, based on the photoreconnaissance techniques CIA officers began working on twenty years ago."

One can then view the U-2 as an instance of technology being used not to wage war but to prevent war. Indeed, the U-2 and its satellite successors have been instrumental in providing the United States with intelligence that has so far ruled out the possibility of Eisenhower's dreaded fear—surprise attack. These have also been products of the Cold War, a war fought by intelligence agencies for world opinion, strategic influence, and territory on the map. Such a cold war of espionage requires cold weaponry, and in that light the spy planes and spy satellites are the coldest weapons of all.

2 THE SPY SATELLITES

Background

Gaining the "high ground" has been a goal of commanders from Hannibal to MacArthur, and for good reason. An arrow fired from the top of a hill will fly farther and hit harder than one let loose from a valley. Even in modern warfare, with highly sophisticated artillery, it is easier to strike from a high point to a low point than the other way around. But holding the high ground has another advantage that has nothing to do with throw-weights or trajectory. Very simply, it is much easier to spy down from a hill, than to spy up from a valley.

In a cold war the high ground, in whatever form it takes, has primarily an intelligence value. For the years 1956 to 1960 the U-2 provided the high-ground advantage, but when Powers was shot down over Sverdlovsk, the Americans again faced the Soviets on a somewhat level plain. In fact, the Soviets enjoyed some measure of superiority, since it was easier for them to put spies in the United States than it was for the Americans to put agents in the USSR. This situation did not last. The United States had been preparing for the time when the U-2 would no longer be effective. One solution was simply to build an airplane—the SR-71—that could fly higher and faster than the U-2. The boldest option, however, was to shoot for the highest ground—space.

To understand why there are spy satellites in orbit today, and how they work, we must begin with a look at the principles of space flight and space technology and at the first series of satellites that began to take shape on the drawing boards almost forty years ago. We will witness the wedding of space technology and spy technology, chronicling the troubled lives of the offspring of that marriage, Discoverer and Samos, the first two American spy satellite series. We will proceed through the successive generations of American spy sats through to today's paramount spy satellite, the KH-11. There will also be a look not only at the other satellites operated by the U.S. military but also at the Soviet spy mission in space. Finally, we will take a glimpse into the future of spy satellites.

A great many dates will be mentioned—the first Discoverer launch, the first Discoverer capsule recovered, and so on—as each one is crucial in its way to the history, and a sense of history is key to a comprehension of the true importance of this technology.

How important is space technology? An example: In the late 1950s American intelligence estimated that the Soviets were shooting ahead in their missile programs and that in the years 1960-1961 a "missile gap" would develop. Khrushchev tried to use this gap as leverage in an effort to pry Berlin loose from the West. The West was resolute but wary. Soon, with Kennedy and Khrushchev at loggerheads, the two superpowers slid close to a confrontation that neither had ever thought would truly come to a pass. Then, in October 1961, the United States, although still determined to keep Berlin from the Soviets, seemed to be suddenly less concerned, perhaps even arrogant about the severity of the Soviet threat. The Soviets backed off Berlin and removed their demands. Why was there such a turnaround?

On October 6, 1961, Kennedy returned from a family vacation for a meeting with Soviet Foreign Minister Andrei Gromyko, during which he let the proverbial "cat out of the bag." While U.S. intelligence had discovered that indeed there was a missile gap, they found that it was in favor of America, not Russia. This was not empty posturing on Kennedy's part. He knew exactly how many missiles the Soviets had and he had concrete proof. Perhaps he even showed his proof to Gromyko—photographs of Soviet missile bases, taken by satellite.

The Early Missile Program

Ironically, the story of the development of spy satellites is inextricably entwined with the saga of the burgeoning of the very missiles that they were designed to monitor. The intercontinental ballistic missile, the main delivery system of modern weapons of mass destruction, had its beginning as a toy rocket in China over 900 years ago.

It was discovered that when a firecracker flared instead of exploded, the hot gas it emitted would propel it. Tying a firecracker to a stick gave it some stability and a relatively smooth trajectory when fired. When aimed upward, these early rockets went hundreds of feet into the air. In the intervening centuries rockets were used primarily for entertainment and not war, for while fiery rockets streaking over the battlefield may have been an effective psychological weapon, they were almost impossible to aim.

A landmark in the development of rocketry came toward the end of the 19th century, a time when only a handful of men had ever dreamed of going into space. The breakthrough came from a Russian schoolmaster, Konstantin Tsiolkovsky, who derived the "ideal rocket equation," which he used to prove that rockets could operate even in the vacuum of space. Tsiolkovsky also conceived of building rockets in stages, an idea that was to be crucial in the early rocket programs, for it allowed for a much more efficient use of energy.

Two other rocket pioneers were Robert Goddard (mentioned earlier for his work with cameras and rockets) and Herman Oberth. Goddard, an American physicist, launched the world's first liquid-propellant rocket on March 16, 1926, at Auburn, Massachusetts. Interestingly enough, even though NASA named a space center outside Washington after him, Goddard himself wasn't much interested in space travel; rather, he thought of his rockets as tools for atmospheric research. Oberth, a German schoolteacher, was more of a theorist than Goddard. His work in the 1930s had a profound effect on the men who designed and built Hitler's V--rockets and who later helped both the United States and the Soviet Union in their own infant rocket programs.

Despite its designation the V-2 bore little relation to the V-1, Germany's first device for unmanned long-range destruction. The V-1 "buzz bomb" was essentially a drone or cruise missile that flew aerodynamically all the way to its target. On the other hand, the V-2 was a ballistic missile: After its rocket engines burnt out, it would just fall to its target like an artillery shell. Like its predecessors on older battlefields, the V-2, which was rushed into production toward the end of the war, was more a psychological than military weapon, for over a 130-mile trajectory (about its limit) the V-2 was likely to miss its target by up to five miles.

After the war, when the United States first considered building rockets, it was this lack of precision in the V-2 that led many within the defense establishment to ridicule the concept of long-range missiles. Even if the V-2's accuracy were improved ten times and its thrust seven times, over an intercontinental distance of 5,500 miles it would still miss its mark by 20 miles. In April 1946, the Air Force, just to be on the safe side, did award a small contract to the Convair division of General Dynamics to study the possibility of such missiles. This was canceled 15 months later, when the decision was made to forgo rockets and concentrate on long-range bombers and cruise missiles instead.

The Army, however, showed somewhat more interest in the idea. It felt that while rockets might not be good for long-range work, they might be suitable as tactical weapons on the battlefield, and so they sponsored a research program by General Electric. Project Hermes relied on a cache of captured German V-2 rockets and captured German V-2 rocket scientists. Among the Germans was Dr. Wernher Von Braun, who would later become the leading figure in the early American space program. Von Braun was enthralled with the idea of space travel and cared little who was funding his research. During the war, in fact, he and a few other rocket scientists were arrested under the suspicion that they were more interested in space travel than the German war effort. Only the influence of Major Walter Dornberger, their supervisor at the Peenemunde V-2 base and himself a space enthusiast, gained their release.

The first test of a V-2 on American soil took place on April 16, 1946, at White Sands, New Mexico, and the last of the sixty-seven captured rockets was launched on June 31, 1951. They were large, unwieldy, and somewhat unpredictable behemoths, but experimentation with them led to the development of Redstone, America's first ballistic missile, which had a range of 200 miles, about 70 miles greater than the V-2.

The USSR too had its own captured V-2s and its own captured V-2 scientists, and their work paralleled what was going on halfway around the world in New Mexico. When the German scientists held in the Soviet Union were finally released, they were quickly snapped up by the United States and debriefed. According to these scientists, while the Soviets were developing limited intermediate range missiles for tactical use, they were, like the United States, concentrating for the most part on cruise missile research. This intelligence that the Soviets were not working on ICBMs must have soothed any fears in Washington, for U.S. funding of ICBM research remained low. As was discovered later, the Americans had been lulled into a false sense of security. The Soviets, it seems, had been very clever. They had built a second ballistic missile development center the German scientists were never told about, and it was there, under the strictest security, that work progressed on ICBMs. Although the Germans never knew about the facility, the Soviets did test certain ideas with the V-2 scientists, but in a way that never aroused any suspicion that there might be a second base.

In the summer of 1952 the U.S. intelligence analysts estimated that the Soviets would be able to strike the Pacific Northwest with a 2,000-pound payload by 1956, and any part of the United States with an 8,000-pound warhead by 1958. For its part America detonated its first hydrogen bomb that fall, and a year later the Atomic Energy Commission indicated that H-bombs could be made much smaller than had been originally thought. This meant that if they were to be used in missiles there would be less of a thrust requirement. In 1954, with smaller warheads possible, the decision was made to go full speed ahead on ICBM development.

As work progressed on the various types of rockets—Atlas, Titan, Jupiter, Thor, etc.—disquieting information came out of the giant U.S. radar station outside the Turkish village of Diyarbakir near the Black Sea. The station's monitoring of Soviet missile tests revealed that they were doing far better than had been hoped.

On January 25, 1967, the first American IRBM to be tested sat on the launchpad at Cape Canaveral, Florida. Seven stories tall, weighing 100,000 pounds, it had rocket engines designed to produce 150,000 pounds of thrust. When the countdown reached zero and the ignition button was pressed, the missile burst into flames and exploded on the launchpad. The next two Thor tests were also failures. Meanwhile, reports from Diyarbakir indicated that the Soviets had been successfully launching two such IRBMs per month since the previous fall.

But those were only IRBMs. U.S. missilemen still felt confident that they were ahead in the ICBM race with Convair's work on Atlas. That confidence was soon shaken. In August 1957 the Soviets announced that they had successfully fired a missile a huge distance and that it had landed in its target area. While this statement was uncorroborated, it was nonetheless worrisome, for it would be a year before the United States would have a successful Atlas test. This panic caused by a sense of being behind made the Americans push all that much harder, and on September 20, 1957, a Thor was finally launched successfully.

The surge of optimism this launch provided gave only a brief respite. Two weeks later, on October 4, the Soviets launched Sputnik 1 (sputnik can be roughly translated as "companion" or, in this sense, "satellite"). Not much larger than a beach ball, Sputnik weighed 184 pounds. It took 96.2 minutes to orbit the Earth, with a perigee (the closet point of its orbit to the Earth) of 142 miles and an apogee (the orbit's farthest point) of 588 miles, all the while beeping out a simple signal that announced its presence and that the Space Age had begun.

The Uses of Space

In the early 1600s the mathematician and astronomer Johannes Kepler described for the first time the laws of planetary motion. Later in that century Sir Isaac Newton proposed that Kepler's laws could all be derived from a Universal Law of Gravitation. In his *Principia* Newton noted an interesting property of the relationship between gravity and the spherical Earth. He wrote that if a projectile launched from the planet were to travel fast enough, 18,000 miles per hour or more, when the object started to fall, one would find that as it fell, the Earth would always be moving out from under it. Thus, it would be in orbit. While Newton's idea of a launch system was a cannon on a mountaintop and not a concrete pad in the middle of Central Asia or in a swamp on the Florida coast, the principle of orbiting a satellite was the same then as now.

In his short story "The Brick Moon," published in 1869 in the *Atlantic Monthly*, Edward Everett Hale wrote of an artificial moon, or satellite, which he thought could be used as a manned military station. Major Walter Dornberger, the commander at the Peenumunde V-2 base in Germany during the war, also put forth an early satellite proposal in his book, *V-2*. He had one rather ghoulish idea. "With our big rockets and step rockets we could build spaceships, which could circle the Earth like moons at a height of 300 miles and a speed of 18,000 miles per hour. Space stations and glass spheres containing the embalmed bodies of pioneers of rocket development and space travel could be put into permanent orbits around the Earth."

The first true satellite was dreamed up by British scientist and science-fiction writer Arthur C. Clarke. In the February 1945 issue of *Wireless World* he proposed that a set of three satellites be set around the Earth at the geosynchronous altitude—22,300 miles, the height at which, if the satellite's orbit is aligned with the equator, the satellite will move at the same speed as the Earth rotates, so that in effect the satellite will stay fixed over one spot on the Earth. Clarke suggested that such satellites could be used to relay communications, and today, forty years later, communications satellites have proved so far to be the only commercially viable application of space technology.

Shortly after World War II, Project RAND was commissioned by the U.S. Air Force to study the feasibility of launching a satellite into orbit. On May 2, 1946, it released a 324-page report which stated that a 500-pound satellite could be launched into a 300-mile orbit by 1951. They saw both military and research applications but cautioned that there was no way one could predict all of the possibilities: "We can see no more clearly all the utility and implications of spaceships than the Wright brothers could see fleets of B-29s bombing Japan and air transports circling the globe. Though the crystal ball is cloudy, two things seem clear: (1) A satellite vehicle with appropriate instrumentation can be expected to be one of the most potent scientific tools of the Twentieth Century; (2) The achievement of a satellite craft by the United States would inflame the imagination of mankind, and would probably produce repercussions in the world comparable to the explosion of the atomic bomb."

The report also presaged the possibility of reconnaissance from satellites: "It should also be remarked that the satellite offers an observation aircraft that cannot be brought down by an enemy who has not mastered similar techniques. . . . Perhaps the two most important classes of observation which can be made from a satellite are the spotting of points of impacts of bombs . . . and the observation of weather conditions over enemy territory." The RAND experts were true to their own original caution, for by thinking only of impact detection and weather forecasting, they had by no means predicted all the possibilities of reconnaissance satellites.

The bottom line of the RAND report was the estimate that it would take five years and $150 million to put a satellite into orbit.

In the years just after the war, as the country sought peace and prosperity, that appeared to be too much to spend on a dubious, quasimilitary project. Although the idea of launching a satellite by no means disappeared, it did not really come to the fore again for eight years.

In June 1954 Dr. Wernher Von Braun presented a report to the U.S. government suggesting that existing military missile equipment in the hands of the Ordnance Corps could be used to launch a satellite into space. Von Braun's proposal was given serious consideration. It was to be a joint Army-Navy project and was given the name Orbiter. In the summer of 1955, however, America scotched the Orbiter project, deciding instead to go with an all-civilian effort—Vanguard—to put an object into space as part of the IGY (International Geophysical Year, 1957-1958). The main reason that Vanguard was chosen over Orbiter, it seems, was that as a civilian project it would not use military equipment, and military secrets would then not be jeopardized by public disclosure. The problem with not using the existing military missile equipment was that Vanguard had to develop its own from scratch, a daunting task.

The first U.S. attempt to launch a satellite came on December 6, 1957, two months after the Soviets launched Sputnik. It was a failure. The rocket engines ignited; the rocket started up but then collapsed back down and exploded on the pad. The tiny silver sphere of a satellite that was Vanguard survived the conflagration, however, and it lay on the debris-strewn launchpad, still obliviously bleeping its telemetric signal. Someone in the control room joked grimly, "Why doesn't someone kick it and put it out of its misery?" Vanguard seemed a disaster.

But the truth was that, as a civilian project, Vanguard had been gravely underfunded. The project engineers had to work in an old airplane factory in Baltimore that had neither heat in winter not air conditioning in summer. What it did have was a score of pigeons fluttering around overhead, at times fouling the blueprint drawings below with their droppings. Nevertheless, Vanguard was responsible for several key innovations in spacecraft design.

With the embarrassing first launch failure, the United States government returned quickly to Von Braun's Orbiter plan and, somewhat miraculously, managed to send up a satellite, Explorer 1, on January 31, 1958. Although thrown together in a flash, the payload, designed in part by Dr. James Van Allen, made the first scientific discovery by a satellite—the Van Allen belts of highly charged particles that surround the earth at distances of from 100 to

30,000 miles. The first successful Vanguard launch put a tiny 3-pound satellite about the size of grapefruit into orbit on March 17, 1958. This was followed by four spectacular failures and then, finally, on February 17, 1959, the launch of a 22-pound Vanguard. In comparison, before the first Vanguard had even been attempted, the Soviets had launched two satellites—Sputnik 1, at 184 pounds, and Sputnik 2, at 1,120 pounds. The disparity escaped no one's attention, and the competition between the two countries was obvious. The space race was underway.

How Satellites Work

The rockets that we have seen standing on launchpads have essentially two components: launch vehicle and spacecraft. The launch vehicle comprises the bulk of a rocket, since a huge amount of power is needed to propel an object to orbital velocity (roughly 18,000 m.p.h.). A launch vehicle can be rated in terms of its "specific impulse," which is the amount of propulsive force produced by a pound of fuel per minute.

There are three basic types of propulsion system—liquid, solid, and hybrid. Liquid-fueled rockets use a combination of two or more liquids that ignite when introduced to each other. The hot thrust gases that are produced are directed through nozzles in the bottom of the rocket, lifting the craft. Liquid-fueled rockets have a very complex design, are more prone to explosion, and consume an incredible amount of fuel (in producing 1.5 million pounds of thrust, the combustion chamber in an F-1 engine on a Saturn 5 consumes 24,811 gallons of liquid oxygen and 15,471 gallons of kerosene *every minute*). A solid-fueled rocket has a much simpler design—a chamber filled with solid propellant and a system to ignite it. The rockets used to boost the shuttle into orbit are solid-propellant boosters. As between liquid and solid, however, liquid-fueled rockets have the higher specific impulse. The middle ground between the two is the hybrid, which utilizes a combination of a solid fuel and a liquid oxidizer to produce thrust.

In the early stage after a launch a rocket is kept vertical, so that the heat generated by the friction of the rocket pushing up through the denser lower atmosphere, and the drag caused by that thicker air, are kept to a minimum. At one point, though, the rocket must veer off onto a horizontal course, or it would never get its payload into orbit—it would just go straight up and then straight down.

During the first few minutes of flight, as the fuel burns and the weight of the craft decreases, its speed increases dramatically, eventually reaching orbital velocity of roughly 18,000 m.p.h. (If a rocket is launched due east, it can take advantage of the speed of the Earth's rotation, reducing its velocity reguirements to 17,000 m.p.h.).

As Tsiolkovsky suggested in the late 1800s, it is most efficient to use rockets built in stages. After each stage burns and is discarded, the fuel in the next stage has less weight to push, hence the rocket's velocity increases. If a satellite is to be put in a low orbit (less than 600 miles up) it can be put there by direct ascent, but if a higher altitude is envisioned, then it must first be put into a lower "parking" orbit. It may remain there for an orbit or two and then, using a process known as the Hohman transfer, when the satellite reaches the apogee (farthest point from the Earth) of its parking orbit, the point where its centrifugal force is the greatest and the restraint of gravity the weakest, the satellite can be boosted into a higher orbit.

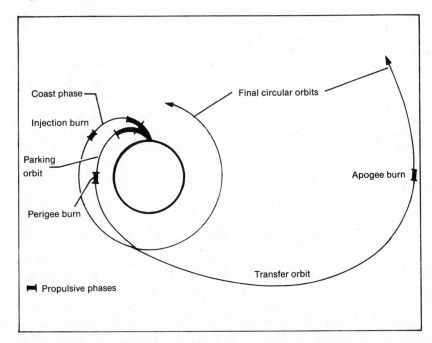

Coast phase

Injection burn

Parking orbit

Perigee burn

Final circular orbits

Apogee burn

Transfer orbit

Propulsive phases

Diagram of two different orbital placement maneuvers.

There are several different types of orbit, each defined by its main orbital elements: perigee, apogee, period, and inclination. Perigee and apogee define the satellite's orbital height, which reflects its mission. The nuclear-detection satellites orbited in the 1960s were put into 60,000-mile orbits—one quarter of the way to the Moon—so that they would get as broad a view possible of space. Communications satellites orbit at 22,300 miles—the geosynchronous height—so that they can remain fixed over one place on the Earth at all times. Weather satellites orbit at 600-800 miles, for coverage of large areas, and spy satellites orbit at 100-300 miles, for close observation. The difference between a satellite's perigee and its apogee may also be indicative of its mission. For example, spy satellites characteristically have very low perigees, as low as 80 miles, so that they can get as close a look as possible.

Except for one notable exception, all communications satellites orbit at 22,300 miles, for at that height the time it takes for a satellite traveling 18,000 m.p.h. to complete its large, circular orbit around the Earth is equal to the rotational period of the planet—roughly 24 hours. If the satellite's orbit is aligned with the equator, then it will be geosynchronous—or geostationary, as it is also known—for it will remain fixed over one spot on the Earth. The notable exception in communications satellites is the Soviet Molniya orbit. A satellite can only be geosynchronous over the equator, yet most of the Soviet Union lies at very high latitudes, and much of it is out of the line of sight of the geosynchronous satellites. For their communications purposes the Soviets designed a highly eccentric orbit with an apogee of 25,000 miles and a perigee of 300 miles. The orbit is not aligned with the equator but is inclined so that a satellite will pass over the USSR in the Northern Hemisphere and Antarctica in the Southern. The orbital period of a Molniya is 12 hours; of that period, eight or more hours are spent above the equator and less than four below. While high over the Soviet Union for eight hours, the satellite is used to relay communications. With a series of four properly spaced satellites, each taking up slightly overlapping eight-hour passes over the Soviet Union, uninterrupted communications coverage can be provided 24 hours a day.

The period of a satellite's orbit is dependent on the orbital height: Since all satellites travel at roughly the same speed, satellites at a lower altitude take less time to travel around the Earth. If a satellite's orbital period is evenly divisible into 24 hours, then it will pass over the same spots each day. If not, then it will fly over new ground each day, slowly shifting over the Earth's surface until it eventually returns to where it started.

Orbits are not perfect Keplerian ellipses, or circles, but rather, because of the perturbations caused by the Earth's gravity, the

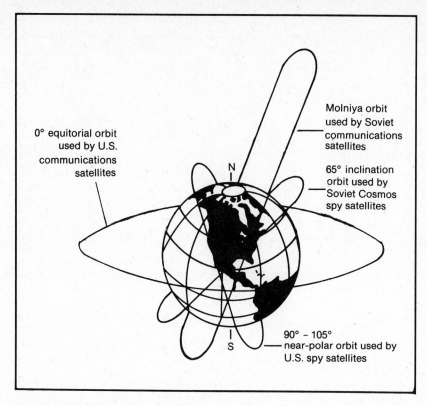

0° equitorial orbit
used by U.S.
communications
satellites

Molniya orbit
used by Soviet
communications
satellites

65° inclination
orbit used by
Soviet Cosmos
spy satellites

N

S

90° – 105°
near-polar orbit used by
U.S. spy satellites

Several key orbital types.

atmosphere, the magnetic fields, the Moon's gravity, and the solar winds, all orbits are imperfect. These perturbations must be countered by the use of stabilizing jets to keep the satellite on course. Some satellites use the calculated effects of these perturbations to alter their orbits in such a way that not only will the satellite pass over the same spot each day, but it will do so at the same time each day all the year round. This is known as a "sun-synchronous" orbit, for in it a satellite will pass over the same spot—the Afghani highlands, perhaps—at the same time—12 noon—every day of the year. A non-sun-synchronous orbit may bring a satellite over the same spot each day, but over the course of a year, the time at which it passes will change.

The last main orbital element is the degree of inclination. This is defined as the angle between the orbital plane and the equatorial plane, and it can range from 0 to 180 degrees. Inclination also reflects a satellite's mission. A 0-degree, or near equatorial, orbit is usually used only for geosynchronous satellites, while in the vicinity of 90 degrees are the polar and near-polar orbits characteristic of reconnaissance satellites. The inclination of an orbit also determines

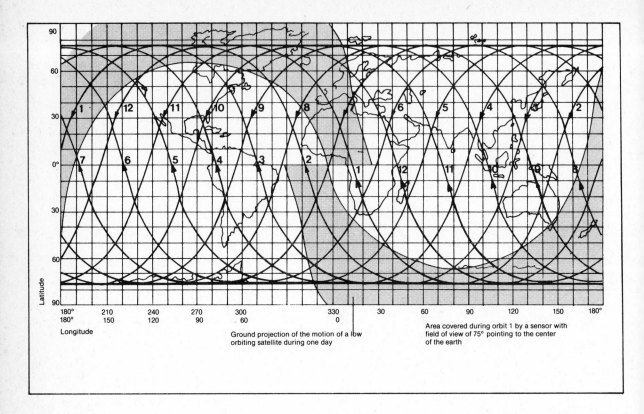

Area covered during orbit 1 by a sensor with field of view of 75° pointing to the center of the earth

Ground projection of the motion of a low orbiting satellite during one day

Ground track of a low-altitude satellite.

how much of the Earth's surface a satellite will overfly. In a 65° orbit the satellite will only cover the Earth between 65°N and 65°S, while a 90° orbit, flying over both poles, will cover the entire Earth.

The satellite itself is of course tiny in comparison to the launch vehicle used to get it into space. The first part of a satellite to be built is often its structure, which must be both lightweight (no more than 15-25 percent of the overall weight of the satellite, so that most of the weight allowed can be taken up by the instrumentation of the payload) and strong (to withstand the powerful forces of vibration and weight loading caused by acceleration during launch and stage separation). Magnesium and aluminum are commonly used as building materials.

The major subsystems on a satellite are power, stabilization and altitude control, thrust system, and telecommunications. Solar panels are the most commonly used source of power, although batteries and nuclear generators have been used when the power demand is higher than solar panels can provide. The way the satellite lies in orbit, its attitude and stability, can be controlled by spinning the satellite, giving it the stability of a football thrown in a spiral or a bullet spun by the rifling in a gun barrel. The attitude and stability can also be controlled with three-axis stabilization, a method that employs inertial wheels, gyroscopes, and jet thrusters to keep the satellite steady. A satellite also has larger jet thrusters, which can be used to maneuver it into a higher orbit, decay its orbit, and correct for injection errors and the perturbation forces.

The telecommunications subsystem is comprised of aerial, telecommand, telemetry, and data storage. Information is received and transmitted through the aerial system. Incoming instructions operate through the telecommand to control the craft. Outgoing information is transformed into digital form and then transmitted to Earth. The number of bits of information (a bit is either a "0" or a "1" in the binary system, corresponding to either a closed or an open electronic gate in a computer) that can be transmitted is limited by the bandwidth (one bit per second requires one Hertz of bandwidth) and the orbital height (as the signal dissipates over distance, the higher the orbit, the fewer bits per second can be relayed). Once on Earth, the telemetry can be translated back into the information it represents, which may be anything from a photograph of a Chinese missile silo to a measurement of magnetic flux. As a satellite will only be in view of a ground station for ten minutes or so, information must be stored, usually on microchip, as it passes around the Earth and then, when it passes over the ground station, beamed to the Earth in a high-frequency burst.

On-board computers are becoming increasingly important in satellites, for it is desirable that as much computation and refinement of information as possible be done in space, so that transmission is as brief as possible. Computers as well as much of the other equipment aboard a satellite, such as telescopes and infrared sensors that tell a satellite where it is, are very sensitive pieces of equipment, and they can easily fail during the rigors of launch or in the harsh conditions of space. For this reason redundant backup systems can comprise up to 20 percent of a satellite's weight.

The overall development of a satellite may take from four to eight years. The design and model test of the craft and of the subsystems may each take a year. Six months will then be needed to integrate the craft and the subsystems, another half-year for the manufacture of a prototype, then a final year of tests leading up to the construction of the first craft and its launch. All of this can be quite expensive. Because of the cost of parts, the complexity of design, the manpower needed for engineering and construction, the nature of the payload, and the length of the mission, it can cost as much as $100,000 per pound to launch something into space.

But with some missions, cost is no obstacle.

Discoverer and Samos

In the early 1950s *Collier's* published a series of articles written by the leading theorists of space travel. In his article, "Prelude to Space Travel," Dr. Wernher Von Braun wrote that one of the great attributes of a space station is that it would be "close enough to the Earth to afford a superb observation post." He elaborated: "Technicians in this space station, using specially designed, powerful telescopes attached to large optical screens, radarscopes, and cameras, will keep under constant inspection every ocean, continent, country, and city. Even small towns will be visible. . . . Nothing will go unobserved. . . . Because of the telescopic eyes and cameras of the space station, it will be practically impossible for any nation to hide warlike preparations for any length of time."

Von Braun was echoing the idea put forward in RAND's 1946 report on the feasibility of launching a satellite—that space would be the perfect place to spy from.

RAND continued to write reports on satellites, some of them solely concerned with the idea of reconnaissance from outer space. Two such secret reports were released in April 1951: *Utility of a Satellite Vehicle for Reconnaissance* and *Inquiry into the Feasibility of Weather Reconnaissance from a Satellite Vehicle.* From these, in the years 1952-1953, RAND gained indirect sponsorship by the CIA to do secret design studies on satellite reconnaissance. The fruit of this labor was a two-volume summary of its work, *An Analysis of the Potential of an Unconventional Reconnaissance Method,* presented to the CIA in March 1954.

As the RAND reports made clear, satellites have much to recommend them for reconnaissance. Traveling at 18,000 m.p.h. at a height of 100-200 miles, a satellite can cover vast areas quickly. As well, floating free in space, there would be virtually no vibration (the bane of aerial photography)—and at that time there was no way to shoot down a satellite.

In late 1954 word from RAND was that satellite reconnaissance was indeed feasible. Richard Bissell at the CIA was at that time starting up the U-2 program, but he was not so preoccupied with the plane that he did not see the tantalizing possibilities in the satellite-reconnaissance proposal. With the life expectancy of the U-2 then set at only two years, Bissell was among those who saw the spy satellite as a possible successor to the high-flying spy plane. On March 16, 1955, the Air Force, with substantial but indirect CIA sponsorship, issued formal operational requirements for a Strategic Satellite System, given the designation WS-117L (Weapons System-117L). Three companies were given one-year design-study contracts in a competition for the contract to build the spacecraft. On June 30, 1956, Lockheed was chosen. The Lockheed project was given the name Pied Piper, and the spacecraft they designed was called Agena.

Lockheed's Agena was to fit atop an Atlas booster that would lift it most of the way into space before its own rockets would kick in and propel it into orbit. Although it was designed to carry almost any kind of payload in its conical nose section (it was used for such nonspy missions as the Lunar Orbiter series and the Canadian Alouette space program), it was, of course, primarily intended to take a reconnaissance package aloft. The craft was to be 19 feet long and five feet in diameter, and most of its volume was to be taken up by fuel and the Bell Aerospace Hustler engine.

For the reconnaissance package two systems were considered—television and film scanning. In the television system, cameras would take pictures of the world below, store the images on tape, and then transmit the images to the Earth as the satellite passed over a ground station. In film scanning, black-and-white photographs would be taken and developed on board the satellite, and then, as the satellite flew over a ground station, a fine white light would scan the photographs, translating the various levels of black and white into signals that could then be transmitted down by radio-telemetry link.

One trouble with film scanning was the estimate that it would take 10 minutes to transmit a 9-by-9-inch photograph; unfortunately, a satellite is only in range of a ground station for ten minutes. While it would take only two minutes to transmit a 70mm-by-70mm (2.75-by-2.75 inch) photograph, there would be proportionately less information in the photograph, as either its resolution would have to be lower or it would have to cover a smaller area. Even with such drawbacks, however, film scanning was chosen over television in August 1957, because television had much poorer resolution. Television would be used by the Army in TIROS—Television and InfraRed Observation System—a satellite program that was first designed for battlefield surveillance but that ended up being suitable only for weather observation, again because of television's poor resolution.

The major contractors for the film scanning system were Eastman-Kodak (photographic equipment), CBS Laboratories (film scanner), and Philco-Ford (signal processing and radio link components).

The camera, as with the U-2, was the most critical element, and as such, it posed the most problems. Resolution decreases with distance, and even if the huge Hycon B camera used in the U-2 could have been reduced in size to meet the weight restrictions of a satellite, the increase in distance from the Earth—from the U-2's 15 miles to a satellite's 100 miles—would have resulted in seven times less resolution. If a U-2 was able to pick out a soldier, a satellite might have trouble spotting a tank.

One way to counter the decrease in resolution by height is to increase the focal length of the camera lens. Several new cameras were developed along these lines. Perkin-Elmer brought out a 48-inch-focal-length panoramic scanning camera. Hycon's K-30 had a 100-inch folding optic lens, and Itek developed a 240-inch lens (these lenses were not 100 and 240 inches long, but they used mirrors to bounce the light path back and forth to produce the same effect). With longer focal length, however, because of the mirrors, lenses, and casing, there is usually greater weight. The folding-optics Hycon K-30, for example, weighed a staggering 665 pounds. In 1958 the largest satellite the United States had launched—the entire satellite, not just the payload—weighed 38 pounds. The program pressed on, however, confident that there would soon be bigger boosters, which would allow heavier payloads.

Meanwhile, RAND continued to compile spy-satellite reports, but in June 1956 they took a completely new tack with *Physical Recovery of Satellite Payloads: A Preliminary Investigation*. This report suggested that an ICBM nose cone, used to carry a nuclear weapon into space and protect it upon its searing reentry into atmosphere, also could be used to carry and reenter a photo-reconnaissance payload. RAND envisioned a mission in which a recoverable capsule crammed with film would disengage from the main satellite and then fire a small retrorocket to slow itself down. The capsule would then fall out of orbit, reenter the atmosphere, deploy a parachute at about 50,000 feet, and float down into the ocean, all the while transmitting a radio signal to indicate its position to the recovery team.

The scheme had many things going for it. It would provide photo interpreters with higher-resolution photographs than the film-

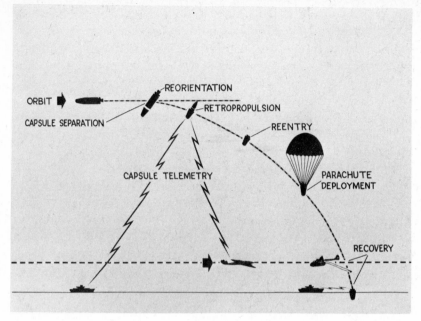

ORBIT

CAPSULE SEPARATION

REORIENTATION

RETROPROPULSION

REENTRY

CAPSULE TELEMETRY

PARACHUTE DEPLOYMENT

RECOVERY

Diagram of recoverable capsule concept re-entry phase.

scanning system could provide because there would be no limitation based on the transmission link. In addition, the PIs would then have the actual photographs to work with, not images that had been beamed down by radio. But the scheme also seemed somewhat farfetched and fraught with difficulties. The entire reentry phase was frightening. If the capsule were not properly oriented when the retrorocket fired, then it could actually be driven up into a higher orbit, from which it would be irretrievable. If it was only slightly misaligned or if the rockets were fired just a little too soon or just a little too late, the capsule would come down thousands of miles away from where the recovery team was waiting. Even if all went according to plan, finding the capsule would be like walking over a football field and finding a pea. For these and other reasons, such as enormous weight, the concept of a recoverable capsule was put on the back burner.

In August 1957 there was an attempt to accelerate WS-117L, the Air Force's spy-satellite program. Additional funding was not forthcoming, however, and the project remained sluggish. But when Sputnik popped into space on October 4, that was all the impetus that was needed. On November 25, 1957, funding for WS-117L magically quadrupled. In that same month RAND released *A Family of Recoverable Reconnaissance Satellites*, its second secret report on what was fast becoming a favorite subject at RAND. The report was so enthusiastic that in January 1958 the Department of Defense (DoD) decided that the theory should be tested as soon as possible.

The first step involved adapting the Lockheed Agena so that it could carry a recoverable capsule, as well as redesigning it to fit atop a Thor booster (designed as an IRBM) rather than the heftier Atlas, which had yet to be completed. The decision to go with the Thor rather than wait for available Atlases meant that the reconnaissance payload would be very small, yet it was reasoned that the first order of business was to test the recoverable-capsule concept as soon as possible, regardless of what the capsule contained.

In the blink of an eye the farfetched idea had been plucked from the back burner and was being pushed forward eagerly. It was given the working name Corona.

When the Senate Preparedness Investigating Subcommittee was informed of the new program it was told that a Thor-Boosted Agena vehicle could be ready to launch by the spring of 1959. At that same meeting Lieutenant General Clarence Irving, the Deputy Chief for Materiel, was queried about reconnaissance satellites by Senator John A. Carroll of Colorado, who wondered if the Russians wouldn't have the same capability. Irving replied that they would. Carroll asked, "And by having such photographic cameras functioning, perhaps each of us would know what the other side was doing; is that possible?"

Irving nodded and said, "I think it would be very healthy. This is the first step toward peace."

The Launching of Discoverer

Vandenberg Air Force Base, on Point Arguello, 150 miles northwest of Los Angeles, was picked as the launch site for the Corona satellites. Vandenberg was chosen for a specific reason. Most reconnaissance satellites are launched into near-polar orbits, so that as the Earth rotates beneath them, they will cover the entire surface of the entire planet in a matter of days. This means that a satellite must be launched in a northerly or southerly direction. But if such a satellite were launched from Cape Canaveral, it would pass over either the heavily populated eastern seaboard or the Miami area before it reached orbit. If something were to go wrong with the launch and the vehicle crashed, it could be an unprecedented disaster. From Vandenberg any such accidents would take place over the ocean.

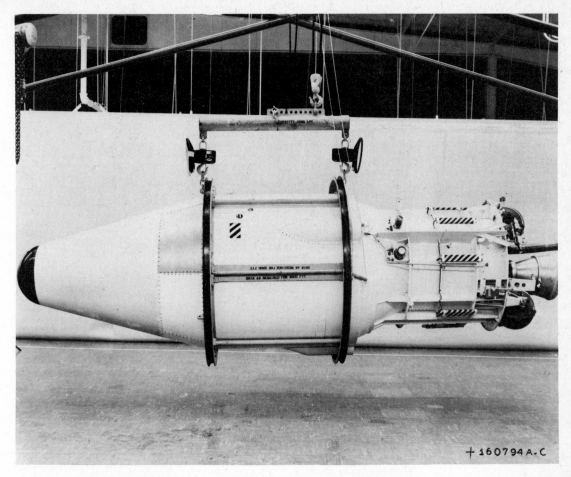

Discoverer spacecraft.

On January 21, 1959, a Thor/Agena sat on a launchpad at Vandenberg. The Agena stage was 19.2 feet tall and five feet in diameter. Fueled, it weighed 8,000 pounds; "dry" in space, it would weigh 1,300 pounds, including the 245-pound reentry capsule. A procedural error caused that first launch to be aborted; a second attempt, also on February 25, was also halted. Finally, on February 28, the third attempt, the first product of the Corona program was launched into a 96-degree highly elliptical orbit, (99-mile perigee, 605-mile apogee). Then, for some unknown reason, the satellite tumbled out of control in orbit, making it impossible to eject the capsule for recovery.

Today, satellites are launched almost daily, but in 1959 any launch at all was a major news event that was impossible to keep secret. For this reason the Corona program was given the somewhat heroic public name "Discoverer." Supposedly, it was a scientific

Discoverer 14 launch.

satellite program designed to benefit all mankind. Later, with the dramatic snatching of capsules from the air, Discoverer became a very popular program. Few suspected then that it was in fact a spy-satellite program, and if they did, they didn't tell anyone about it, for fear of tainting the innocent image of international, peaceful, scientific cooperation that was such a part of the space program in those days.

In April 1959, with Discoverer 1 useless in orbit, Discoverer 2 was sent up into a 90-degree, 152-mile perigee, 225-mile apogee orbit. Unlike its predecessor it was controlled from earth. In preparation for the most difficult part of the venture, the reentry of the capsule, the Agena spacecraft was rotated 180 degrees so that it was properly oriented for the ejection of the capsule. The gas jets were then used to tilt the Agena 60 degrees downward, so that after the capsule was separated from the Agena and its retrorocket was fired, the capsule would be driven down into the atmosphere. Everything was going according to plan, and the ground crew was understandably excited. Perhaps one person was just a little too excited, for the capsule was ejected prematurely. It was sighted coming down over the northern tip of Norway, but despite its brightly colored parachute it was never recovered, at least not by the United States.

Diagram of air-recovery technique.

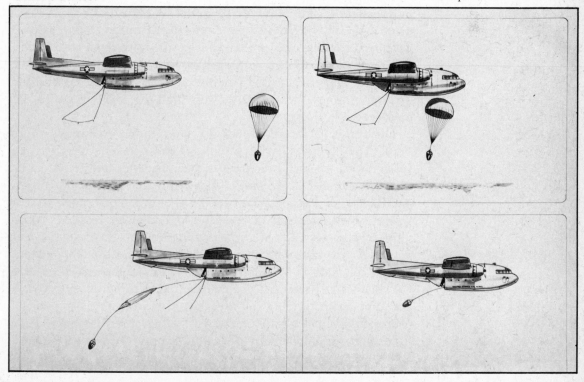

In May 1959 the Air Force outfitted Fairchild C-119 cargo transport planes with midair recovery equipment designed by the All-American Engineering Co. Flying out of Hickam Air Force Base in Hawaii, crews practiced their technique by snagging dummy capsules dropped from high-flying aircraft, and by June they were deemed at least moderately efficient at the task. Unfortunately, the Hickam recovery crews did not have a chance to test their skill on an actual reentering capsule for the rest of the year, as one launch after another proved to be a failure. Of the next eight Discoverers, four didn't even reach orbit, three ejected capsules that were never recovered, and one reached orbit only to tumble out of control just as Discoverer 1 had. To aid in the recovery procedure certain equipment, such as a stroboscopic light for sighting and tiny strands of foil to be ejected as chaff (easily picked up on radar), were added to Discoverer 11—all to no avail. Discoverer 11 was not spotted in the recovery area.

These were indeed faltering steps in America's race to seize the high ground. A year had passed since the tentative, limited successes of Discoverers 1 and 2. Perhaps, it was thought, recovery of a capsule from space would always be simply too difficult ever to be feasible. The designers went back to their drawing boards. The entire system was tested and checked by Arnold Engineering, an independent testing center in Tennessee. A certain amount of relief greeted their discoveries that the retrorocket in the reentry capsule developed troubles after prolonged exposure to the cold of space and that there was a problem with the parachute design. Heartened that they now knew where the troubles lay, the engineers made the necessary improvements. Hopes were high that there would finally be success.

Discoverer 12, launched June 29, 1960, didn't even make it into orbit. The unbroken string of failures had not gone unnoticed by Eisenhower, who had been promised an operable satellite system by the spring of 1959. He was furious with Allen Dulles and Bissell, and Bissell, in turn, was angry about the technology problems. "It was a most heartbreaking business," Bissell later recalled. "If an airplane goes on a test flight and something malfunctions, and it gets back, the pilot can tell you something about the malfunction, or you can look it over and find out. But in the case of a recce [reconnaissance] satellite, you fire the damn thing off, and you've got some telemetry, and you never get it back. There is no pilot, of course, and you've got no hardware. You never see it again. So you have to infer from telemetry what went wrong. Then you make a fix, and if it fails again, you know you've inferred wrong. In the case of Corona [Discoverer] it went on and on."

There was a suggestion that because of its unlucky number Discoverer 13 should be changed to Discoverer 14, but superstition was set aside, and on August 10, 1960, number 13 was launched into a 153-mile perigee, 375-mile apogee, 93-degree orbit. The Satellite Test Control Center at Sunnyvale, California, monitored the satellite and as it came over the North Pole on its seventeenth orbit, the order went out from Sunnyvale to the ground station in Kodiak, Alaska, to signal the capsule to eject.

Kodiak signaled for ejection. The capsule retrofired on schedule and reentered the atmosphere. It jettisoned its heat shield and deployed its parachute at roughly 50,000 feet. It was heading for the recovery area 300 miles northwest of Hawaii, and the recovery ships and C-119 airplanes maneuvered into position.

To catch the capsule in midair a C-119 was to fly just over the capsule's parachute, snagging the parachute lines with a trailing, trapezelike device so that the capsule could then be reeled in. The C-119s circled, waiting for the dropping prize. There was heavy cloud cover at 10,000 feet that day, though, and while some of the planes caught sight of the capsule as it dropped, they could not get to it before it hit the clouds and disappeared. But at least this time they had a good idea of where it would be floating in the water. It was spotted bobbing in the sea, and within a few hours a ship was alongside. Frogmen pulled the capsule out of the ocean, the first man-made object ever to be recovered from space.

Discoverer 13 capsule pulled from the sea.

Eisenhower boasted of Discoverer's success, saying it demonstrated that the United States "leads the world in the activities in the space field that promise real benefits to mankind." Not all agreed. In the bulletin put out by the USSR Academy of

Sciences there were laudatory remarks on the peaceful nature of the Soviet space program, but the United States was scorned for open "espionage." It seems the true intentions of the Discoverer program were apparent to more than just the few Americans in the know. For its part, the Air Force stated that Discoverer 13 had carried no sensor equipment, and one assumes that they were telling the truth.

Eight days later, on August 18, Discoverer 14 was launched from Vandenberg. It, too, orbited and ejected its capsule according to plan. At 7:53 A.M. Hawaiian time, the recovery team received the first strong signal from the descending capsule, indicating that it was heading into the recovery area. Captain Harold E. Mitchell was the commander of the C-119 closest to the dropping target. He made the first visual sighting of the capsule at 8:06 A.M. Even with its parachute deployed, the capsule was dropped at about 1,500 feet per minute, or 25 feet per second. Mitchell lined up his target and headed in.

The trailing trapeze missed its target by inches, almost touching the top of the parachute. He circled back and dropped to 10,000 feet for another pass. This time he was not quite so close, missing by several feet. Mitchell had only one more shot before the capsule hit the clouds at 7,000 feet and disappeared. He pulled around quickly, dipped to 8,500 feet, and sped back to meet the plummeting capsule. As he came in, it must have seemed like he was going to collide with it. Instead, the plane skimmed over the top of the parachute canopy, its trapeze neatly catching up the parachute lines and securing the capsule. Understandably jubilant, the crew reeled it in. Undoubtedly, there were cheers in Washington, too. Discoverer was substantially operational at last.

This time the Air Force issued no statement either way about whether or not Discoverer 14 had any sensor equipment aboard. It had already been three months since Gary Powers had been shot down, and the Iron Curtain had been drawn tight. There was a growing need for information, and while it is doubtful that Discoverer 14 had cameras aboard (because of weight limitations), it is likely that Discoverer 15 was so equipped. Unfortunately, it came down in rough seas outside the recovery area and was not recovered.

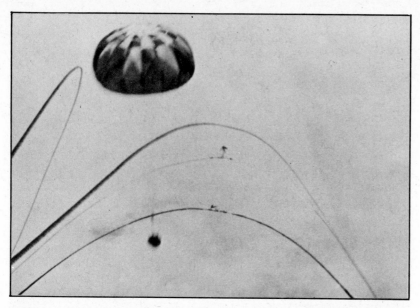

Sequence of photographs depicting the air-recovery of the Discoverer 14 capsule.

The trailing trapeze about to hit the parachute lines.

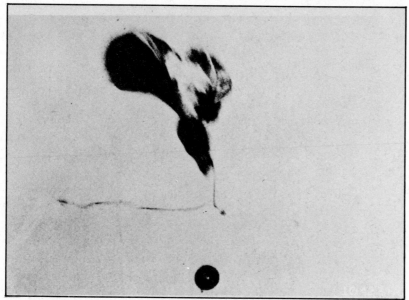

The lines are snagged.

Samos

In early September 1960 a new name was added to the list of designations in the reconnaissance satellite program. It was Samos—Satellite And Missile Observation System—and it was the only American spy satellite ever to be actually publicly identified as such. It was, in fact, just the new name given to the Air Force and CIA's WS 117-1/Pied Piper/Sentry film-scan/radio-transmission

The capsule is reeled in.

The capsule is brought aboard.

satellite, the program that had been slowed as Corona/Discoverer shot ahead. The camera and film scanner had been successfully tested aboard airplanes, and with some extra funding—inspired, perhaps, by Discoverer's successes—Samos was given a boost. Control of Samos was put in the hands of the National Reconnaissance Office, the top-secret agency that Eisenhower had created in late 1959 to supervise all spy-satellite activities.

The first launch of a Samos came on October 11, 1960. Following the trend of bad luck established by Discoverer, Samos 1 failed to achieve orbit. After several tests on the Atlas booster, Samos 2 was launched on January 31, 1961, and sailed up smartly into its desired orbit (295-mile perigee, 343-mile apogee, 95-degree inclination, 95-minute period).

If the camera on board that Samos had a lens with focal length of only 40 inches—such as the Perkin-Elmer—and film with a resolution of 100 lines per millimeter, then photographs taken from Samos 2 would have been able to resolve objects as small as 20 feet across on the ground. This resolution would have easily spotted huge, 100-foot-long ICBMs and their facilities—the most pressing reconnaissance mission at the time.

For all of its successes Discoverer was ultimately only a test program. Because of the short period in orbit and because of the weight restrictions that meant a big camera could not be taken up,

The Samos spacecraft.

Discoverer did not perform true reconnaissance. Samos, however, with its film-scan/ radio-transmission system had no complicated reentry phase that needed to be tested. As soon as a Samos reached orbit, it was operational, able to send back photos within hours of its launch. Discoverer 13 had been the first victory, but with Samos 2 America truly seized the high ground.

The cameras on Samos could photograph an area 50 by 50 miles (2,500 miles square), and as such only needed to take 4,000 photos to cover the entire Soviet Union, or only 1,000 to cover the areas presumed to be of strategic interest. During the time that Samos was operational it completed 500 orbits in less than a month. Then it was deactivated, perhaps because it ran out of film. Somewhere in that 500 orbits worth of film was the information that had been so long sought—the true level of Soviet ICBM strength. Estimates based on the U-2 photos had set the number at 120 missiles. The Samos photos cut this back to 60, and by September 1961, when the photo interpreters had more pictures to study, the estimate was decreased even more.

Work continued on Discoverer. Discoverers 16 and 17 were the first to use the larger Agena-B spacecraft (6 feet longer), which had been built to accommodate heavier payloads, and both missions were successful. Discoverer 18 was the first to use a Thor booster with improved thrust (10 percent more), which allowed for even heavier payloads. From launch through ejection and a midair recovery on the first pass, Discoverer 18 was a perfect mission. Discoverers 19 and 21 were Midas—(Missile Detection And Surveillance)—early-warning tests and did not require reentry of the capsule (more on Midas later).

Discoverers 20, 22, 23, and 24 were all failures for one reason or another, and insecurity returned to the missilemen. Suddenly the idea of tossing a capsule up into space and then catching it again did not seem so matter of fact as it had begun to appear.

Discoverer 25 was an ocean recovery but, nonetheless, a success. Of the next six Discoverers (26-31) only three were successes. Nor was Samos faring that well. The attempt to launch Samos 3 on September 9, 1961, ended abruptly when the Atlas/Agena rocket exploded on the launchpad.

All in all, though, in spite of so many failures, the few successes in the nascent spy-satellite program had brought back invaluable information.

Benefits and Consequences

After analyzing more satellite-acquired information in September 1961, the American estimate of the number of operational Soviet ICBMs was revised. In December 1959 it had been estimated that the Soviets would have 400 ICBMs by the middle of 1961. However, satellite photos taken during this time revealed that the Soviets didn't quite have 400 missiles—they had only 14. The United States already had three times that many Atlases. In addition, it had 80 submarine-based Polaris missiles, 600 SAC B-52 bombers, and even more B-47s. The missile gap was confirmed, but contrary to expectations, it was the United States that enjoyed the overwhelming superiority.

It was at this time, as the Berlin crisis heated up in the fall of 1961, that Kennedy revealed to Gromyko that the United States knew the true level of the Soviets' ICBM strength. The decision to show the Russians what America knew must have been a difficult one to make. Telling your enemies what you know about them—even worse, telling them how you know what you know—can render your intelligence sources obsolete. As soon as someone knows that they are being watched, that their phone is being tapped, or that there is a spy satellite overhead, then the key elements of candidness and surprise are lost and the information perhaps invalidated. Kennedy, however, had no choice. He had to let the Soviets know that he knew the true number of their missiles and he had to show them his proof.

Having apprised the Soviets of his country's satellite reconnaissance capabilities, Kennedy was in a delicate situation. He knew that if the matter were kept within diplomatic circles, the Soviets might just learn to live with spies overhead. Kennedy feared, however, that if spy satellites became a public issue, as the U-2 had become, then the Soviets, with their well-known obsession for privacy and keeping face, might move quickly to develop a means to bring down the offending satellites. Kennedy decided, therefore, to drop a blanket of complete secrecy over the satellite program in 1961.

After Samos 3 exploded on the launchpad, the entire Samos program ceased, officially, to exist. Discoverer, however, had been far too public an enterprise to end abruptly without arousing some suspicions, so it was phased out slowly. Of the final set of Discoverers (32-38) five made it into orbit, and four of those successfully ejected capsules, all of which were recovered. The last

Discoverer was launched on February 27, 1962. The final tally for America's first venture into space-based spying was 34 attempts, 26 satellites placed in orbit (23 of those with recoverable capsules), and 12 capsules recovered (8 from the air, 4 from the ocean).

While the early spy satellites played a crucial role in closing the missile gap and in defusing the Berlin crisis, it can also be said that to some extent they precipitated the Cuban Missile Crisis, for one of the reasons that the Soviets decided to put IRBMs and MRBMs (medium-range ballistic missiles) into Cuba was because they knew that the United States knew that they were behind in their intercontinental capability—something the early spy satellites had discovered. The counterargument, of course, is that without the information the satellites provided, the arms race at the time might have accelerated at an even more panicky, uncontrolled rate.

Another problem with the early spy satellite was the question of legality. Was a spy satellite like a U-2 violating a nation's airspace, or was it more like a ship at sea, watching a country from international waters? The United States naturally sided with the ship-at-sea analogy, but how would the Soviets—with their jealous guarding of privacy—respond?

According to one statement, it might have seemed, rather surprisingly, that the Soviets were somewhat indifferent to the reconnaissance satellites overhead. Eisenhower wrote in *Waging Peace: 1956-1961* that at the short-lived Paris Summit Conference of 1960, which disintegrated because of the U-2 fiasco, when de Gaulle questioned Khrushchev about satellites flying over France with cameras, "Khrushchev broke in to say he was talking about airplanes, not about satellites. He said any nation in the world who wanted to photograph the Soviet areas by satellite was completely free to do so."

But Kennedy knew that he could not take Khrushchev's offhand remarks as a statement of policy. In May 1962 he asked Secretary of State Dean Rusk to set up an interagency committee to review the political ramifications of reconnaissance satellites. The committee fully expected the Soviets to demand their prohibition, regardless of what Khrushchev had said in Paris.

On July 23, 1961, an editorial in *Red Star* (the Soviet Armed Forces newspaper) exclaimed that "A spy is a spy, no matter what height it flies." The Soviets' official demands for a ban on spy satellites came out during the negotiations for the peaceful uses of outer space. Yet an editorial in *Red Star* and a few quiet invectives over the bargaining table were hardly akin to the roar of indignation that swelled up around the U-2. The reason for such restraint on the

Soviets' part may have been that they were quietly working away on their own spy satellites.

The major corroboration of this came from Khrushchev himself. In July 1961 Belgian Foreign Minister Paul Henri Spaak reported to C.L. Sulzberger of *The New York Times* that Khrushchev had said that there was no need for on-site inspection of nuclear tests. "Anyhow," Khrushchev is reported to have said, "that function can now be assumed by satellites, Maybe I'll let you see my photographs." In May 1964, when Khrushchev was interviewed in Moscow by U.S. Senator William Benson, he asked that U-2 flights over Cuba be halted. Khrushchev said that satellites were more adequate and less provocative. "If you wish," said the Soviet premier, "I can show you photos of your military bases taken from outer space. I will show them to President Johnson, if he wishes." Then, joking, "Why don't we exchange such photos?"

In 1963, the Soviets stopped calling for an end to American satellite reconnaissance. They had developed their own spies in space. Thus, eight years after Eisenhower had first suggested it, a de facto Open Skies relationship between the two superpowers was in effect.

The struggle for the high ground continued, and the only way for the United States to maintain its advantage was to build bigger and better spy satellites.

The Next Generations

By the time the Soviets had their first spy satellites, in late 1963, the United States had a second generation of both their film-scan/radio-transmission and recoverable-capsule satellites ready to launch. From the moment Kennedy slapped down the secrecy order on satellite reconnaissance, the satellites were launched unidentified. By international agreement, however, the orbital characteristics of every object launched into space must be released to the United Nations, which lists them in a directory. Quite often, however, both the United States and the Soviet Union conveniently ignore this requirement. In such cases the orbital characteristics may be listed in the independent British Royal Aircraft Establishment's *Table of Earth Satellites*. Even though the satellites are not identified as such, if their orbital characteristics are listed, their spy satellite mission can be discerned.

The specific spy-satellite characteristics are low-perigee, near-polar orbit and a short life. As the names Discoverer and Samos faded into history, spy-satellite watchers named new generations of reconnaissance satellites after the type of mission they performed. As the Samoslike film-scan/radio-transmission satellites provided relatively low-resolution images and were best suited for broad search-and-find missions, they were known as area-survey satellites. The recoverable-capsule satellites, on the other hand, which orbited at lower altitudes and provided photographs of higher resolution, were known as close-look satellites.

Area-Survey Satellites

In 1962 the payload in area-survey satellites was refined and the weight reduced. This meant that the smaller Thor rocket, rather than the Atlas behemoth, could be used to boost the Agena into space. The second generation of area-survey satellites used a Thrust-Augmented Thor—a Thor with a cluster of three 50,000-pound-thrust rockets strapped on—and the new Agena-D spacecraft, which was distinguished by the ability to restart its engine in space so that it could boost itself back up when its orbit started to decay. The new Thrust-Augmented Thor/Agena-D combination could lift 2,000 pounds of usable payload into space, twice what the previous Thor/Agena could manage.

The first two launches of TAT/Agena-D area-survey satellites were failures, but in keeping with superstition, the third attempt, on May 18, 1963, was a success. Six more TAT/Agena-D area-survey launches were made that year, and through 1964 and 1965 an average of one per month blasted off from Vandenberg Air Force Base in California, each spending three to four weeks of active duty in space. They were usually launched between 1:00 and 3:00 P.M., so that when they passed over their targets in the Soviet Union, it would be just when the sun had passed its zenith, so that tall objects would cast slight shadows. The early fruits of these missions were the discoveries that the Soviets were building their own Polaris-type submarines and that they were digging underground silos to hide their SS-7 and SS-8 ICBMs.

To gain an understanding of how these film-scan/radio-transmission area-survey satellites work, one need only look at the equipment used in the five Lunar Orbiter satellites launched in 1966 and 1967. President Kennedy had assigned NASA the responsibility of all manned missions in 1962, giving the NRO the job of managing all unmanned "special projects"—i.e., spy satellites. NASA's main goal was to fulfill Kennedy's dream and to put a man on the Moon by the end of the decade. As such, they were in desperate need of information on the lunar surface so that they could select landing sites for the Apollo missions. They needed to put a craft in a lunar orbit that could radio back high resolution images of the Moon's surface. NASA turned for help to the NRO and, through them, to the CIA, which had built such equipment for their own uses. Willing to do their part to help America win the space race, the CIA agreed to help NASA by lending it some technology.

The system the CIA donated to NASA was the one designed for Samos, the first generation of area-survey satellite. The same contractors were used: Eastman Kodak (film and camera), CBS Laboratories (film scanner), and Philco Ford (signal processing and radio link). Each 850-pound Lunar Orbiter carried a 150-pound camera system. Two lenses were used; a 3-inch-focal-length lens for wide survey and a 24-inch lens for close looks. Like cameras in reconnaissance aircraft, those aboard the Orbiters had a motion-compensation system that moved the film past the camera's aperture at a speed corresponding to the angular velocity of the terrain below, so that the photographs would not be blurred. The CBS film scanner/converter used a fine white light 0.0002 inches in diameter (1/20th the diameter of a human hair) to scan back and forth over the developed film, converting the light and dark areas into separate signals that could be sent to Earth for translation back into photographs. Because of the limited power on board the Orbiters, and because of the 238,000 miles between the Moon and the Earth, it took forty minutes to transmit just one 70mm frame of film.

Despite the fairly small amount of film carried (to keep the overall weight to a minimum), it took only five Orbiter missions to photograph the entire surface of the Moon, from pole to pole, which roughly equals the entire landmass of the Soviet Union. From its orbital height of 28 miles above the Moon's surface, a Lunar Orbiter's 24-inch lens would photograph a 43-square-mile area, a 3-inch lens, a 400-square-mile area. From a 112-mile orbit above the Earth, a 24-inch lens would cover 700 square miles, a 3-inch lens, 7,000 square miles.

From 28 miles above the Moon's surface, the 24-inch lens, camera, and film could resolve objects as small as 3 feet across. The same lens in use above the Earth, therefore, would have a ground resolution of 12 feet. If a 40-inch lens were used—a conservative guess for the second generation of area-survey satellites—then

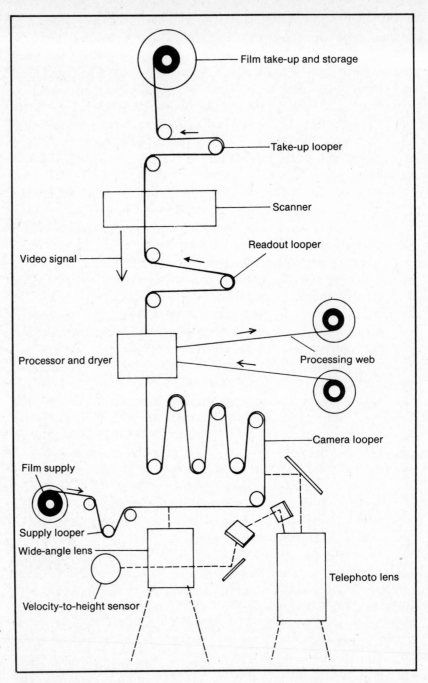

Film take-up and storage

Take-up looper

Scanner

Readout looper

Video signal

Processor and dryer

Processing web

Camera looper

Film supply

Supply looper

Wide-angle lens

Telephoto lens

Velocity-to-height sensor

Diagram of the film-scan/radio-transmission system used in the area-survey satellites.

anything larger than 7 feet across could be picked out. In the search for Soviet ICBMs 7-foot ground resolution would have revealed not only where launch facilities were, but whether or not missiles were in place, and what kind they were.

Such information from a spy satellite would be beamed down to one of the ground stations all around the globe within one hour of the pictures having been taken. The pictures, stored as blips on magnetic tape, would then be dispatched as quickly as possible to NPIC in Washington for interpretation.

Close Look

The second generation of close-look recoverable-film-pack satellites was first delivered to the Air Force in 1962, and was in use soon after. It is believed that these satellites employed several cameras, which fed film onto 36-inch-wide take-up reels in the new General Electric reentry capsule. This new capsule differed from the old ones in that it did not have its own retrorocket, but instead used the restart capability of the Agena-D to slow it down for reentry.

The close-look satellites were launched less frequently than the area-survey satellites—only four to ten per year from 1963 to 1965. Since they were heavier than the area-survey satellites, they had to use the heftier Atlas boosters to get them into orbit. As well, in order to obtain the highest resolution possible, their orbits were extremely low, so that they decayed faster—hence, the short mission life of only three to five days. They were launched just before noon so that the sun would be at its zenith when the satellites flew over their targets. Fewer launches were made during the winter, possibly because the harsh Soviet climate limited new construction at that time, with the result that there was little for the satellites to see.

In August 1963 the LG-77, a giant camera made by Hycon of California, was tested in a high-altitude balloon over the deserts of New Mexico. It took pictures with a frame size of 4.5 by 4.5 inches. Thus, if the film used had the then possible resolution of 200 lines per millimeter, from 100 miles in space the LG-77 would have been able to discern objects as small as 2 feet across. This camera did indeed weigh a monstrous 400 pounds, but the Atlas/Agena-D was capable of lofting 4,000 pounds into space. It is presumed that it was this Hycon LG-77, or a very similar model, that was sent up on the second-generation close-look missions.

While the consumers of satellite-generated intelligence were pleased with what the second generation of area-survey and close-look satellites were providing, they were by no means satisfied. Their appetites were whetted, and they wanted more. If they could spot something the size of a toolbox, they wanted to be able to pick out a tool. This quest for even greater specificity of information had a strategic beginning, for as the Soviets began to put their missiles in hardened silos, there was a perceived need for ever more precise targeting. If an attacking missile landed within 400 yards of a silo, it would have only an 80 percent chance of destroying the missile in the silo—farther out, the percentage dropped swiftly.

The Third Generation

The third generation of American spy satellites roared into space on July 29, 1966, on a mission to provide ever more precise targeting. The first of this generation to orbit was of the close-look variety. It went up atop a Titan 3B/Agena-D, which was able to orbit a 6,000-pound payload. These satellites had two recoverable film-pack capsules, which meant that they could carry more film into space, thus prolonging each mission. While the second-generation close looks could only orbit for three to five days, the third generation began at eight days and increased to fifteen or more by 1968. A key advantage here, of course, is that the longer a satellite can stay up, the fewer have to be launched.

These third-generation close looks orbited at a slightly higher altitude than their predecessors, again to prolong mission life. On these satellites extra care was taken to maintain a regulated temperature, since heating or cooling the film by only a few degrees could distort the photographs, making the prized targeting information drastically inaccurate.

A major new addition to the close-look configuration was a multispectral camera, built by Itek, that took photographs in six different light bandwidths. Multispectral photography operates on the principle that objects reflect light differently for different bandwidths of the spectrum. For example, on panchromatic film (all visible bandwidths) a new-mown lawn will appear the same as one that hasn't been cut for a week. If photographed in red light however, the new-mown grass will appear to be lighter in color than the uncut grass. The use of other bandwidths—yellow, green, blue, orange, etc.—will present other information.

The summer of 1966 saw the inauguration of the third generation of area-survey satellite. On August 9 of that year a Long-Tank-

Thrust-Augmented-Thor/Agena-D boosted a 2,600-pound intelligence payload—20 percent larger than the previous payloads—into space. The new area-survey satellite undoubtedly had higher resolution than its predecessor, and it could stay up longer, but the most important new feature of the satellite was the addition of an infrared (IR) sensing package.

Sensitive to light below the red end of the spectrum, IR photography not only picks up light that is just beyond being visible to us, it also registers thermal radiation, or heat. For this reason IR scanners can be used to make photographs of objects even in darkness, just from the heat they give off. These IR scanners are composed of an array of sensing elements, each one of which registers the intensity of the IR radiation striking it, much in the same way that each silver-halide grain in black-and-white film records the intensity of light striking it. The information that a scanner receives from all of its detector elements can then be combined to form a coherent photograph. Although the resolution of IR scanners in the 1960s was quite low, they did at least provide the first satellite view of Earth at night.

The slowest part of area-survey spy-satellite work was the transmission stage, when the photo information was beamed to Earth. This was revolutionized with the introduction of the SLGS—Space Link Ground System—which provided transmission of images at a far faster rate. As more pictures could be beamed down in the ten minutes that a satellite was within range of a ground station, the satellite's coverage could be increased. Another leap forward in data relay was made in 1967-1968, when communication satellites were first used to relay picture data from ground stations to Washington rather than having the tapes of data transported there by plane.

A Manned Mission?

While the CIA and Defense Department's secret satellites were being tossed up into space from Vandenberg Air Force Base, across the country another government project was also shooting capsules out of the atmosphere. This work, however, was far from secret. Whereas the payload in the tip of an Atlas/Agena-D launched from the sandy coast of California was a collection of cameras, the payload sent up from the swamp-encircled Cape Canaveral was often a human being.

For some time there had been thoughts of uniting the previously separate reconnaissance and manned space missions. When Dr. Wernher Von Braun wrote of using space as the high ground for observation, he thought of it as a manned mission. Sending a person into space is of course a far more complicated and costly venture than just sending up a collection of transistors and wires, which don't need to eat, breathe, or stay warm. Still, despite the cost and difficulty, the Pentagon and the CIA were still very much interested in flesh-and-blood spies in space.

It had been thought that the limit of resolution of the human eye from an orbital height of 100 miles would be about 200 feet, but tests indicated that visual acuity may improve in zero gravity. Astronauts in the Mercury program in 1963 said that they could easily spot large landmarks from space, and Gordon Cooper said that he actually saw individual streets and houses as he passed over Tibet. With this discovery a new thought arose: What if astronauts were equipped with binoculars and telescopes? Couldn't they be spies?

There are two crucial problems with unmanned reconnaissance satellites: They don't always get the information that one desires, and if they break down, they are 100 miles up in space and there is nothing that anyone can do about it. The idea of people up there, picking out targets and pointing equipment, and perhaps fixing anything that breaks—the idea of agents in orbit—was just too enticing to ignore. On January 23, 1965, the Pentagon announced that it had approved studies for a manned orbiting laboratory, or MOL (pronounced "mole").

On the Gemini 4 mission, launched June 3, 1965, the astronauts took up a simple Hasselblad camera equipped with a 3-inch lens. The pictures they took showed surprisingly good detail. On Gemini 5 three cameras, two with telephoto lenses, were used. A few of these pictures were released, and although they were intentionally blurred to disguise the camera's true resolving capability, they are quite remarkable. In one picture of Love Fiild, near Dallas, buildings and runways can be easily seen. That would have been enough resolution to spot missile sites and even some of the larger missiles themselves.

On August 25, 1965, the Soviet military newspaper *Red Star* accused the Gemini 5 astronauts of spying. That same day President Johnson gave the go-ahead for the development of MOL. It was to cost $1.5 billion to build and launch the first five MOLs. Each one was to weigh 25,000 pounds, with 5,000 pounds being devoted solely to reconnaissance systems and the rest to the structure and to life-support and subsidiary systems. Each MOL was to orbit for one month at a time, and each had a Gemini-type capsule attached for the crew's use in getting back to Earth. Later versions of MOL were to be designed to stay up much longer, and replacement crews would come up in Gemini capsules that the retiring crews then would use for the trip back home. The last crew to go up would come back to earth in the Gemini capsule built into the MOL.

Artist's conception of a MOL in space.

MOL was in trouble from the start. The CIA felt that it was theirs to control because, like the U-2, it was a manned spying mission. The Air Force argued that as a military mission in space it was theirs. President Johnson eventually decided that the CIA would have to share it with the USAF and other interested parties.

The biggest problem with MOL was the simple question of its utility. Washington journalist and author Philip Klass recalled a time when he and a few other military and space watchers in the capital were asked to help brainstorm possible uses for men in space. As the unmanned satellites were all working so well, about all they could come up with was maintenance, and while that was undeniably important, what had to be weighed was the incredible cost of launching a repairman into space.

It was eventually this cost that killed MOL. Within a year of Johnson's go-ahead MOL's size had ballooned to 30,000 pounds, and the date of the first launch had slipped back from 1968 to 1969 and then to 1970. All the while the projected costs kept rising, from $1.5 to $2.2 to $3 billion. The United States was at that time deeply involved in another very costly military venture—the war in Vietnam—and anything viewed as possibly extraneous was cut loose. President Nixon's Secretary of Defense, Melvin H. Laird, announced the cancellation of MOL in June 1969. By that time $1.62 billion had already been spent (by comparison, the entire cost of developing the first generation of spy satellites, from 1957 to 1960, was $1.5 billion).

When MOL was canceled, the military and intelligence communities took it with surprising quiescence. Usually, when a program is cut, there are outraged cries that the national security will be threatened. Not this time. One reason for their seeming indifference was that the third-generation area-survey and close-look satellites were performing splendidly. They also knew that the fourth-generation spy satellite on the drawing boards would be ready within two years, and when this "Big Bird" flew, there would be no need for flesh-and-blood spies in space.

Big Bird and Key Hole

Over the thirteen years area-survey spy satellites were in use, from Samos 1 to the last launch in 1972, they were remarkably successful—98 satellites placed in orbit out of 109 attempts, a 90-percent success rate. Close-look satellites, from the dissolution of the Discoverer program in 1962 onward, had also had a success rate of roughly 90 percent. The only thing better than having a successful reconnaissance program with coverage from both close-look and area-survey satellites would be to have both capabilities in one satellite—a satellite that could make both a general search of an area and could also zoom in on items of particular interest. That one satellite was Big Bird.

Top secret, the satellite was given the official designation Program 467 but was nicknamed Big Bird because of its enormous size (in the CIA it's known as the KH-9). With its protective launch shroud it was 50 feet long, and 10 feet wide,—almost as bulky as a railway freight car—and it weighed roughly 29,000 pounds. When it became operational, it was the largest military satellite in space. Built by Lockheed from a design based on the inimitable Agena, it rode into space atop a Martin Marietta Titan IIID booster. Together, on the Vandenberg launchpad, a Titan with a Big Bird on top towered over 17 stories.

In combining area-survey and close-look missions, Big Bird had both an Eastman Kodak-CBS Laboratories film-scan/radio-transmission package and a giant high-resolution Perkin-Elmer camera that fed film into one of four recoverable capsules. The film-scan information was transmitted to Earth over a 20-foot antenna, and the recoverable capsules, as they had been since Discover's day, were ejected into the atmosphere and then recovered from the air by C-130 transport planes flying out of Hickam AFB in Hawaii.

Along with these two main reconnaissance packages, Big Bird reportedly carried a high-resolution television camera with a zoom lens that could be operated and directed toward items of interest by observers on the ground, allowing for an even speedier area survey. Big Bird most likely also had multispectral and IR scanners aboard. It may also have been the first spy satellite to be equipped with synthetic aperture or side-looking radar (SLAR for Side Looking Airborne Radar), which can see through clouds and form images of the ground with a much higher resolution than regular radar.

The satellite was to be test-launched by the end of 1970, but development problems with the Perkin-Elmer camera delayed the inaugural liftoff until June 15, 1971. The first two launches were tests. Big Bird became operational on July 7, 1972, with its third launch.

Big Birds were sent up into 100-mile perigee, 170-mile apogee, 96-degree, 88-minute, sun-synchronous orbits. One remarkable feature of the Big Bird is that even at such a low orbit it could remain up for as long as six months because of its maneuverability; it was able to boost itself regularly back up into a higher orbit when the drag of the atmosphere began to slow it down. Its maneuverability also allowed it to pass repeatedly over one particular area day after day, instead of just shifting slowly over the globe, as it did when it was not maneuvered. The cost of such versatility was weight, since extra fuel had to be carried up in order for it to perform such stunts. At the end of a mission, when all the capsules had been ejected and the satellite had run out of film and fuel, the Big Bird was exploded in space rather than run the risk of having it survive reentry and crash somewhere in the world.

Big Birds were launched at a rate of roughly two a year from 1972 through 1976, then only one (or none) a year until 1983 when the program came to an end.

Artist's conception of an unidentified defense satellite of the early 1970s. Both the Big Bird and KH-11 satellites are of this size and general shape.

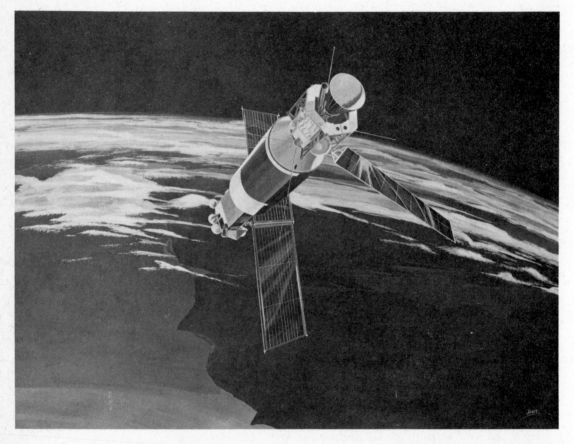

While Big Bird took over all the responsibilities of the area-survey satellites, the close-look program was not completely abandoned, with individual close satellites launched on missions that required an orbit lower than Big Bird could handle. Now reports indicate that there are not that many close-looks left in the inventory either. But when Big Bird expired at the end of 1983 and the close-look program for the most part wrapped up in 1984, how does America continue to spy from space? The answer: The fifth generation of spy satellite, given the inscrutable designation 1010 and the code name Key Hole, now most commonly known as the KH-11, is currently the main U.S. spy satellite.

The KH-11

On December 19, 1976, what was first thought to be a Big Bird was launched from Vandenberg AFB into a 153-mile perigee, 331-mile apogee orbit—unusually high for a Big Bird. Even more strangely, four days after launch this satellite was boosted still higher, only to be lowered again three months later. But the most striking thing about this supposed Big Bird was that it remained in orbit for two years; the longest any previous Big Bird had stayed up was a little over six months.

The first inkling of the true nature of this satellite was made public during the espionage trial of William P. Kampiles in 1978. His crime was selling a copy of a satellite's operation manual to the Soviet embassy in Athens for a paltry $3,000. Even though the manual was a critical piece of evidence, it was not made public during the trial. The satellite was identified only as the KH-11. This was the true identity of the Big Bird with the strange behavior—it was the operationa test of project 1010, the CIA's new spy in space.

The KH-11's weight and size have been estimated to be similar to those of Big Bird—roughly 28,000 pounds, 50 feet long, and 10 feet wide. A KH-11's apogee remains somewhat consistent throughout its life, while its perigee can vary from an initial height of 150 miles to a boosted height, after four days, of 175-210 miles. Other in-flight modifications of its orbit indicate that the KH-11 is at least as maneuverable as Big Bird.

The KH-11 differs from all its predecessors in satellite reconnaissance in one major respect: There is not one inch of film on board. The KH-11 takes pictures with a sensing system that converts light images into digital information, which it then beams to a ground station. Although there has been no publicly released information on how a KH-11 works, we can figure out what goes on inside one by examining a well known public cousin—the Landsat satellites—much as we looked at the Lunar Orbiter series in order to understand how the area-survey satellites worked.

How a KH-11 Works

The Landsat satellites (known first as ERTS—Earth Resources Technology Satellite) began orbiting in 1972. Using multispectral scanning techniques, a Landsat satellite surveys the Earth's surface, detecting drainage patterns, healthy and diseased crops, snowfall coverage, weather systems, soil aridity and arability, and mineral deposits, all from the specific spectral signature that each type of surface radiates. Again, no film is used; the pictures are taken digitally.

The Landsat satellite's telescope focuses light onto an optical plane that, if in an ordinary camera, would be covered with a sheet of film. In a digital imaging system the optical plane is an array of light-sensitive detectors, each one of which registers the level of intensity of light that strikes it. It works in a manner similar to the human eye. In our eye the focal plane is the retina. The retina, at the rear wall of the eye, is covered, almost like a carpet, with tiny detectors known as rods and cones. Each part of the image that falls on these detectors is given its own electrochemical value, and all of this input is fused together by the brain to form one coherent image. While humans see in color, both Landsat and KH-11 satellites see in black and white, or, to be more precise, in levels of gray. The computers that process this digital information fuse all the tiny dots of gray into one image, much as our brain fuses together the information from all the rods and cones.

Just as NASA's Lunar Orbiter cameras had lower resolution than their secret counterparts, so the Landsat satellites see with less acuity than the KH-11. Landsat 4, the most recent, has a gray scale of 256 gradations (compared to 64 levels in its predecessors), which means that each detector can register 256 different levels of light intensity. The KH-11 is sure to have an even finer, more highly graded gray scale, perhaps registering as many as 1,000 separate levels of gray. The KH-11's big advantages over Landsat lie not just in its gray scale, however, but in the size of its optical plane, the density of detector elements per square inch, and the power of its telescope.

To understand how the Landsat 4 optical system operates we can follow the path of light through it. An optical mirror positioned at the front of the telescope swings back and forth, scanning the surface of the Earth below. The mirror reflects an image through the optical magnification system of the telescope onto two focal planes. Each focal plane has a different arrangement of detector elements covering a different group of bandwidths. There are seven bandwidths covered, with four in the visible spectrum comprising one focal plane, and the three others, operating in various IR (Infrared) bandwidths, making up the other. Each bandwidth is provided with 16 detectors, each composed of thousands of light-sensitive elements, tuned to register light only in the specific bandwidth the detector has been assigned. The visible bandwidths monitored by Landsat 4 are, in microns (one millionth of a meter), 0.45-0.52—bluish on the spectrum; 0.52-0.60—green; 0.63-0.69—yellow; 0.76-0.90—red. In the shortwave IR, the bands are 1.55-1.75 and 1.80-2.25, and, in the longer wavelength IR region, elements detect in the 10.4-12.5 micron range. For reference, all the colors we can see in the rainbow fall into the 0.30-1.00 micron range.

Silicon chips are used as detector elements on the focal plane devoted to the visible light bands, while the detector elements for IR are made out of antimony because of that metal's special sensitivity to IR radiation.

Each light-sensitive element corresponds to one picture element, or pixel. A pixel is like one of the thousands of dots that make up a photograph printed in a newspaper, or one individual cell of light that, when combined with the thousands around it on a television screen, forms a TV picture. Each pixel, when struck by light, is assigned a numerical or digital value that represents the location of the pixel and the intensity of light—the level of gray—striking the light-sensitive element. These digits can be transmitted to a computer, which can assemble the pixel information and translate all the individual levels of gray back into an image.

Then the reconstructed image can be viewed on a TV screen, or it can be printed out in the form of a photograph. As it is difficult for the human eye to distinguish one finely divided level of gray from the next, the levels are assigned colors. This is why Landsat photographs are called "false color" pictures, for the hues assigned to the gray levels can be arbitrarily chosen and may not have anything to do with the color of a surface as a human eye would perceive it. Vegetation may come out red, snow blue, and water yellow.

Inside the KH-11

The question of resolution is always the bottom line when discussing satellite reconnaissance. Can they read license plates, newspaper headlines, spot a ball on a golfing green?

Landsat 1 satellites had a ground resolution of only 260 feet, although they could detect long objects as narrow as 30 feet if there was a sufficient contrast between the object and its background—a cleared black asphalt road running through snow-covered countryside. Landsat 4 has a ground resolution of 90 feet for most objects, 11 feet for long, narrow features. With such resolution Landsat 4 can pick out anything larger than a house—highways, airports, large airplanes on runways, and oceangoing ships.

The KH-11's ground resolution has been estimated to be as low as six inches. As a Landsat 4 scans an area 600 by 600 miles and has a ground resolution of 90 feet, this means that in each picture it takes there are approximately 45 million pixels (a TV screen has roughly a quarter of a million pixels). If a KH-11 were to take a picture of that scope, with its much higher resolution, it would have to have over 8 billion pixels. It is more likely, however, that instead of such a huge number of pixels and the enormous processing demands that such a number would entail, the KH-11 simply takes a more microscopic view of the world. For instance, 100 by 100 miles would require 1 billion pixels, 45 by 45 miles, 45 million pixels. In any case, the KH-11 is sure to have many more pixels per square inch than a Landsat 4, and this heightened density of light-sensitive elements is one of the advanced areas of technology that the spy satellite uses.

Another important technological breakthrough is the KH-11's telescope. While the first spy-satellite cameras had focal lengths of not more than 50 inches, the newest telescopes, with folding optics, may have a focal length of 240 inches, or 20 feet. Another reason for its high resolution is an advanced technology known as active optics, which can be used to negate the blurring effects caused by atmospheric distortion. The Itek active-optics equipment aboard the KH-11 essentially analyzes the distortion in front of the aperture and then guides the Perkin-Elmer mirrors in the telescope to adjust for it. Ultimately, this means that the resolution of an optics system is only limited by the size of its aperture. With a lens opening wide enough, a focal length long enough, a focal plane large enough, enough light-sensitive elements to fill it, and enough processing capability to handle the data, an optics system in space could have resolution limited only by the cost of putting it up in space.

It is likely that the KH-11, like the Landsat 4, has two separate focal planes, or one for visible light and another for IR radiation. The individual bandwidths in which it senses may be much more narrowly defined than those in the Landsat, with dozens of bandwidths covered on each focal plane, each one only a tenth of a micron wide. While the visible-light focal plane can only be used in daylight conditions, the IR plane can also be used at night to detect the thermal radiation of objects. If, for example, the Soviets were to try to hide a new missile-launching site by constructing it only at night, the KH-11's IR sensors would pick up the thermal radiation of trucks, jackhammers, perhaps even individual men as it flew over at night. However, even IR sensors cannot see through clouds. Radar is useful under these conditions, since it is unaffected by water vapor—which is what clouds are made of.

Radar operates by beaming out tiny microwave pulses that travel out to an object, bounce off it, and return to the radar antenna. In the early radar systems developed before and during World War II, little more than the distance and general location of the object could be determined from the returning pulses. Now, however, the most sophisticated radar can provide information on the shape, size, and contour of an object and can even be used to form pictures. Of course, to obtain high-resolution pictures, the radar device must emit a high number of pulses per second and have a large antenna. The high number of pulses can be produced in space, but the antenna would have to be too big—several miles long. Fortunately, there is a way to get around building such a prohibitively large antenna: One must fool the radar.

It was found that if a radar system was pointed out the side of a moving airplane, the returning pulses could be processed as if the antenna were as long as the distance between the point the radar pulse was released and the point at which it returned. This is synthetic aperture, or side-looking radar (SLAR), and the first work on it was performed in the early 1950s. SLAR was first used in space in 1978 aboard the Navy's Seasat satellite. It released 2,000 pulses per second and from an altitude of 500 miles produced radar images with a ground resolution of 80 feet. At that height and with that resolution, a normal radar antenna would have to be roughhy 4.3 miles long. The antenna on Seasat was only 33 feet long.

One goal of spy-satellite observation is to achieve "real-time" capability—the ability to see what the satellite sees as it sees it. With Discoverer and the other reconnaissance satellites with recoverable capsules, weeks might pass before a picture taken by a satellite was returned to Earth and analyzed. Even with Samos and the other radio-transmission satellites, days might elapse before a photograph taken in space ended up on the light tables at NPIC. One obstacle to real-time analysis is the length of time that it takes to transmit information from space to Earth. A way around this obstacle is to do as much information processing in space as possible, so that the data transmitted are more refined and will take up less transmission time. This is one of the applications of the DoD's support of VHSIC (Very High Speed Integrated Circuit) research. A VHSIC microprocessor on board a satellite could process the information from the sensors almost instantaneously and transmit it to Earth so that a photo interpreter could receive an image almost immediately. The next generation of KH-11s will have this capability.

It is unlikely that there will ever be real-time radar images from space. Because each pixel in a radar image needs 3,000 pulses per second to provide it with the required information about what it is seeing, billions and billions of operations would have to be carried out each second for the images to be seen. The amount of energy required to perform such a feat would be next to impossible to provide in space with existing technology, and the bottleneck that would develop before the transmission phase would bring such an operation to a halt. Thus, for the foreseeable future, imaging radar information will continue to be transmitted to Earth unprocessed. While there is then something of a wait for the radar images, it seems to be worth it. Seasat and space-shuttle tests of SLAR have revealed its ability to see, not only through clouds, but down several fathoms into the ocean and up to 30 feet through sand. SLAR can also be used to create exceptional 3-D images.

What Can the KH-11 Really See?

While one may speak of 6-inch ground resolution or the ability of a satellite to pick out a golf ball from 100 miles, there is, unfortunately, no official indication of just exactly what the satellites can and cannot see. The various statements about their purported prowess makes the situation all the more confusing.

In the February 6, 1978 issue of *Newsweek*, CIA Director Stansfield Turner was reported to have told White House aides that the quality of American satellite photos was such that one could tell a Guernsey cow from a Hereford. There is also the perhaps apocryphal tale of the KH-11's role in plotting the tragically abortive attempt to rescue the American hostages in Iran. The story is that the KH-11 was used to plot the route into the occupied embassy, and in some of the pictures the resolution is so good that a PI can tell one mullah from another. According to other rumors, satellites can tell whether a cat crossing the road is male or female, and there are satellite photos that indicate there are still American prisoners being held in Southeast Asia. Perhaps the most popular tales—the ones most often quoted in the press—are that satellites can tell which side of a 50-cent piece is facing up when the coin is lying on the ground, that there is a satellite photo of a man on a street in Siberia holding a newspaper and that one can make out the name *Pravda* on it, and that satellites can read license plates.

What some of these claims, true or not, have in common is that they say little about the satellites' resolving power. In many instances they say more about advances in photogrammetry, the science of determining the dimensions of objects in photographs.

Because a Guernsey and a Hereford have different overall coloring, and because one is generally larger than the other, a KH-11 could tell the difference between them with no better than a 1-foot ground resolution. Similarly, it has been said that the KH-11 could tell one mullah from another by the size of their beards. And while the claim of satellite's being able to determine the sex of a cat may suggest that they can take a quick peek at the animal's behind, it has been suggested that a male cat can be told from a female cat by the size of its head. In the same vein, the presence of American prisoners in Southeast Asia is said to have been indicated by the length of the shadows cast by workers in a field, as North Americans are on average taller than Asians.

It is highly doubtful that the resolution of satellite photography is high enough for one to read the logotype on a newspaper or to tell which side of a coin is faceup on the ground. Perhaps such information could be detected with multispectral scanning. It is possible that one side of a coin, because of its design, has a slightly different spectral signature than the other side, or that *Pravda*, with its own specific layout, design, and ratio between black ink and white page, registers its own specific level on the gray scale. As for license plates—in the words of Victor Marchetti, former executive assistant to the deputy director of the CIA, such claims are "pure unadulterated bullshit."

Beside the fact that license plates are mounted vertically, which would make them very hard to read from space, even if one were laid out flat on the ground, the resolution of a spy satellite would not be good enough to read it. A ground resolution of 2 inches does not mean that one can read letters 2 inches tall but, rather, that an object 2 inches wide can be distinguished from its background. A ground resolution of 15 feet would not be enough to indicate whether a car was a Ford or a Chrysler, but just that there was an object the size of a car.

According to Dino Brugioni, former photo interpreter at NPIC, when these rumors start up, no one moves to correct them because in doing so they might reveal the satellites' true capabilities. Victor Marchetti thinks there is another reason for why the intelligence community doesn't quash such speculation. "They have a tendency to try to make themselves look good. They want people to think they can do these incredible things. It gives them more support. In clandestine affairs they like to be able to say, 'We've got a man in the Kremlin with his hand on the premier's more sensitive anatomical area.' The same is true for satellite reconnaissance. If the public is led to believe that they can read license plates from outer space, then that is just fine with them."

How high, then, is the resolution of spy-satellite pictures? A reliable source who has seen one says that he was able to clearly read the identification numbers on the wings of an airplane on a Soviet airstrip. This prompts a question: For all practical purposes, how high does the resolution have to be?

To monitor compliance with a missile treaty, resolution no better than that needed to read the identification numbers on a plane's wing—a resolution of about a foot—would be needed. With atmospheric compensation systems, resolution may get down to the millimeter level, but with other systems such as infrared and side-looking radar able to provide other types of information, such high resolution may not really be necessary.

Further Advances

While the KH-11 may be America's premier spy in space, it is not the satellite of choice on all missions. When the United States discovered in June 1983 that the Soviets were constructing a new radar base near Abalakova in south-central Siberia, they did not send the KH-11 over to get pictures. Instead, they sent up a KH-5, one of the last few close-look satellites in the inventory, to get photographs of the highest resolution possible. If, then, the KH-11 is not called upon when it comes to a need for the highest resolution, and, if the inventory of close-look satellites is depleted, what will the United States do when images of very high resolution are required?

The answer: yet another generation, the sixth, of spy satellite. This new spy sat will have digital sensing equipment that is supposed to provide images that will match, if not surpass, the resolution provided by film satellites. The new KH-11 will at first be launched atop a Titan IIID booster, and later by the space shuttle when the DoD's shuttle facilities at Vandenberg AFB are complete.

One attraction of shuttle-launching a KH-11 is that if the satellite fails, a new one can be taken up into space to replace it, and the defective one retrieved and taken back to Earth for repairs. A costly complication is that the new KH-11's weight has ballooned to 32,000 pounds, 4,000 pounds heavier than its predecessor and more than the shuttle is designed to carry. To solve this problem an extra booster, an Aerojet LR-87 module, is to be added to the shuttle for these launches.

In an interview in the September 1983 issue of *Omni*, Secretary of Defense Caspar Weinberger, said, "I can't go into details about surveillance satellites, but we are looking for greater accuracy and what the technical people call specificity. The products will be more useful, I am told."

Specificity is essentially the ability to get just what's needed from the satellite and nothing more. As Marchetti has said, "More and more collection does not necessarily increase the quality of your information. Photographs of an installation taken every minute are probably worth no more than a photograph taken every week. But there is that temptation—'We can get a picture every minute!'—that appeals to the moneyspenders in the Pentagon. It's so dazzling, it's hard to resist. We have to be careful. There is a tendency to collect more and more of the same information, and it becomes superfluous." To Marchetti, an increase in specificity is a move in the right direction—improving the quality of the coverage, not the quantity.

One quality that will be improved is the KH-11's ability to provide information in close to real time..As mentioned before, an obstacle to getting real-time images is the amount of time it takes to transmit the information from each pixel to Earth. A partial solution is to employ on-board processing, which can section off blocks of pixels that register the same level of gray, then transmit the blocks as if they were single pixels. Also, if the satellite were to store in its memory a record of the pictures it took of an area, when it passed over that area again, it could compare the new pictures with the old and then transmit to Earth only information on the pixels that showed a change.

The new KH-11 is at this point the most sophisticated remote-imaging satellite. It will completely replace and render obsolete the last of the remaining spy satellites that use film. And how does the intelligence community feel about its mechanical spies in space? A technical collection expert at the CIA remarked to Victor Marchetti in the fall of 1983, "It's unbelievable. You'd be just delighted."

Other Military Satellites

The KH-11 is not alone in space. Along with the hundreds of civilian and Soviet satellites in orbit there are other American military satellites up there as well. Some of these satellites are sunk in secrecy as murky as, or murkier than, that which surrounds the KH-11. Some are watchdogs; some are simply military communications and weather satellites; others are nothing less than electronic eavesdroppers in space. These satellites were spawned in response to many of the same concerns that prompted the spy-satellite program, and so their story begins about the same time Corona/Discoverer and Samos began to take shape.

Early Warning

The string of lonely outposts across the arctic wastes of Alaska and the Canadian north are another reminder of the post-Pearl-Harbor fear of surprise attack. The DEW line of radar stations, built by the United States and Canada in the early 1950s, was designed to provide advance warning of a Soviet bomber attack over the North Pole—the shortest route from Russia to America. In 1953, as the DEW line of defense was being erected, it was estimated that it would provide four hours' warning and that, when coordinated by computer with F-102 fighter/interceptor squadrons, the barrier across the north would be impenetrable.

However, in Moscow on May 1, 1954, the Soviets unveiled their new M-4, 600-m.p.h. swept-wing bomber. Suddenly, before the DEW line was even finished, its warning margin was cut to two hours. This was a serious but not devastating development, as even two hours would be enough time to mobilize air defenses and intercept an attack before it reached the populated areas of Canada and the United States.

Less than a year after the DEW line became operational, however, the U.S. radar station and electronic listening post in Diyarbakir, Turkey, picked up some disturbing information: The Soviet rocket test telemetry they intercepted indicated the Russians' missile development was progressing much faster than had been expected.

By late 1956 the Soviets had already begun testing long-range missiles, and in the summer of 1957 they announced the first successful test of an ICBM. The introduction of missiles into the equation of surprise nuclear attack didn't merely cut further into the DEW line's warning time—it effectively rendered the entire string of frozen outposts obsolete, since the DEW radar equipment was incapable of picking up missiles hurtling down from space at over 5,000 miles per hour.

Obviously, another alarm system was needed to replace DEW, and so in 1958 the go-ahead was given to build two massive radar stations—one in Thule, Greenland, and the other in Alaska. This Ballistic Missile Early Warning System (BMEWS) cost $800 million and provided only 15 minutes' warning of a missile attack. With the new Minuteman missiles, though, that would be enough time to launch a retaliatory strike before a surprise attack obliterated American missile sites.

But 15 minutes might not be enough time to confirm that the attack was a real one, and the U.S. President would be put in the horrifying position of having to decide whether or not to launch what might turn out to be unprovoked nuclear war. And so work began on another system that would give 30 minutes' warning; combined with the BMEWS' 15-minute alarm, this would provide confirmation of attack. The new 30-minute warning system was not to use radar technology, nor was it to be ground-based—it would be a satellite.

Midas

The Midas (Missile Detection And Surveillance) project was included along with Discoverer and Samos in a contract awarded to Lockheed in the summer of 1958. Lockheed contracted to build a satellite with a thermal infrared detecting array that could pick up a massive missile launch by spotting the intense heat of the burning gases emitted during the burn phase of the launch. There were to be eight to twelve such satellites in 2,300-mile orbits, so that at least one would be over the Soviet Union at all times.

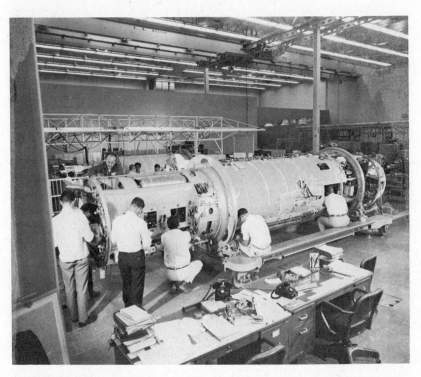

A Midas spacecraft being constructed.

The first Midas, launched February 26, 1960, exploded before it reached orbit. Midas 2, launched soon after, did make it into space, however, and its IR detectors tested well for two days before the craft developed an unknown malfunction. Further tests of Midas early-warning technology were carried out successfully aboard Discoverers 19 and 21.

At this point Midas seemed to be progressing well, and the USAF pressed for an acceleration of the program. With the optimism for Midas apparently running high, it came as something of a surprise when the new Kennedy administration's Secretary of Defense, Robert McNamara, said before a congressional hearing, "There are a number of highly technical, highly complex problems associated with this system. The problems have not been solved, and we are not prepared to state when, if ever, it will be operational."

What went wrong? McNamara was not referring to the explosion of Midas 1 or the unexplained malfunction of Midas 2, for those types of problems come with putting anything into space and are expected. What disturbed McNamara and others were the flaws found at what was really the center of the whole program—Midas's IR detection system. It appeared, among other things, that the Midas detectors could mistake sunlight reflecting off high-altitude clouds for a missile attack.

Although there was a Midas 3 (July 12, 1961) and a Midas 4 (October 12, 1961), after which the operational launch segment of the Midas program was severely curtailed, as of 1966 there were only four more test launches of early-warning satellites, and only two of those reached orbit. Although the launches were cut back, work continued in the research of IR detection technology.

A step forward in the development of early-warning satellites came when it was discovered that a virtually foolproof device for detecting missile launches was the human eye. Astronauts in Gemini 5 spotted the test firing of a rocket sled in New Mexico and a Minuteman launched from Vandenberg, while Gemini 7 astronauts found they could detect submarine-launched Polaris missiles as well. More important than the human eye was the human brain, which could distinguish between the flare of a rocket's plume and light reflecting off clouds. Although this was used as an argument for the construction of the Manned Orbiting Laboratory, it was reasoned that instead of putting a man in orbit, it would be more efficient and just as effective to put up a TV camera with a high-power lens along with an IR detection system. Thus, ground observers could double-check any IR warnings. In 1966 there were three launches to test the new TV camera and the new, designed to be more trustworthy, IR technology.

While Midas satellites were originally to orbit at 2,300 miles, with this new generation of early-warning satellites the geosynchronous orbit was to be used. However, unlike the geosynchronous communications satellite, which stays fixed over one spot on the equator, an early-warning satellite would be launched into an orbit with a slight inclination—no more than 10 degrees—which would cause it to trace a figure eight over the equator. This would be a necessary aberration, since much of the Soviet Union would be out of the line of sight of a satellite that remained over the equator. With a 10-degree inclination, however, half of the time the satellite would be above the equator, with a better view of the higher Soviet latitudes. The satellites would have to be launched in pairs in complementary 10-degree orbits, so that while one was below the equator, one would be above it.

Defense Support Program

Program 949 was the designation given the testing phase of these new geosynchronous early-warning satellites. The improved IR technology, which would no longer mistake sunlight reflecting off clouds for attacking missiles, was sent into geosynchronous orbit by an Atlas/Agena D rocket. The first of the four Program 949 satellites was launched from Cape Canaveral on August 6, 1968. It was later joined by a second satellite that complemented its 9.9-degree orbit, so that at all times there was one satellite with a view of all of Russia. The third 949 satellite failed to make orbit, while the fourth was launched September 1, 1970, into position over Singapore.

At that point the new early-warning satellite program was deemed operational. It was given a new designation, Program 647, and name, Defense Support Program. As seemed to be the rule with most military satellite efforts, the first launch, on November 6, 1970, was a failure. There was a malfunction in the booster, and the satellite did not reach the desired orbit. On May 5, 1971, the first operational DSP satellite was set in place, 22,300 miles above the Indian Ocean. A year later another DSP satellite was put into place, this time over Panama.

A DSP satellite is composed of an electronics, power, and control module and a Schmidt infrared telescope. The module is a cylinder 9.5 feet long and 9 feet in diameter. The outer wall of the module is covered with 204 square feet of solar cells, which, combined with four 15-square-foot hinged solar panels, provides the satellite's power. The entire satellite rotates five to seven times a minute on its long axis, which points toward Earth. Closest to Earth is the 12-foot-long Schmidt telescope, which is angled out from the axis of the satellite 7.5 degrees. This, combined with the spin of the satellite, means that the telescope traces a circular ground track on the Earth, covering more ground than if it were just to stare at one small spot.

The Schmidt telescope is kept aligned by a 400-pound inertial-momentum wheel. The telescope uses a system of mirrors to focus the light that enters its 3-foot-wide aperture onto a detector array containing 2,000 detectors. The telescope is filtered to admit light at 2.5 microns—in the near infrared area of the spectrum, which is where the emissions of rocket plumes peak. While each detector covers a 1.5-square-mile area on the Earth, that resolution is sufficient for its purposes.

One big difference between the IR detection system of the DSP satellite and that of the Midas a decade before is that the Schmidt

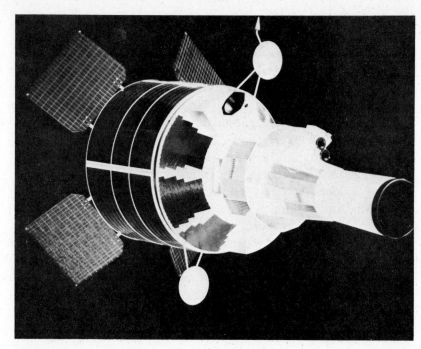

Model of a DSP early warning satellite.

telescope takes a reading of an individual area every eight to twelve seconds. If it picks up a hot object, it can determine if it is stationary—such as light off clouds, a forest fire, or a blast furnace—or moving. A moving, burning missile will move from detector to detector in the telescope. This movement from detector to detector will also give an indication of where the missile will land, for by knowing the missile's azimuth (heading) and how long it was under thrust, it can be guessed with relative accuracy where it will come down. One thing the DSP satellites are unable to do is track a missile after burnout, for then it is too cool to register on the detector array inside the Schmidt telescope. A DSP satellite can pick up a launch within 60 seconds of blast-off and can relay the message to Earth within 90 seconds. Radar stations can then search for the missile and give accurate target data—when and where the missile will strike—within six minutes.

The full DDP system consists of pairs of satellites in three positions: over the Indian Ocean to detect Soviet and Chinese missile tests and launches, over the Pacific Ocean, and over South America, the latter two to detect SLBMs (submarine launched ballistic missiles).

There are three areas in early-warning satellite technology that are under improvement. The first is information processing and handling. The DoD would like to have simple, mobile ground stations, in order to reduce the reliance on the existing fixed—and therefore vulnerable—ground stations at Buckley Field in Colorado, and Pine Gap, Australia. Second, American officials are concerned with the vulnerability of early warning satellites to blinding by lasers as the satellites' sensitive IR detectors can be destroyed by bright light. One protection method developed by Martin Marietta is a laser light detector which, when triggered, instantly activates quick shutting doors which snap shut over the aperture to protect the IR sensors (of course, the satellite would nevertheless be rendered inoperative for as long as the laser was fixed on it).

The final area of improvement desired in DSP technology is in the area of midcourse tracking—the ability to follow the missile throughout its entire trajectory, not just during its burn. Accomplishing this goal will require highly advanced computer and detector technology which will be discussed further at the end of this chapter. As we will see then, advances in early-warning satellite systems are vital to American military and intelligence plans for the next 20 years.

Nuclear Detection

One way to control the proliferation of nuclear weapons is to ban their testing. In the 1950s, while the United States was confident that atmospheric tests could be detected through a combination of seismographic and airborne radiation sensors, there were fears that the Soviets might take their bombs into outer space, perhaps behind the Moon, where they could conduct tests with impunity. In the fall of 1959, the Pentagon initiated a program to study the means available for policing a test ban in space. In December 1961 TRW received the contract to build the spacecraft. Assigned to construct the X-ray, gamma, and neutron radiation detectors that could detect a nuclear explosion in space were the Atomic Energy Commission's Los Alamos Laboratory and Western Electric's Sandia Corporation. On October 16, 1963, less than three months after the signing of the Nuclear Test Ban Treaty, the first pair of these Vela (Spanish for "watchman") satellites were launched.

The Vela satellites, each weighing only 300 pounds, orbited at the exceptionally high altitude of 60,000 miles (one quarter of the way to the Moon) and were positioned one on each side of the Earth for complete coverage of space. It was determined by what they

A Vela nuclear detection satellite.

detected of natural phenomena such as solar flares and cosmic ray radiation that the Velas would be able to detect a nuclear detonation as far away as Venus. During its period of operation the Vela program underwent two major changes. In 1965, after China exploded its first nuclear weapon, it was decided that the Vela should be capable of detecting explosions in the atmosphere as well as in distant space. The first pair of these new 500-pound Velas (also built by TRW) with this added capability were launched into 70,000 mile orbits on April 28, 1967. The second major development with Vela began on May 23, 1969, for from that launch on, Velas began to carry instrumentation to detect

EMP—ElectroMagnetic Pulse (the wave from a nuclear explosion that can erase computer memories and disrupt electrical equipment).

Early in 1970, the Pentagon announced that Velas 11 and 12 would be the last of the series of nuclear-detection satellites. It seemed strange that perhaps the most unquestionably successful of American military satellite programs (the Test Ban Treaty was never violated in outer space) was to be terminated. As is customary in the DoD, however, while the Vela name may have disappeared, the program was simply continued in a slightly altered form. It had been decided that as the Vela instrumentation was comparatively light, it could be included in the DSP early-warning satellites. Although the Defense Support Program (DSP) satellites orbit at a much lower altitude than the Velas, because there were many more DSPs, the same coverage could be maintained.

On September 22, 1979, nuclear-detection equipment aboard 647 satellites caught two bright flashes over Antarctica. The State Department issued a statement saying that the flashes were an "indication" of a low-yield, 2-kiloton, clandestine nuclear test and accused South Africa of the deed. Radiation tests of the area proved negative, however, and Prime Minister Botha denied the allegation, saying that the United States should get its facts straight. As yet there has been no completely satisfactory explanation of the incident, although it has been suggested that a small meteoroid may have hit the satellite, momentarily disrupting its sensors. Because of this, satellites are now equipped with impact sensors that indicate when a satellite has been struck.

Those in the DoD who plan for the contingencies of nuclear war would like to see one further improvement made in nuclear detection capability. They want IONDS—the Integrated Operational Nuclear Detection System. IONDS will tell them the exact location of a nuclear detonation, so that after the first exchange in a nuclear war, the survivors will know where to send the second barrage, so that the remaining bombs are not wasted on targets that no longer exist. It is ironic that technology originally designed to prevent nuclear proliferation is now being included in plans for nuclear war.

ELINT Satellites

While the U.S. intelligence community has been somewhat secretive about its photoreconnaissance satellite program, there is

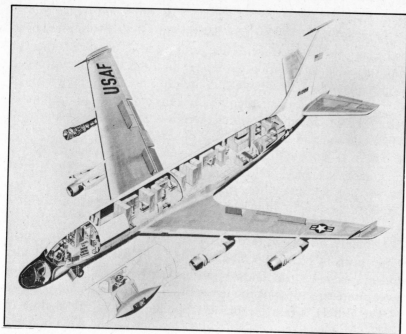

Artist's rendering of an EC-135 ELINT surveillance aircraft.

another type of satellite about which it is even more closemouthed—the ferret/ELINT. The ferret satellite is used to gather ELINT—ELectronic INTelligence—by monitoring Soviet and Chinese air and missile-defense radar systems, missile and satellite telemetry, and radio and microwave transmissions.

For the most part ELINT gathering is carried out aboard airplanes such as the EC-135. These planes fly along the Soviet and Chinese borders, occasionally violating their airspace in order to trigger defense systems, so that they can catalog the operating frequencies of the radar as well as find out how fast the antennas rotate, the rapidity of the "pulse rate," and the length of each pulse. In time of war invading bombers would use this information to program their ECM (Electronic CounterMeasures) equipment to jam or to fool the radar. (The radar stations of course have ECCM—Electronic CounterCounterMeasures—which the bombers would also have to contend with.) The role of the ferret, then, is to gather information that can be used to plot a route into a country. However, as there are likely to be radar stations far behind a country's borders, far beyond the reach of the short border sorties of an EC-135, ferret/ELINT satellites are needed to provide the full picture.

The first launch of a ferret/ELINT satellite took place on May 15, 1962; in the ensuing nine years 16 more were put in orbit. They were all sent into roughly circular, 300-mile, near-polar orbits, with 94- to 95-minute periods. Starting in 1965 the satellites began to be launched in pairs, with one orbiting lower than the other for more detailed information gathering. In 1963 the program began using subsatellites. A subsatellite, usually quite small, piggybacks a ride into space aboard a larger satellite. In comparison to the regular ferret/ELINT satellites, which weigh 2,000-4,000 pounds, a subsatellite may weigh only a few hundred pounds.

The first subsatellite was carried into space by an area-survey photoreconnaissance satellite on August 29, 1963. By 1971 a total of seventeen subsatellites had been ejected from area-survey satellites, and eight from close-look satellites. These subsatellites were used in a general survey capacity, monitoring and cataloging Soviet and Chinese radio and radar signals, while the heavier main ferret/ELINTs picked up more detailed information, such as radar pulse rate and length. The orbital characteristics of the subsatellites were similar to those of the ferret/ELINTs.

The ELINT satellite program appeared to come to a close in 1971. Although some subsatellites continued to be put up, there seemed to be no more new larger ferrets being put into the characteristic 300-mile ELINT orbit. On March 6, 1973, at Cape Canaveral, an Atlas/Agena-D launched a payload into geosynchronous orbit. As it was unidentified, hence military, it was assumed to be an early-warning satellite. By 1973, however, early-warning satellites were no longer using the Atlas as a booster. Also, an early-warning orbit is usually inclined 10 degrees and is not circular, while the orbit of this satellite was very nearly circular.

Four years later, on May 3, 1977, there was another such mystery satellite launched; another on December 11 of that year; yet another on April 18, 1978. No details of their orbits were released.

It was a spy trial that first told the public of the KH-11 (Kampiles, prosecuted for selling the satellite's manual to the Soviets in 1978), and it was a spy trial that answered the question of what these satellites really were. In April 1977 Christopher Boyce and Andrew Daunton Lee went on trial for selling spy-satellite secrets to the Soviets. It was eventually revealed in the trial that the secrets they sold concerned the Rhyolite series of satellite built by TRW, where Boyce worked. These were the mystery satellites, and they were the latest generation of the ferret/ELINTs.

There are still four of these 600-pound Rhyolites in orbit, and their primary duty is to monitor Soviet missile tests. One pair is stationed over the Horn of Africa to monitor the solid-fuel rockets launched from Plesetsk, north of Moscow, and any SLBMs that might shoot up from the White Sea. The second pair of Rhyolites is farther east, over the Indian Ocean, where they can monitor three things: the liquid fueled rockets launched from Tyuratam, the ABM test center at Sary Shagan by Lake Balkash, and test warhead impacts on the Kamchatka Peninsula. Of each pair of satellites, one is operational and the other is a spare, ready to kick in if the other fails.

Although some orbital data can be gleaned from the U.N. registry and the Royal Aircraft Establishment's Table of Earth Satellites, the information can often be misleading and contradictory. And, as satellites at the geosynchronous altitude cannot be spotted from the ground, they are, in effect, hidden in space. As they primarily monitor telemetry, the Rhyolites do not entirely replace the full duties of the earlier ferret/ELINTs. It is believed by some observers, therefore, that the KH-11, as well as performing its digital imaging responsibilities, also does some ELINT eavesdropping as well.

Some observers feel that too much weight has been put on the shoulders of Rhyolite. With the fall of the Shah, America's crucial missile test listening posts in Iran were lost. Those posts were only 700 miles from Tyuratam, while the Rhyolite now responsible for monitoring Tyuratam is 22,300 miles up in space. As the strength of telemetry signals declines with distance, Rhyolite receives approximately 1/1,000th the strength of signal that reached the Iranian posts. Presidents Nixon, Ford and Carter have been blamed for not having provided proper backup if the Iranian posts were to fall. Ford has received the most criticism on this account, as it was his administration that canceled Argus, the proposed advanced ferret/ELINT that was to have replaced Rhyolite.

The problems facing ELINT satellites now is one of timing. The new follow-up to Rhyolite, Project Aquacade, is not to orbit for several years, and in the interim new Rhyolites are ready to be used if needed. The combination of Rhyolites already in place and the ELINT capabilities of the KH-11 would seem to provide adequate eavesdropping resources for the United States until the more advanced Aquacade makes it into space.

Ocean Surveillance

The Navy has long been interested in surveillance from space, but the technical problems involved in spying down on the ocean are far greater than those presented by spying down on land. There are no fixed targets, the area is larger, and since the mission is more tactical than strategic, real-time information is more desperately needed. Imaging radar is the desired spying mode, but as the discussion of the KH-11's radar capabilities and limitations revealed, there are many difficulties with space-based radar (power requirements and information-processing bottlenecks) that have yet to be solved.

The Navy has been far behind the Air Force in satellite work, for while the USAF was lofting payloads into space, the Navy was concentrating on design studies. The Navy's satellite reconnaissance effort, Program 749, didn't start until 1968, and the first launch didn't come until December 1971, when a satellite atop an Atlas/Agena D was boosted into a 610/620 mile, 70-degree orbit. The next launch was not to come until 1976.

The Navy intended to initiate two satellite programs, White Cloud and Clipper Bow. White Cloud, first launched on April 6, 1976 into a 650/680-mile orbit, is a passive radar satellite—it picks up the radar pulses emitted by ships navigating at sea and from those can roughly determine their position. The 2,200-pound main White Cloud satellite ejects three subsatellites into orbits separated by less than 100 miles, a maneuver that suggests that they use interferometry to determine the positions of the ships more precisely. It is also speculated that White Clouds use IR detection equipment in an effort to track submarines by the slightly warmed water they leave in their wakes. Spaced 120 degrees apart, three White Clouds, with accompanying subsatellites, are enough to cover all the seas and oceans.

Clipper Bow was to be an active radar satellite. Like Seasat and the space shuttle, it was to use SLAR to take pictures of the ocean surface and the craft crossing it. It was eventually realized, however, that the technology needed to make it work was well beyond present capabilities, so the project was canceled in 1980. Yet, while Clipper Bow was put to sleep, the idea of putting up an active radar ocean surveillance satellite was not. The new project is ITSS—Integrated Tactical Surveillance System—which is intended to employ satellites capable of tracking not only surface ships but airplanes, such as the Soviet Backfire bomber, as well. There is no sure prognosis yet on the probable success or failure of ITSS, but one thing is certain: A surveillance system with such capabilities will be of great interest to all branches of the military, not just the Navy.

Communications

The main U.S. military-communications satellite systems are DSCS, FLTSATCOM, AFSATCOM, MILSTAR, and TDRSS. DSCS—Defense Communications Satellite; the acronym is pronounced "discus"—II satellites can relay over superhigh-frequency channels (which are harder to jam and can transmit more bits per second—100 million—than lower frequencies) and can handle 1,300 two-way voice communications at one time. Its successor, DCSC III, first launched in 1982, has the added features of nuclear hardening (protection from the effects of electromagnetic pulse—EMP) and has greater jam resistance, not to mention the fact that it can handle the equivalent of 10,000 two-way voice communications simultaneously.

Artist's rendering of a DSCS II defense communications satellite in orbit.

FLTSATCOM—FLeeT SATellite COMmunications system—the acronym is pronounced "fleetsatcom"—can relay Navy communications among over 600 ships at sea. In 1977, however, in an effort to save money, Congress instructed the Navy to stop building FLTSATCOM satellites and in their place lease channels from the Hughes commercial LEASAT communications satellites, which were then scheduled to be launched from the space shuttle beginning in 1982. By 1981 it seemed that neither the shuttle nor

Hughes would be ready on time, and the admirals went back to Congress to ask for both revisions in the Hughes contract and more money to resume FLTSATCOM production. They received both. Navy satellite communications over LEASAT channels began in 1984 and will continue into the 1990s. In addition, three new FLTSATs are being built to ensure that the Navy's requirements are met.

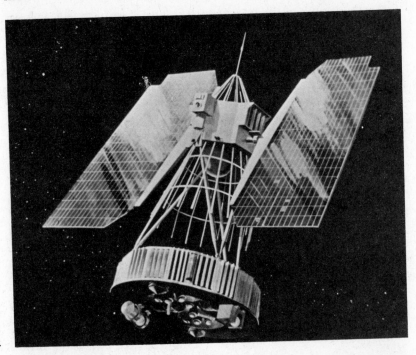

Artist's rendering of a FLTSATCOM satellite in orbit.

AFSATCOM is the satellite communicattons system used by the Air Force. Operational in late 1983, AFSATCOM uses other host satellites—FLTSATCOM, DSCS III, and even DSP early-warning satellites—to provide command and control of the nuclear forces. The entire system is supposed to be nuclear hardened and survivable. The system to replace both FLTSATCOM and AFSATCOM is MILSATCOM or Milstar, and it will service air, sea, and ground mobile terminals. The multiservice system was defined and its engineering began development in 1983. It will be durable, jam-resistant, nuclear hardened, survivable, and secure, and it will be America's key defense communications system for the 1990s and the early 21st century.

The TDRSS—Tracking and Data Relay Satellite System—defense communications satellite system has been designed to relieve vulnerable ground stations of their responsibilities. It will transmit information received by satellite, from satellite to satellite back to the United States, instead of being routed through a ground station first. The first launch of a TDRSS satellite from the shuttle in 1982 was almost a failure. After being sprung from the cargo bay, its thruster failed to kick in, leaving it stranded out of its intended orbit. Somehow, over a period of months, clever and adroit ground technicians managed to boost the satellite into its proper orbit using only its tiny stabilization and altitude thrusters.

The Global Positioning System

GPS (Global Positioning System—also known as Navstar), scheduled to be fully operational in 1987, will be a navigational satellite system employing up to eighteen satellites in 12,500-mile-high orbits. It will replace the now seemingly rudimentary Transit navigation satellite system. With GPS any mobile receiving station, whether at sea, in the air, or on land, will be able to determine its own location to within 50 feet and its velocity to within a fraction of a mile per hour.

The GPS's navigational acumen is an offshoot of the Doppler effect. When we hear a train approach with its whistle blowing, the

Artist's conception of a full complement of Global Positioning System satellites in orbit.

whistle may seem to have a very high pitch, but as it passes, the pitch drops. The reason for this is that as the train approaches, the sound waves emitted by its whistle are compressed by the forward motion—increasing their frequency and heightening the pitch—but as the train passes, the waves are stretched out by the movement away, hence lowering the pitch.

This principle applies to light and radio waves as well. A GPS satellite will beam a radio signal to an airplane or a ship, and when the signal is bounced back, the satellite will compare it to what the signal should be if the airplane or ship were motionless. The difference between the two will give an indication of the craft's velocity. An airplane's altitude will be determined with the use of very precise atomic clocks that measure the time it takes for the radio signal to go from the satellite to the airplane and back to the satellite again, hence indicating how far the aircraft is from the satellite and, by extension, from the ground.

The latitude and longitude of a ship, plane, or unit in the field will be determined by cross-referencing four GPS satellites simultaneously.

A fully operational GPS may not only be a boon to the navigational needs of airplanes, ships, and ground troops, it may make the so-called smart weapons obsolete. A cruise missile, for example, would not need its own terrain-following capability if it could simply get a reading of its position every few seconds from the GPS, which could direct it to within 50 feet of its target. As the premier navigation system, the GPS will also have its civilian applications, although the DoD is, of course, wary about allowing anyone outside of the military to use it. As a final note, it seems that the GPS will carry IONDS—Integrated Operational Nuclear Detection System—the system designed to tell nuclear warriors what they have hit and what to aim for in the next barrage.

It should be remembered that all of this impressive American military and intelligence technology is focused primarily on the Soviet Union. It should also be remembered that the Soviet knows who their enemy is as well, and while they have been matching the Americans weapons system for weapons system, they have also been matching United States spy satellite for spy satellite as well.

The Soviet Spy Mission In Space

"The Soviet program gave off an aura of secrecy. The Soviets released practically no figures, pictures or diagrams. And no names; it was only revealed that the Soviet program was guided by a mysterious individual known as the 'the Chief Designer' . . . {and} his powers were indisputable! Every time the United States announced a great space experiment, the Chief Designer accomplished it first, in the most startling fashion."

Tom Wolfe, *The Right Stuff*

On October 4, 1957, when Sputnik was launched into orbit, the Space Age began. That Sputnik flew at all was primarily the result of the efforts of two men. First, the almost mythical Chief Designer, Sergei Pavlovich Korolev. He was a pilot, engineer, Gulag survivor, true rocket magician, and father of the Soviet space program. The other man behind Sputnik was Nikita Khrushchev, the head of the Communist Party and the leader of the Soviet Union.

In the mid-1930s Korolev was a promising young engineer working under the tutelage of Tupolev, the legendary Soviet aircraft designer. Korolev was quickly gaining status of his own with his work in the field of liquid-fueled rockets. Such status, however, was no protection from the purges of the day, and he, along with many of his fellow workers, was sent to a prison camp. Intellectuals of high status were prime victims of Stalin's notorious paranoia, and even Tupolev himself was imprisoned. Because of the legend surrounding him, however, Tupolev managed to retain some power and influence even within the camps. When he heard of Korolev's incarceration, he managed to have him moved to a camp that housed other rocket and aircraft engineers, and there they engaged in an exchange of ideas that kept at least the theoretical side of their work alive.

After the war, Korolev was still a prisoner to some extent, but he was released to help with the study of the V-2 rockets that the Soviets had captured from the Germans. Korolev and his engineers used the expertise of the German scientists accompanying the rockets to check their own work, and from this, in 1947, they fashioned the first all-Soviet rocket, the R-1.

In 1948 Korolev was again imprisoned as a suspect intellectual and was not released until 1953. From then on he rose quickly in Soviet aerospace engineering, one of the beneficiaries of

Khrushchev's program of promoting Gulag survivors above Stalinists. This policy was not so much in recompense for their previous hardship as it was a way to gain instant loyalty from a significant number of the Soviet Union's intelligentsia. Khrushchev took a particular interest in Korolev and saw early that the man was destined for greatness. As he expressed it in his memoirs, "We had absolute confidence in Comrade Korolev. When he expounded his ideas, you could see passion burning in his eyes. He had unlimited energy and determination, and he was a brilliant organizer."

As much as Khrushchev may have praised him in his memoirs, in life it seems he never entirely trusted Korolev. To the world Korolev was kept in anonymity—only referred to by his title, Chief Designer—and in print, when writing for scientific journals, he was only allowed to use the name Sergeyev. Typically, Korolev was never allowed to travel outside of the Soviet Union, and when Western aerospace scientists and engineers came to his country, he was never allowed to meet with them. For much of his adult life the key figure in the Soviet space program—one of the scientific and engineering geniuses of the 20th century—was kept under house arrest.

The Soviet Space Program

In 1956 the United States announced its plans to send up a civilian satellite, Vanguard, as part of the coming International Geophysical Year. Korolev was inspired. He knew that with the rockets he had developed for the Soviet military he could send up a much larger payload than could the Americans. Although initially rebuffed by the Central Committee, Korolev continued to work on a rocket that was to have three times the thrust of the American Atlas booster—and the Atlas wasn't even going to be ready for use with Vanguard. Such a rocket would be too much for the facilities at Kapustin Yar, so a new launch site was constructed at Tyuratam in Central Asia. Although Tyuratam became the home of their space program, the Soviets would continue to insist that all launches came from the Baikonur Cosmodrome, several hundred miles away. This was part of their strategy of preserving secrecy through disinformation.

After several successful tests of the R-7 rocket, Khrushchev gave Korolev the go-ahead to send up a satellite. He felt that such a feat might lend greater credence to his boasts of military might.

Throughout the summer and fall of 1957 Korolev lived at Tyuratam in a small house he had constructed near the launchpad. It was his enthusiasm, guidance, and drive that brought the program together so quickly. By the beginning of October that year they were ready. The rocket, consisting of five long pods fired in unison, rose off the launchpad on the night of October 4. As the space vehicle followed its intended arc, the pods were consumed and dropped off, but not before they had boosted the tiny Sputnik satellite to 18,000 miles per hour. Finally, the little globe started to fall. It fell and fell and fell, but as it did, the horizon kept receding under it. It was in orbit. In Korolev's words: "Today the dreams of the best sons of mankind have come true. The assault on space has begun."

It has been said that the success of Sputnik was something of a fluke, that the Soviets really didn't know for sure if it would work or not. Nevertheless, Korolev did get it into orbit, and he did it first. Not only that, but over the next few years, as the Russians began to launch ever larger satellites, the American space program seemed to be mired in failure. The rockets that didn't explode on the pad finally made it into space usually months after a similar Soviet vehicle. For all the world it seemed as if the Russian bear was striding boldly into the future, leaving the American eagle in the dust. But this image of Russian superiority was something of an illusion, for the Soviet program was not without its own catastrophes.

In the fall of 1960, although he liked the "fireworks," Premier Khrushchev expressed a desire for both greater practicality and more propaganda leverage from his country's space shots. In October of that year he was to attend the UN session in New York, and he put pressure on Field Marshal Mitrofan Nedelin, one of the heads of the Soviet space program, to see to it that a probe was sent to Mars while Khrushchev was in New York, or failing that, immediately upon his return to the Soviet Union.

Nedelin and his engineers failed to deliver while Khrushchev was in America, and when he returned to Moscow the pressure mounted. Finally, on the night of the launch attempt, when the countdown reached "O" and the button was pressed, the engines failed to ignite. Nedelin was furious. He needed a success—now. So, instead of first having the rocket defueled and then checked, Nedelin ordered an inspection of the rocket as it stood on the pad. He and his crews went out, set up scaffolding, and proceeded to inspect the rocket. Suddenly, without warning, ignition resumed and the engines flared. Fouled by the scaffolding, the huge rocket toppled over on its side and exploded, killing everyone in the immediate area. The only survivors were a man who happened to be having a cigarette in a fireproof hut and those, including Korolev, who had remained in the control bunker. In *Red Star in Orbit*, a history of the Soviet space program, James Oberg estimates that forty people died in the tragedy, making it the single greatest disaster in the history of spaceflight.

Korolev's next major rocket design was the Vostok booster used to launch the first man—Yuri Gagarin—into space, on April 12, 1961. An interesting side note is that this first flight was essentially an unmanned mission with Gagarin along for the ride like a monkey or a dog. He had no capability whatsoever to control the spacecraft. There had been fears that weightlessness would disorient a man, perhaps even drive him insane, so all the manual controls were disconnected in case a crazed Gagarin tried to interfere with the mission.

Still, the Chief Designer had done it again. During his life Korolev was responsible for the first satellite in orbit, the first animal in orbit (the dog Laika in Sputnik 2), the first lunar probes, the first interplanetary probes, and the first man in space. Yet, when he died in 1966, few outside of the Soviet Union—indeed, few in the Soviet Union—had ever heard his name.

Of interest here is another first with which Korolev can be associated: On April 26, 1962, a Vostok rocket designed by the unsung hero of the Space Age was used to launch the first Soviet reconnaissance satellite, Cosmos 4.

Soviet Spy Satellites

While deducing the existence, configuration, and capabilities of U.S. satellites is by no means easy, it is a simple matter when compared to figuring out what the Soviets are up to in space-based reconnaissance. In 1963 amateur satellite trackers began to notice that the Soviets were tossing up more and more short-duration satellites while at the same time releasing less and less scientific information from these missions. As well, these satellites were disappearing from orbit long before natural orbit decay would dictate.

To Geoffrey E. Perry, a science teacher at the Kettering Grammar School in England, this suggested that the satellites were most probably military and that they might be on reconnaissance missions. Intrigued at this possibility, he assigned the tasks of monitoring the Soviet satellites' shortwave radio transmissions to his students. It is a class project that has continued for two decades, and the work of Perry and his students over the years is unrivaled in the history of amateur spacewatching. Much of the unclassified information on the Soviet space reconnaissance program has been derived from their studies, and for his efforts Perry was awarded an M.B.E.—Member of the British Empire.

The monitoring of the telemetry of these satellites both in orbit and during reentry has allowed four distinct generations of Soviet spy sats to be discerned. The first generation began with their first spy satellite, Cosmos 4. What was suspicious about that satellite was that, unlike its nonmilitary predecessors, Cosmos 1, 2, and 3, which were launched from the small Kapustin Yar facility into 49-degree orbits, Cosmos 4 was launched from Tyuratam into a 65-degree orbit. It stayed up for eight days, longer than its predecessors.

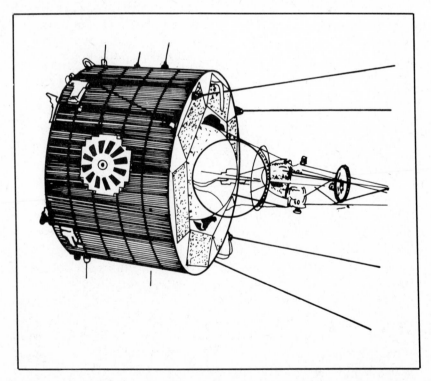

Illustration of a generic Soviet Cosmos spy satellite.

Externally, on the launch-pad, these first-generation missions would have appeared the same as a Vostok launch. The booster was an SL-3, and the nondescript payload that sat on top consisted of a

5,100-pound spherical reentry capsule and a 4,800-pound instrumentation and retrorocket package. The mission length of these satellites averaged eight days, with the longest being ten. Their orbital inclinations varied from 65 to 51 degrees, according to the mission requirements. The last of the first generation, Cosmos 153, went up April 4, 1967.

The second generation used the SL-4 booster, which was capable of lifting 12,000-13,000 pounds into orbit. There were three subdivisions within the second generation: low-resolution, high-resolution, and extended-duration. Both low- and high-resolution satellites were similar to the first generation in that they stayed up for only eight days and were not maneuverable in orbit. The extended-duration model, although considered part of the second generation because of its telemetry, was in many ways a generation unto itself for it was maneuverable in orbit and could stay up for all of 12 days. As well, while the low- and high-resolution satellites of the second generation were terminated in 1970, the extended-duration sats continued in operation from March 21, 1968, to May 5, 1978.

The third generation began to appear in October 1968. Still in use, they are characterized by their maneuverability and a mission length of thirteen days. There are three subdivisions in this generation, each with its own mission: low-, medium-, and high-resolution satellites. There are only one or two launches a year of the low-resolution variety. They weigh slightly under 13,000 pounds and stay in orbit for two weeks at an altitude of 130 miles perigee, 150 miles apogee. Their inclination and very low resolution suggest that they may be used more for mapping than for spying. The medium-resolution satellites, at 14,500 pounds, weigh the most of the three. They also have a two-week orbital life, circling the Earth at an initial height of 110-160 miles perigee, 150-240 miles apogee. They then use their maneuvering capabilities to boost up into an orbit 200-220 miles in perigee, 230-260 miles in apogee.

The high-resolution satellites use all orbital inclinations and perform many maneuvers in their two-week lifespan. They weigh 13,500-14,000 pounds, with initial orbital heights of 120-130 miles in perigee, 145-230 miles in apogee. In subsequent maneuvers the apogee remains fairly constant while the perigee may be boosted up to 160 miles, presumably to remove the craft from the effects of atmospheric drag. The maneuverability and the variation in orbital height and inclination suggest a satellite that has great flexibility in mission assignment.

The fourth generation is composed of only one type of satellite. While in the first three generations the entire capsule was reentered, in the fourth there are recoverable film packs (like America's Discoverer or Big Bird), which are ejected, reenter the atmosphere, and are recovered (on the ground, though, not in midair like the U.S. models). The fourth generation also has a digital imaging system like the KH-11, although not of the same level of sophistication or capability. First launched in 1975, the fourth generation was probably not fully operational until 1980. These satellites usually orbit for four weeks, although one has been reported to have been in operation for as long as forty-four days. They are launched into an initial 105-mile perigee, 215-mile apogee orbit, and then, after their orbit has decayed somewhat, are boosted back up to their initial orbit. After all the film packs (like Big Bird, it has between four and six) have been ejected, the main craft is deorbited, being allowed to burn up in the atmosphere.

A. Diagram of a Soviet Soyuz spacecraft.

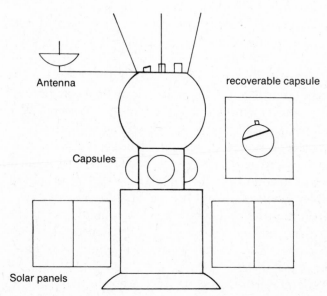

Antenna

recoverable capsule

Capsules

Solar panels

B. The Soyuz craft adapted to serve as a fourth-generation spy satellite with recoverable capsules.

In 1984, Soviet satellite reconnaissance coverage was provided by three third-generation satellites and one fourth-generation satellite. It is likely that all of these are based on the technology of Soyuz (the manned program of the late 1960s and early '70s). Experts believe that the docking section of the Soyuz manned spacecraft may simply have been replaced with a camera package. In the case of the fourth generation it is likely that an extra section has been inserted into the satellite's midsection to carry the film packs. All of these satellites are most likely powered by solar cells.

When Cosmos 112 was launched on March 17, 1966, the young satellite watchers under Perry's guidance at Kettering noticed something strange. It didn't seem to have been launched from either Tyuratam or Kapustin Yar. When four more satellites had a similarly mysterious launch origin, the picture began to take shape. It indicated a new launch site at Plesetsk, a town north of Moscow and within the Arctic Circle. Although Plesetsk has been the most frequently used of the three launch sites within the Soviet Union since 1966, its existence has never been officially acknowledged. While Tyuratam, with its mix of military, scientific, public-service, and manned missions, is the Soviet equivalent of Cape Canaveral, Plesetsk, used to launch military satellites into polar orbits, is the Russian Vandenberg. The Soviets have not only denied the existence of the Plesetsk site, they have also insisted that their launches come from Baikonur when in fact the "civilian" shots come from Tyuratam, 215 miles to the south. As one might expect, they have also completely denied that they have been using spy satellites at all.

While it is even more difficult to judge the resolving power of Soviet satellites than it is to judge that of American satellites, there are rough ranges within which the satellites' powers probably fall. As has been mentioned, the low-resolution satellites may be used just for general survey and mapping missions, since their ground resolution is probably somewhere between 50 and 100 feet. The satellites of medium resolution, akin to the old American Samos area-survey satellites, probably have a resolution of between 4 and 8 feet. Their high-resolution satellites, like their American close-look counterparts, may well be able to spot something as small as 8 inches across. The fourth generation would also have similar resolving capabilities.

Like the Americans, the Soviets do not limit their intelligence role in outer space to photo reconnaissance. Since 1970 the USSR has been operating heavy ferret/ELINT satellites. Like their American counterparts, these satellites catalog and analyze radar defenses and monitor and pinpoint the origin of military radio communications. The first such Soviet ferret/ELINT was first thought to have been a failed satellite of the Meteor class (a weather satellite). But then a constellation of similar satellites began to appear, with each orbit separated from its neighbor's by 60 degrees.

Further, as these satellites were replaced regularly, and as no scientific results were ever attributed to them it was deduced that they were military, and from their orbit (81.2-degree inclination, 97.7 minute period), that they were ferret/ELINT satellites.

Soviet ocean-surveillance satellites that track ships by their radar signals began to be launched from Tyuratam atop SS-9 boosters in 1974. They have almost circular 65-degree, 93.3-minute orbits and are launched in pairs, with the orbit of one satellite exactly dovetailing with its partner's, providing complete coverage of the earth's oceans from 650 S to 650 N.

A second type of ocean-surveillance satellite orbits at the same inclination but has a shorter period, indicating that it flies over at a lower altitude. This satellite remains attached to the second stage of the rocket while in orbit, using the second stage's rockets to counter the drag. Once the satellite has completed its mission, part of the payload is boosted up into a higher orbit, where it will remain for several hundred years.

It is believed that this type of ocean-surveillance satellite may have active side-looking radar to use in attempting to spot ships at sea. As SLAR requires a great deal of power for its operation—more than solar cells alone could provide—it has been deduced that this satellite must carry a nuclear generator and that it is this generator that is boosted up into a higher orbit at the end of its mission, where it will remain until the radioactivity of its nuclear fuel has decayed to a safe level.

Confirmation of this hypothesis came in January 1978, when Cosmos 954, an ocean-surveillance satellite, made an uncontrolled reentry into the atmosphere, flinging pieces of radioactive debris across a section of the Canadian arctic. The Soviets had apparently tried to boost the nuclear generator into a higher, safer orbit, but for some reason they failed, and the generator came down. Because of the hail of international protest (especially from Canada, which has still not been entirely compensated for the cost of the cleanup), the Soviets did not orbit another nuclear-powered ocean-surveillance satellite until 1980. Since that time there has been another uncontrolled reentry, but in this case the pieces fell in the ocean.

In 1972 the Soviets began launching satellites similar to their Molniya communications satellites (with their eccentric near-polar orbits—perigees of a few hundred miles and apogees of approximately 25,000 miles), but different enough to suggest a new mission. On one pass of the Molniya orbit, a satellite will spend approximately eight hours high over the Soviet Union. On its next pass, however, the high part of the orbit will be over North America. Although useless to the Soviet Union for communications at this point, it would be in a perfect position to detect missile launches from North America. There are nine of these early-warning satellites, each spaced 40 degrees apart, so that at all times there is at least one Soviet launch-detection satellite somewhere high over the United States, at an altitude from which it can beam its findings directly down over the North Pole to command and control centers in the Soviet Union.

Satellite For Satellite

The Soviets may have a counterpart for every American intelligence satellite, but, one may ask, how do they compare?

In the quest for higher defense spending in the United States, figures about Soviet military superiority have been lobbed about like grenades. These grenades often turn out to be nothing more than smoke bombs. Such is the case with figures about Soviet military satellites. In an interview in the November 1982 issue of *Military Electronics/Countermeasures*, Dr. Eberhardt Rechtin, president of Aerospace Corporation, the major research and development wing of the USAF's Space Division, was questioned about American versus Soviet military/civilian ratios in satellites. At that time the U.S. ratio between military and civilian satellites was 50:50, while in the Soviet Union it is 90:10 military over civilian.

According to Rechtin, "This does not say that some of the Soviet military satellites couldn't be used for civilian purposes, or that some of our civilian satellites, like commercial communications satellites, aren't used by our military forces, because they are. . . . [but] while the actual ratio may not be exact, the emphasis is quite clear. The next question is therefore, how many launches does each nation perform? The Soviets unquestionably launch many more satellites than the United States. The weights of individual satellites are approximately the same as those of comparable U.S. satellites. In other words, the Soviets aren't launching lots of little ones while we launch a few big ones. The missions they are trying to accomplish are approximately the same as U.S. missions: communications, meteorology, surveillance. So why do they launch so many more? The principal reason the Soviets have to have more satellites is that theirs don't work as well."

While the KH-11 can stay up for two years, its Soviet counterpart is useful for less than two months. Other smaller American military satellites function for five or more years, while the Soviets are striving for a two-year lifespan for similar satellites. Consequently, while the Soviets may launch many more satellites each year, of the 300 satellites now operating in space, 180 are American, 100 Russian, and the remaining 20 belong to a mix of other nations. This disparity has little to do with orbit, as anything above a few hundred miles can orbit for decades without decaying. It is more a function of the disparity between the reliability of the two nations' hardware. While not seeking to bolster that old (and demonstrably wrong) propagandistic myth about Soviet technological backwardness, in this particular area, primarily because of computer sophistication, the United States is ahead by some five to ten years. Currently, though, the Soviets have an advantage in mission flexibility because of the number of launches they make each year, but when the space shuttle becomes fully operational, going up every two weeks, that advantage will be erased as well.

The Soviets do have a definite lead over the Americans in the race to construct an operational antisatellite weapon (ASAT). The Soviets began testing their FOB—Fractional Orbital Bombardment—system in 1968, and it is now considered operational (in the FOB system the ASAT maneuvers in close to an enemy satellite and explodes, wiping them both out). The United States has only recently begun testing its ASAT, the Prototype Miniature Air Launch System (PMALS). To take out an enemy satellite, a PMALS projectile, which is about the size of a basketball and loaded with sensing equipment to guide it, is launched into space from an airborne F-15 fighter plane. It homes in on the enemy satellite and destroys it, not by exploding but simply by hitting it at a speed of 40,000 feet per second. Even though the Soviets have the jump on the United States, the FOB is considered to be far less sophisticated than the U.S. PMALS. The Americans enjoy another advantage too. While both types of ASAT can only strike at lower altitude-satellites such as surveillance satellites, the Americans will actually be able to take out Soviet communications and early-warning satellites in their Molniya perigees, when they are only a few hundred miles above Antarctica.

Are Satellites Necessary for the Soviets?

One question often asked about the Soviet reconnaissance mission is: Why do they bother? In the United States an incredible amount of military information is relatively easy to obtain; as well, the Soviets have over a thousand agents in the United States gathering all that is not so openly available. It would therefore seem unnecessary for them to orbit satellites, at a cost of many billions of rubles over the years, just to peek into American backyards.

One reason that they have engaged in this endeavor is that in the early 1960s when they developed their first spy satellites, they didn't trust the information their agents were sending. The Soviets had long been following a course of disinformation, and they suspected that the United States might well be doing the same thing, so they wanted to find out for themselves.

Even after their satellites had corroborated available information, the Soviets continued to orbit these craft—a great many of them—every year. The primary reason for this would be to monitor other areas of the world—China, for example—especially, to be ready for any armed conflict. Tactical information on how, and how well, other forces perform is the goal, as is ELINT information on other countries' battle codes and radar signals. Whenever any conflicts arise, there is a distinct increase in Soviet reconnaissance satellite activity. An illustration of this is their response to the heavy fighting between Iran and Iraq in November 1982.

On November 1, 1982, Iran launched a major offensive into Iraqi territory, heading toward Basra and Mandali. On November 2 the Soviet Union launched Cosmos 1419, a photoreconnaissance satellite, and within eighteen hours had maneuvered it into a 70.3-degree, 140/175-mile orbit that would give it worldwide coverage within 70 degrees either side of the equator in two weeks. On November 5 the satellite passed to the east of Basra and continued on over western Iran. Several hours later its apogee was lowered and its orbit maneuvered so that on November 6 and 7 it made continuous passes over the region. Finally, its apogee was raised and it was sent off again on its global reconnaissance mission. On November 13, however, when it returned to the same region, its apogee was again lowered. Cosmos 1419 continued to pass over the region for the next two days, until it was finally deorbited and recovered on November 16.

On November 18 Cosmos 1421 was launched into a similar pattern. After four days in orbit it was maneuvered to make continuous passes over the Baghdad-to-Basra area. After repeating this several days later, it was brought back to Earth on December 2, 1982. This surge of activity generally accompanies any such conflict, from the Falklands War to the U.S. invasion of Grenada.

Finally, one can feel a sense of reassurance in the knowledge that at this point there is a rough parity between the space-based reconnaissance efforts of the two superpowers, and truly it has been because of this basic equivalence that strategic arms talks have been possible. When we look at the future of strategic reconnaissance, however, we see that this balance may be in jeopardy.

The Future

At the heart of the intelligence satellites of the future will be infrared detection technology. The goal is to produce a highly sensitive IR detector array that will be able to perform the integrated tasks of launch warning, missile tracking, and intelligence surveillance. The concept of integration, in fact, is vital to almost all future space efforts. Integrating systems and constructing space platforms rather than individual satellites is expected to be more efficient, since it will centralize the information gathering. Also, strange as it may seem, even in the vast expanses of space there is the potential for orbital crowding in the not too distant future, and integrating satellites and building space platforms will save space in space.

In a thermal IR detection system the temperature of the detector elements is a crucial factor. All a detector does is sense heat levels, so it must be cooler—very much cooler—than the heat-emitting objects it observes. There are two ways to cool the detectors in space: active and passive. Active cooling uses battery-powered refrigerators to cool the detectors, while passive cooling simply uses the low, 180 K temperature of space to do the job. In the 1960s, when IR space technology was first being developed, passive cooling was chosen because it was easier. However, passively cooled elements are not as cold as those using active cooling, so that the detectors could only spot high-temperature sources such as a missile's rocket plume. The detectors then could only pick up emissions in the relatively short IR wavelengths, the 2-3 micrometer region. It was known, however, that the longer wavelengths would be the key to any advanced IR detection system.

In 1974 two projects were initiated at DARPA—Defense

Advanced Research Projects Agency—to test and develop active cooled sensors to detect the longer IR wavelengths. The projects were P80-1 (Teal Ruby) and P80-2 (SIRE). SIRE—Satellites InfraRed Experiment—was the first to get underway. The goal of these experiments was to test the possibility of detecting and tracking a missile after burnout against the cool background of space. Basically, this was to be the next generation of early-warning detection. In March 1976 Hughes Aircraft began work on the sensor package and cooling system, which was to weigh approximately 500 pounds. The contract to build the spacecraft to house the sensor system was awarded to Lockheed in November 1977. According to Lockheed plans the spacecraft would be a modified version of their all-purpose Agena, and the booster to be used was to be an Atlas-F rocket. It was to launch from Vandenberg into a sun-synchronous, twilight, 98-degree, 469-mile-high orbit. The Lockheed contract commenced in 1978 and was to run until the first scheduled launch in 1981.

By 1979, however, the weight of the SIRE payload had ballooned to over 1,000 pounds. A major portion of that weight was the heavy refrigeration unit, which required the power from 600 square feet of solar cells to operate. The comparatively lightweight IR sensor system was composed of ninety-five detectors arranged in twelve linear arrays, each array tuned to a different band of the IR spectrum. At this time the entire spacecraft would have weighed a gargantuan 5,500 pounds. It was overweight—and over budget.

By 1979 the Air Force was becoming alarmed by Lockheed's overruns. Originally, it had been thought that the spacecraft would only need to be a modified Agena. But the farther they got into it, the farther the craft got away from the original Agena design. Costs rose, and ultimately the Air Force canceled the spacecraft development, deciding that the SIRE would be carried into space aboard the shuttle. Because of shuttle delays, however, this decision essentially shelved SIRE.

Teal Ruby

With the decline of SIRE came the rise of Teal Ruby. While SIRE was to pick out a post-burnout rocket against the cool background of space, Teal Ruby was given the more difficult task of detecting aircraft against the IR clutter of Earth. In 1977 Rockwell (also general contractor for the shuttle) received the contract for the Teal

Ruby sensor package, and in 1978 they were awarded the spacecraft contract as well.

Teal Ruby, like most recent space work, has been dependent on advances in the field of integrated circuitry. In the DSP (Defense Support Program) early-warning satellites the arrays of detectors are assembled, mounted, and wired by hand. Not only are single-satellite arrays very expensive—$4 million each—but they are also limited as to the number of detector elements each can contain; in a DSP array this is roughly 2,000, limiting the resolution of the detector system to roughly 1.5 square miles (the area that each detector covers at any given time).

Teal Ruby uses new integrated-circuit technology that with batch processing instead of hand-wiring allows for cramming hundreds of thousands of elements onto a single chip. The key to this miniaturization is VLSI—Very Large Scale Integration—which basically entails getting as much circuitry as possible into a very small space. The Defense Department has issued specifications for a circuit only 0.5 microns wide (a micron is one one-millionth of an inch). Currently, the state of the art is around 5 microns, though IBM has a prototype circuit of 2 microns, Honeywell 1.25 microns, and TRW 1 micron. *Aviation Week* offered this analogy of the true meaning of such dimensions: If a map of the United States were to be drawn with lines 0.5 microns wide, every street in the country could be represented in a map only 20 inches wide.

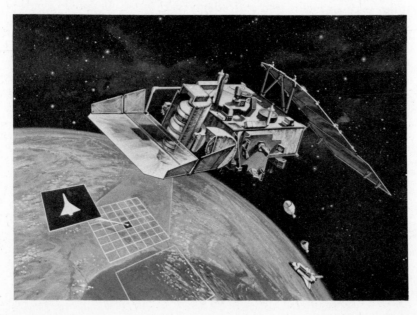

Artist's conception of Teal Ruby in operation, detecting and identifying an aircraft.

VLSI provides many advantages. Because of the high density of elements, the satellite need not be spun to afford greater coverage; rather, the telescope can operate in the "staring mode." This means that as each detector stares at one area on the ground, rather than scanning a whole circle of areas several times a minute, the computer-processing requirements are greatly reduced. The processing needs can be further reduced if the computer is instructed to process and transmit information only if there is a change in what the detector sees. Also, because of the higher density of detector elements the resolution is much higher, with each detector covering (from a geosynchronous altitude) only 0.03 percent of a square mile (900 by 900 feet) or less. The new Honeywell detector chip for DSP satellites has 80,000 elements on each chip; its predecessor had only 2,000.

The specifications for Teal Ruby call for 150,000 detectors in each of its thirteen subarrays, with each subarray sensitive to a different band of wavelengths in the IR spectrum. The detector elements are made of mercury cadmium telluride, a substance that is particularly sensitive in the region of the IR spectrum known as the "blue spike." Aircraft engine emissions peak at the blue spike, and atmospheric absorption of IR radiation is modest in that region.

A telescope is used to focus the light onto the focal plane containing the detector arrays. The telescope can be operated in three different ways. As the Teal Ruby satellites are to orbit at 460 miles with an inclination of 75 degrees, they will be moving quite swiftly in relation to the ground. The first mode of operation for the telescope is to lock into an area on the earth and, by slowly angling the telescope, keep that target area in its sights. The second mode is for the telescope just to stare straight down, following the ground track. The third mode has the telescope pointing forward to observe the limb region of the Earth.

Teal Ruby was to go into orbit aboard the fifth shuttle flight, originally scheduled for 1980, but because of a series of setbacks and delays both in Teal Ruby and the shuttle, all did not go quite according to plan. So far, at over $110 million, the sensor package of Teal Ruby is already more than 100 percent over budget, and the entire project is at least four years behind schedule.

DARPA

In a way one can expect projects at the Defense Advanced Research Projects Agency (DARPA) to go off schedule and over budget—not because of poor management or sloppy project supervision, but simply because of the nature of DARPA's work. Established February 12, 1958, by Public Law 85-325, DARPA's basic mission was outlined by Secretary of Defense Neil McElroy: The agency is to engage in high-risk/high-payoff projects that, if successful, would put the Soviets in the position of having to play catchup in the high-technology race.

In size DARPA is comparable to the CIA. Its budget request for 1984 was $867.7 million: $11.4 million for administration, $108.6 million for basic research (testing alloys, studying space structures, experiments in high-speed aerodynamics, etc.), and $747.7 million for exploratory development of advanced strategic and tactical defense projects. This represents approximately 18 percent of the DoD's investment in science and technology research.

Along with Teal Ruby, another major DARPA project is the space-based laser program, composed of ALPHA, LODE, and Talon Gold. ALPHA is the chemical laser itself; LODE is the optics system that would direct the laser beam; Talon Gold—very much a reincarnation of the abandoned SIRE, as it is supposed to detect missiles against the cool of space—is the target-acquisition, tracking, and pointing component of the triad. Other DARPA projects include the X-29 Forward Swept-Wing aircraft, charged-particle-beam weaponry, advanced materials science, and information-processing research.

Teal Ruby is part of the Infrared Surveillance Technology Program at DARPA, the goal of which is to produce a staring-mosaic IR array that is highly sensitive in the long IR wavelengths. To support Teal Ruby HICAMP—Highly Calibrated Airborne Measurement Program—was initiated in 1981. HICAMP I took staring-mosaic IR arrays up in U-2s to measure and catalog the Earth's background clutter of IR radiation. (HICAMP II now in operation is simply an improved, more precise HICAMP I.) HICAMP is vitally necessary to the whole program, for only with precise measurements of the Earth's background IR radiation will Teal Ruby be able to detect aircraft and missiles. In 1984 Teal Ruby was scheduled to undergo critical design review and to be tested for its integration with the shuttle.

As was mentioned in the discussion of the KH-11's technology, the VHSIC—Very High Speed Integrated Circuit—program is crucial to the next wave of space-based surveillance technology. VHSIC technology will allow expanded on-board processing so that the information can be brought home in close to real time. Westinghouse has said that they could be on the threshold of a processor capability of 40 million complex number operations per second on only two 6 by 8-inch printed circuit boards. In effect, a computer the size of a shoebox will be able to perform the functions of an already miniaturized room-sized computer. VHSIC technology is seen as vital to all aspects of defense. In the DoD's statement on research, development, and acquisition for 1984, it was very simply stated that "VHSIC is our highest priority technology."

HALO

Although Teal Ruby, when in operation, will be an exceptionally advanced reconnaissance system, able to track missiles and aircraft, it is in fact only the first step to an even more advanced system, HALO—High Altitude Large Optics. HALO, set to operate in the mid-1990s, will be perhaps the ultimate space-based reconnaissance platform. In recent years there has been a great deal of effort applied to integrating and unifying space missions. HALO will be the end result of that effort. It will combine aircraft, missile, and ship tracking with strategic and tactical surveillance.

One of the key components of HALO will be the IR detection technology provided by Teal Ruby. Just as the HICAMP airborne flight tests and IR measurements support Teal Ruby, so Teal Ruby will support HALO. According to Dr. Robert S. Cooper, director of DARPA, "Teal Ruby will provide proof-of-concept for other multi-mission surveillance functions, develop a comprehensive and global radiometric background data base, and space qualify first generation advanced IR sensor surveillance technology. The Teal Ruby experiment represents the first large-scale implementation of a two-dimensional, staring mosaic IR detector array and will also use the lightweight techniques developed in the HALO technology program for design and manufacture of the Teal Ruby telescope."

HALO has been given high priority at DARPA since studies began in 1977. Many private contractors are involved: Rockwell is responsible for the mosaic detector array; Perkin-Elmer, Hughes, and Itek for lightweight optics; Hughes and Garrett AiResearch for cryogenics; TRW for data utilization; Science Applications for IR phenomenology; Charles S. Draper Laboratory for structural dynamics; and Aerodyne Research for mirror sensor technology.

The HALO Revolution

One obstacle to receiving real time information is the regular movement of satellites. A photo interpreter at the NPIC who wishes to take a close look at the Murmansk shipyard as it rebuilds after the 1984 explosion may have to wait several days before the KH-11 passes over Murmansk. In the book *Satellite Spies* there is an interview with someone only identified as a "highly classified person" from the DoD. In reference to the reconnaissance satellites of the future this man is reported to have said, "We have television so perfect that the next time this country goes to war, field commanders will be able to sit in front of a television console and see everything that moves. A satellite will be right overhead, and it will show them everything that is happening while it is happening. They will have live coverage of hundreds of square miles of the battlefield sector. . . . Nothing will escape the satellite's eyes."

An interesting claim, considering that it was published in 1976, at a time when the KH-11 was just becoming operational. Presumably by "television" the "highly classified person" meant digital imaging. As for his claim that a satellite would be directly overhead future battlefields, providing real-time information, it seems that this highly classified person was not so highly scientific, for satellites cannot hover over a battlefield. As soon as they stop moving, they fall. In 1976, in fact, the best that could be expected of satellites was that they could provide repetitive coverage of an area every ninety minutes or so.

The key to HALO's operations is found in its name—High Altitude Large Optics—for when it flies, HALO might well be geosynchronous, orbiting at the very high altitude of 22,300 miles. If that proves to be the case, then the man quoted in *Satellite Spies* may turn out to have been correct, although the satellite will not hover over any one battlefield, but will cover roughly a third of the Earth's surface in one sweep. Of course, at such an altitude resolution would be greatly diminished. That is where the Large Optics part of HALO's name comes into play.

As mentioned in the section on the KH-11, recent developments in adaptive optics have virtually nullified the distorting effects of the atmosphere, so that, in practice, resolution is limited only by the size of the aperture and the resolution of the receptors on the focal plane. The plan for HALO therefore would be to construct very large optics, with aperture and focal length measured in meters, so that even at the geosynchronous altitude the visual precision would be equivalent to that of the KH-11.

There are of course great weight penalties in boosting a payload into geosynchronous orbit. It has been suggested that the optics be constructed out of very thin glass or metal membrane mounted on high stiffness-to-weight-ratio support structures. Another major obstacle is that the liquids used in the cooling system will simply evaporate over time. Enough liquid could be carried up for a two-year stint, however, and replacements could be taken up into space by shuttle and then ferried out to the HALO platform by interorbital tug.

There would be great advantages to having a geosynchronous spy satellite. At 22,300 miles it would be almost impossible for personnel on the ground to spot the satellite or to hit it with an antisatellite weapon; that altitude would also increase its nuclear survivability. For the intelligence community and the Pentagon, though, HALO's greatest attribute will be its ability to stare down at any area of the Earth under its gaze and beam that information back to Earth in real time. There could also be a revolution in the quality of information derived that could match the advancements in space technology. Not only will there be improved computer manipulation and enhancement techniques, but in addition, researchers at TRW (responsible for the data-utilization part of HALO) are working on highly sophisticated artificial-intelligence programs that will be able to identify what HALO sees—in some respects replacing photo interpreters.

HALO will probably also have on-board processing capabilities that will produce information so refined that it will be suited for use by small mobile stations on the ground, in the air, or at sea. A demonstration of the concept, a mini-HALO, is scheduled to be launched by shuttle in 1988, and will operate for two and a half years.

The Return of MOL

Military and intelligence satellite programs sometimes seem to be supernatural, for all the ghosts that can be seen and all the

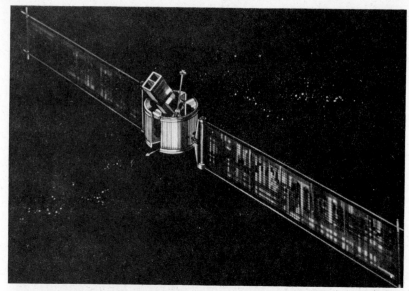

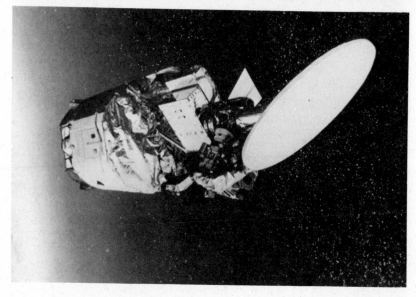

reincarnations that occur. Whenever a program is put to rest, it always seems to rise from its grave at a later date in a superficially different body, sometimes stronger than ever. The Navy's Clipper Bow active radar satellite was interred in 1980, only to reappear miraculously a short time later as ITSS—Integrated Tactical Surveillance System. The SIRE project, canceled in 1979, seems to have resurfaced as the Talon Gold segment of the space-based laser program. Now the ghost of MOL—the Manned Orbiting

Laboratory—perhaps the biggest of the defunct programs (by the time it was put to sleep, in 1969, over $3.5 billion had been spent) is beginning to rattle its chains.

The National Aeronautics and Space Administration has only survived, has only received high funding, when it has been engaged in a major project. From the time of President Kennedy's commitment to put a man on the Moon by the end of the 1960s to December 7, 1972, when the last Moon launch was made, NASA existed only because of the Apollo program. When Apollo was finished, NASA faced the possibility of disintegration. For their continued existence the NASA chiefs turned to the space shuttle, which has served them well.

With the fifth flight, in November 1982, the shuttle became operational—a mixed blessing. As is the nature of such programs, development and production require a lot of people and a lot of money. When the program becomes operational, fewer people and less money are needed. So NASA is in a predicament similar to the one it faced at the end of Apollo: "What do we do next?" In searching for another project to provide a reason for its continued existence through the rest of this century, NASA seems to have settled on the notion of a space station.

In the 1960s it was enough just to get a man on the Moon—it was a feat accomplished merely to prove that it could be done. In the 1970s, however, some practical benefit had to be demonstrated before development of space could continue. Eventually, the shuttle is supposed to pay for itself through the revenue it receives for carrying communications satellites and other commercial packages into space. Similarly, a space station would be expected to have some commercial applications that would let it pay for itself.

While the idea of a space station may conjure up images of the spinning wheel under construction in Stanley Kubrick's film *2001: A Space Odyssey,* NASA's plans are much more modest: a large cylindrical midsection to house four to six people, with attached minifactories and ports for shuttles and interorbital tugs. The station would be modular and could expand to accommodate up to 18 people. The minifactories would be the commercial venture, using the microgravity environment to develop such things as exceptionally pure medicines, precisely doped silicon chips, and perfectly round ball bearings. To many, however, it seems highly unlikely that a space station, with a startup cost of $9 billion and an overall cost of $20-$30 billion, is likely to pay for itself making perfectly round ball bearings.

The truth of the matter is that the military now seems to be the key to the viability of the station plan, as it was with the shuttle. The shuttle was only developed because the DoD gave NASA its support, and now NASA is back at the Pentagon, hat in hand once again.

In an interview in the November 22, 1982 issue of *U.S. News & World Report,* NASA Administrator James M. Beggs was asked if there would be a role aboard a space station for the military. Beggs replied: "Actually you would start with a very few men, who would certainly enhance our surveillance capability." Here indeed is the ghost of MOL—flesh-and-blood spies in space. Of course, the duties of these agents in space would not be so much active espionage as the maintenance and direction of the reconnaissance equipment. In answer to the vibration problems of manned reconnaissance (the breathing and movement of the astronauts would disturb the cameras), it has been suggested that the reconnaissance station be an unmanned station in a polar orbit, serviced by astronauts operating out of the main station on interorbital tugs. Alternatively, the reconnaissance platform could fly close enough to the space station to be serviced by astronauts on simple space walk maneuvers.

It appears that the DoD perceives the idea of manned space-based reconaissance as a not entirely appealing carrot that NASA is holding out to entice their support. DARPA Director Cooper has been quoted as saying, "In ten years of groping, we haven't figured out how to use a man in space. We think it is a good idea, but we aren't sure why." The DoD is happy with their unmanned craft, and the only thing that is likely to swing them around in favor of the station is that the Soviets are likely to have one soon.

According to a report in *Aviation Week* of July 15, 1974, the 33-foot-focal-length telescope aboard Salyut-3, described by the Soviets as a "solar telescope," was, strangely enough, not aimed at the Sun at all, but at the Earth.

There has been murmuring over the years that the overall Soviet manned space mission, from Soyuz to Salyut to the space stations and space colonies they plan for the near future, has always been and always will be military in nature. The Soviets accused the Gemini astronauts of espionage and have been only slightly more restrained in criticizing the shuttle flights; indeed, their accusations that the shuttle is used for spying may not be entirely off-base. It was the imaging SLAR operating from the shuttle's cargo bay that uncovered archaeological sites beneath the Saharan sands. Obviously, such a device could just as easily be used to make radar maps of warhead impact sites in Kamchatka or submarine pens in Murmansk.

Will NASA get its space station into orbit? Will there be James Bonds in orbit? As of December 1984 the issue was still undecided. Signs for station enthusiasts are promising, though, as President Reagan supported initial funding of the project for the 1985 fiscal year.

The Forecast

In all likelihood the spies in orbit in the future will continue to be machines, not people. The trend through the 1990s seems to be to build large, high-resolution detector systems satellites with high-speed on-board processing. These satellites will have highly refined sensing capabilities in both the visible and infrared wavelengths. They will be integrated platforms in space, quite possibly in geosynchronous orbit, able to perform the tasks of launch detection, missile and aircraft tracking, and general surveillance—all in real time. SLAR will also be improved, though it seems that processing demands will prevent its use in real time; nevertheless, SLAR will remain invaluable for its ability to penetrate cloud cover. HALO may or may not replace the KH-11 and its ilk. It seems likely that some low-orbit, close-look capability will be maintained, although perhaps more for ELINT purposes than for photographic intelligence. Once DoD shuttle launches from Vandenberg begin, this chore may be carried out either directly from the shuttle or by satellites launched from the shuttle. It also seems likely that the military will rebuild some form of expendable rocket capability to supplement shuttle launches.

Perhaps the most important development will be the mobility and portability of ground stations. Combined with continuous overhead coverage, these stations will provide, for the first time, real-time, "live" tactical battlefield surveillance. While the Vietnam War has been called the first televised war, the conventional conflagrations of the future are likely to be fought using television. HALO will give commanders what they have so long sought after—the ability to look over the hill.

3 THE USE OF SPY SATELLITES

Operations

While spy satellites are the single most important means for gathering intelligence, they have by no means put every secret agent out of work. U.S. satellites are for the most part only used over countries such as the Soviet Union, China, Bulgaria, North Korea, and Albania, all of which are virtually impenetrable by agents. Although a great deal of what goes on in the Third World is of strategic interest to the U.S. intelligence community, most of it is observable by agents. A standard chauvinistic joke at the CIA is that there is no need to send satellites over the developing world, since "a used Chevy will get you a Foreign Minister and a Buick the Prime Minister."

Even where satellites are used, they are not automatons that operate by themselves, they are machines operated by people. A satellite will not take a picture unless it has been instructed to do so. The request for a satellite picture to be taken may start with a low-level analyst in the CIA's Intelligence Directorate, who, upon reading intelligence reports and after looking at a collection of satellite photographs taken before, may decide that it is time for a new series of photographs of, for example, the Soviets' Tyuratam space and missile launch facility in Central Asia.

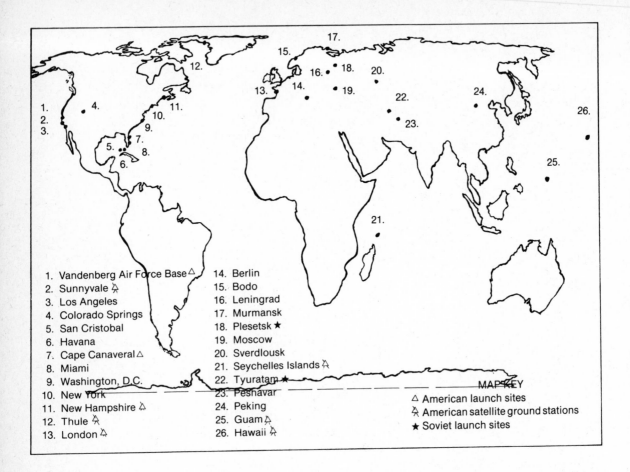

1. Vandenberg Air Force Base △
2. Sunnyvale ⋏
3. Los Angeles
4. Colorado Springs
5. San Cristobal
6. Havana
7. Cape Canaveral △
8. Miami
9. Washington, D.C.
10. New York
11. New Hampshire △
12. Thule ⋏
13. London ⋏

14. Berlin
15. Bodo
16. Leningrad
17. Murmansk
18. Plesetsk ★
19. Moscow
20. Sverdlousk
21. Seychelles Islands ⋏
22. Tyuratam ★
23. Peshavar
24. Peking
25. Guam ⋏
26. Hawaii ⋏

MAP KEY
△ American launch sites
⋏ American satellite ground stations
★ Soviet launch sites

Map of key spots discussed, including American satellite control ground stations and American and Soviet launch sites.

The analyst's request for more Tyuratam photos will pass upward through the hierarchy, being evaluated for priority at every level, until it finally reaches the national intelligence officer responsible for the junior analyst's area of concern. (In this case it might be Soviet Central Asian missile sites or Soviet military space activity.) With the proper support and priority, the request will go on to the reconnaissance committee of the U.S. Intelligence Board (USIB). The reconnaissance committee—or Comirex—is composed of members representing the various agencies that request photo reconnaissance data. If the board members agree that the request is warranted, they will pass it along to the National Reconnaissance Office (NRO).

The NRO (established August 25, 1960) has for a long time been the most secret of U.S. intelligence operations, even more hush-hush than the equally colossal National Security Agency (which monitors communications and makes and breaks codes). Although its budget is almost $3 billion annually, and its personnel numbers perhaps 50,000, the NRO is neatly hidden away in Air Force Intelligence. Only recently has the public been made at all aware of this spy-satellite operations agency—indeed, as late as 1981 many congressmen and senators had never heard of it.

The NRO's budget is controlled by the National Executive Committee for Reconnaissance (Excom), which is composed of the Assistant Secretary of Defense for Intelligence, the Director of the CIA, and the President's National Security Adviser. As mentioned, the NRO receives operational requests from Comirex, and it is from those requests, and the priority assigned each, that it draws up the Joint Reconnaissance Schedule, which sets down what the satellites will gather and when.

Master Control

Once a satellite mission request is posted in the Joint Reconnaissance Schedule, it will find its way to the Big Blue Cube. Located in Sunnyvale, California, the Big Blue Cube is a nine-story, pale-blue, windowless block of a building in the middle of an industrial park. The only hints of its true business are the telltale white satellite dishes in the parking lot. Housed inside the Cube is the Satellite Test Center, the headquarters of the Satellite Control Facility (SCF). The SCF comprises a system of eight ground stations (including the Big Blue Cube) located around the world that are used to monitor and control the NRO's secret satellites. The other stations are at Thule, Greenland (800 miles from the North Pole), the Seychelles Islands (in the middle of the Indian Ocean), Guam, Hawaii, Vandenberg AFB, New Hampshire, and England (just south of London).

The SCF monitors and controls the roughly fifty military satellites that are in orbit at any one time, making five contacts with each satellite each day. It is within the Big Blue Cube at Sunnyvale, however, that the true control of the satellites is maintained. There are seven mission-control centers inside the Cube, each assigned to a different type of satellite (reconnaissance, navigation, communications, etc.). Each mission control has its own line of communication to the various tracking stations, so that it can instruct the personnel at each station what commands are to be transmitted to the satellite when it passes over that station. These stations can command the satellite to do any number of things, from turning on a camera to firing a thruster to boost the satellite into a higher orbit. The stations also receive information from the satellite in the form of telemetry, information that ranges from the mundane (the satellite's report on its position and condition) to the dramatic (a picture of a new Soviet radar site in Siberia). This information is sent back to that satellite's mission-control center in the Cube, then finally on to whichever agency or service requested the information.

Hardening and Safeguarding

Recently, questions have been raised concerning the vulnerability of the Big Blue Cube and the network of ground stations to nuclear attack, terrorist attack, or earthquakes. Key words now tossed around in the preparations afoot for war in the future are "survivability" and "hardening." Defense planners want to harden systems against the effects of a nuclear detonation—not so much against the blast as against gamma radiation and EMP (ElectroMagnetic Pulse), both of which can wipe out computer and electrical systems. Gamma radiation causes "leaks" in semiconductors; EMP can erase computer memories and, if strong enough, permanently damage semiconductors. To make systems survivable on Earth, a first step is simply to dig them into the ground. It is with this in mind that an underground, nuclear-hardened, earthquake- and terrorist-proof backup headquarters for SCF has been built into the new Consolidated Space Operations Center near Colorado Springs. This is not merely an STC backup, for it will serve as mission control for the DoD shuttle launches and any new military satellites. The CSOC is under the control of the U.S. Space Command, which, since its inception in the fall of 1982, has been overseeing all of America's military efforts in space, from the preparations for DoD shuttle flights to military satellite operations.

The Big Blue Cube is, of course, not the only installation in the SCF system that is vulnerable. Every one of the other seven tracking stations is in an equally precarious position. Intelligence officials still shudder over the loss of American electronic listening posts in Iran when the Shah fell, and there are similar fears for the security of the tracking stations. For this reason there is a move to eliminate the ground stations as a step in the intelligence-gathering process.

To accomplish this, more processing of the information must be done on board the satellite (using the new VHSIC technology). Most important, though, is the link between the satellite and Sunnyvale

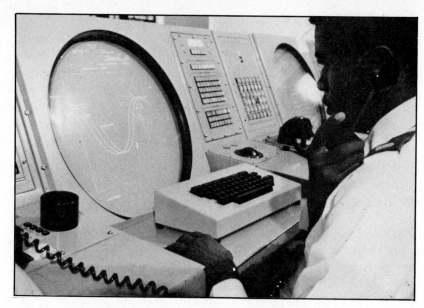

Tracking an orbiting satellite at Colorado Springs.

or Colorado Springs. When the new TDRSS—Tracking and Data Relay Satellite System—becomes operational, satellites will be able to transmit and receive information directly to and from the United States, relaying it from satellite to satellite rather than through a tracking station on the ground.

At this point, however, the stations are still used, so that an order for a picture series of the Tyuratam launch site in Central Asia would go out from the Big Blue Cube to the ground station in the Seychelles. The staff there would wait for the satellite to come within range, then beam up the order for it to activate its digital-imaging system at a precise time over a given set of coordinates. The satellite would then sail out of sight, flying high above the Indian Ocean, then on over Iran and the Soviet Union. If the satellite were one of the few remaining close-looks, it would take its pictures when directed to, then eject the recoverable film pod when it was full, and the pod would be recovered from the air off Hawaii. If the satellite used were a KH-11, then it would store its images, then beam them down to the Mission Ground Site at Fort Belvoir, near Washington. From either type of satellite, the pictures would end up at NPIC (National Photographic Interpretation Center) in Washington.

Principles of Photo Interpretation

NPIC was started under Art Lundahl's direction in the 1950s and is now located in the Washington, D.C. Navy Yard, at the corner of 1st and M streets in the Southeast section of the city. Building 213 in the yard is the home of NPIC. It is a five-story, yellow cement building notable for the fact that most of its windows have been cemented over, in an effort, it is supposed, to prevent eavesdropping. To gain an understanding of what goes on behind those closed windows, it is necessary to look at some of the principles of photo interpretation.

The most basic aerial photo interpretation is done with a single black-and-white photograph. The first step in interpretation is to learn the nature of how objects on the ground appear from the air. In day-to-day life we usually see objects on the ground from a height of 5-6 feet. And we are used to seeing cars and buildings and landmarks from the side, not the top. Accurate identification of objects depends of course on the size of the object itself and on the resolution of the photograph (from above, a haystack may look the same as a small tree or a shrub).

In general, long, thin objects like roads are the easiest to identify. Unpaved roads are lighter in color and are easier to spot then paved roads, which usually have more regular, controlled curves. Similarly, railway lines, which appear dark and narrow and are difficult to spot, can be distinguished by their long, smooth curves. While power lines themselves are too fine to be resolved, individual power line towers can be spotted, and the route of the lines can be plotted when they cut a swath through a wooded area.

In identifying other objects, such as buildings, vegetation, and landmarks, shadows play an important role—they may be either a help or a hinderance. They can help by giving a sense of the height of an object, but they hinder interpretation when the shadow can be confused with the object that casts it (from above, the shadow of a house with a black roof and the house itself may together just look like one big house). Shadows can also fall on other objects of interest, blacking them out.

The most helpful tool for a PI is a stereoscope. Most aerial photographs are taken with 60-percent overlap, so that a feature on one photograph will also appear either on the photograph before it or on the one after it in line. As the airplane or satellite is at a different point over the feature when the first picture is taken than it is when the second is snapped, the two photos will show two slightly

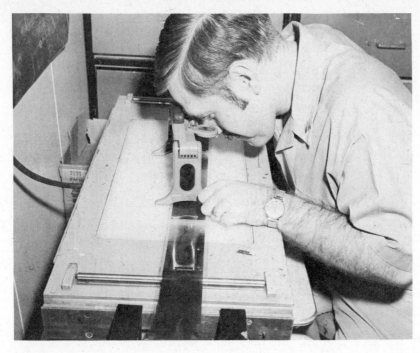

An Air Force intelligence photo interpreter at work.

different angles on an object. The stereoscope exploits this slight difference in angle so that the object can be viewed with the illusion of three dimensions.

A stereoscope is a pair of special magnifying glasses that are set 3-4 inches above a pair of overlapping photos. The matching features on the photographs are separated by the distance between the viewer's pupils—roughly 2 inches. By looking at photographs through the stereoscope, the brain is tricked into thinking that these separate images are the slightly different angled images that each eye normally sends to the brain. It takes some patience and concentration, but once the brain is fooled, it fuses the two flat images into one with three dimensions of startling, exaggerated proportions.

The stereoscope is essential in gauging the contour of terrain, something that is almost impossible to judge without a sense of depth. Through a stereoscope one can tell if a road is following a stream, a valley, or a ridge, or whether a feature is being obscured by a shadow, as the feature will pop up while the shadow remains flat. Objects viewed through a stereoscope will be vertically exaggerated by two to three times, so that a two-story building may appear to be six stories in height through a stereoscope. If, however, one happens to know the true height of at least one object in a photograph, even with the stereoscope's exaggeration, one can then calculate the height of other objects shown.

The use of infrared-sensitive film is another boon to the photo interpreter. Because of chlorophyll's specific absorption spectrum, green vegetation, which appears dark on regular panchromatic film, is quite light in infrared. Thus, one can tell the difference between true vegetation and something only painted to look like vegetation, such as military camouflage. Infrared is also very handy in plotting the precise location of water (water appears black in IR photos) and of paths and roads through fields (the vegetation appears light while the track comes out dark), and in separating a shadow from the object that cast it.

While film cannot pick up the longer-wave IR emissions from objects, detectors (like those used in the KH-11) have this capability. The information can then be translated into photographs for use by the PIs. The great advantage in detecting longer-wave IR is that it includes thermal radiation—heat. It is said that the thermal IR detectors available during the Vietnam War were so sensitive that they could pick out footprints in the jungle at night, since the footprints were warmer than the ground around them. For the PI, however, the great advantage of thermal IR information is that it can give indications of what goes on inside buildings—previously completely inaccessible terrain. By analyzing the heat patterns that emanate from a building, one can figure out the building's internal structure, traffic flow, energy consumption, and level of activity.

The partner of IR photography is multispectral photography. Just as vegetation has its own specific absorption spectrum in IR, so it does in every other band of light. This applies to all objects. A road may appear very light in the blue band and very dark in the yellow. By comparing photographs of the same terrain taken in different bands, one may distinguish between features that in panchromatic film may have appeared to be exactly the same. An example is a well-traveled road versus an unused one. Through comparison of photographs multispectral photography can provide information on the shape, size, texture, color, hue, and contrast of an object, all areas that are very hard to determine with black-and-white or even color photography.

Computers have revolutionized photo interpretation just as they have everything else. Photographs can be stored digitally, making such things as comparing different multispectral photographs easier and more exact. For example, a computer can process a picture taken in the blue band and simply superimpose it on one taken in the red. The PI is then able to see instantly the differences and similarities between the two photographs. A thermal IR picture of a missile site taken one night may indicate activity in one area, while a picture taken the next night may reveal work going on in a slightly different place. By comparing the two pictures in a computer, the PI can find out where the activity is concentrated.

Of crucial strategic value is the computer's ability to measure exactly. Its precision in photogrammetry allows the PI to judge, for example, whether or not the gauge of a rail line is wide enough to support the transport of missiles or, indeed, if a new missile's size violates a treaty. The computerized viewing screens at NPIC allow PI to move a cursor around on a photograph and get an exact measurement of an object instantly.

With the KH-11's digital imaging system, the data already exist in a form compatible with a computer, making the use of such information that much simpler. The computer is able to manipulate the image in ways that one is unable to do with pictures taken on film. If there are several different pictures of the same terrain taken from slightly different angles, the computer can fuse these images to form a graphic composite model that can be manipulated on all three axes. Suddenly, one is able to examine a three-dimensional model of a missile site that is not exaggerated like a stereoscopic image. Thus height, depth and contour become ever more measurable.

The computer is also able to scan back through a history of digital images of one target site so that it can determine what developments and changes have occurred at the site over the years. Computers can also enhance images by removing any static, by increasing or decreasing the intensity of the light, and by enlarging and highlighting certain areas, all at the touch of a key.

The new technology has in many ways made the job of the PIs easier (they can quickly scan for patterns, check old pictures, measure objects, and perform other tasks almost instantly), but it has also made their jobs harder by increasing the amount of information that each PI has to digest. Essentially, though, computers or not, the PIs' duties have remained the same since the days of Art Lundahl in the 1950s and '60s: They are supposed to figure out what is going on on the ground by examining pictures taken from as far as 100 miles above the Earth.

What Can Be Learned

Dino Brugioni, once a photo interpreter at NPIC, explains the basics of how a PI works:

If I had never even seen an area in photographs before, there are certain things I could tell. You see, in most areas of the world— Latin America, Africa, Russia, China—a man lives his life within 25 miles of where he was born. I can tell the man's diet. If there are cattle, he eats beef, and if there are barns, that means he drinks milk. Pig sties mean he will eat pork—which also tells me something about his religion—and pens indicate he raises chickens. I can tell the amount of health care in a rural area by the size of the hospitals—it's the building without a playground. I can tell whether there is education provided if there is a school or not, as the school is the building with a playground. I can tell the prevalent type of religion by the number of mosques, churches or temples.

The size of the roads, their surface, the number of railway lines into a neighborhood plant tells me the level of industrial activity in the area. I can look at a house and tell if it has indoor plumbing by whether or not there is a well or an outhouse in the yard. I can tell how the house is heated—is there an oil tank, a chimney, or a coal box? And I can tell how wealthy a man is by the car, or lack of one, in front of his house. Finally, I can tell what the death rate is by the number of new graves in the cemetery. I can track a man from birth to death.

If I see a strict pattern, then a flag goes up. That's the sign of the military. Everything will be evenly spaced. They won't put one gun battery here, the next 33 feet along, and then the other after that 57 feet further. They'll all be 60 feet, or whatever, from each other. At NPIC, it was that regularity that we were always on the lookout for.

During World War II PIs began to specialize. There were those who knew how to identify decoys, while others specialized in aircraft or radar stations or shipyards. The trend toward specialization continued, so that now at NPIC one PI might be responsible for just one or two missile sites. The PI must know every inch of his assigned area, so that he can detect the subtlest change (here of course computers are a great help, able to compare photograph to photograph in a split second).

The hardest job for the PI is to identify something new. To do so requires a "convergence of information." Pictures of the new feature, whether it be a building or something else under construction, are first analyzed in terms of what, if anything, is already known about the area. Then any related previous experience comes into play. Perhaps it has been shown in the past that a certain level of "track activity" (the disturbance of the Earth by feet or vehicles), or a certain manner of clearing vegetation, indicates that a certain type of installation will be built. The PI must also check to see if the United States has any similar sites to use for comparison. In analyzing any new site, the abilities of many may be brought to bear. In the case of the Soviet missile sites in Cuba in 1962, it was John Wright, a Soviet missile-site specialist at the Defense Intelligence Agency, not an NPIC PI, who first recognized that the configuration of SAM batteries in Cuba was similar to the deployment around IRBM sites in Russia.

PIs need encyclopedic minds. They need to know everything they can about the area they study. Brugioni recalled one instance at NPIC when they were confused by some photographs of a Himalayan village. "A short distance outside of town there was a cleared, skinned area of ground and we didn't know what it was used for. Was it a playing field? Did they play baseball there? I read up on the customs of that town and its neighbors and found that when a person dies, the town undertaker takes the body out of town to the cleared area, cuts it up and throws it around for the carrion birds and carnivores to get. The activity of the birds and animals cleared the land."

The PIs work closely with the analysts at the CIA, who also have their specialties and areas of expertise. To the PIs, the analyst is one more person who can help them identify the objects in a picture. To the analysts the PI is the person who provides the photographic information that they use (along with all the other forms of intelligence available—communications intercepts, embassy reports, HUMINT, telemetry analysis, etc.) to write their reports. In the example several pages back of a junior analyst who requests a picture series of the Tyuratam launch site, the PI will inform him of any new developments that are apparent from the pictures. The analyst may then use that information in the report he prepares for his superiors.

The Final Steps

The analyst's report will eventually serve as just one piece of input in another report on a broader issue. The closer to the President that the information gets, the broader its base, until by the time it reaches the NIE stage—National Intelligence Estimate, which is the most highly refined intelligence product, and what the President sees—dozens, perhaps hundreds of people, including PIs, analysts, and leading experts outside of the intelligence community, have added their contributions.

If the NIE makes it all the way through the CIA Director and the National Security Council to the President's desk, the final result of the junior analyst's request for a picture series of Tyuratam may be that one morning in the Oval Office the President reads one line that says: ". . . and photographic evidence of the Tyuratam launch site in Central Asia indicates that the Soviet space shuttle program may be nearing an operational capability." That one line is the result of the long process of gathering, handling, and processing the information derived from America's spy satellites.

Ramifications of Satellite-Surveillance Technology

What have been the ramifications of this satellite-surveillance technology, and what is it likely to mean in the future? This is a question that is easy to miss when one is immersed in the sophisticated technology of spying from space. Sometimes it is hard to remember that these satellites are not designed to read license plates (which they can't do) or to spot golf balls on putting greens—rather, they are designed to read the identification numbers on a Soviet missile, to monitor the speed of submarine production in Murmansk, or to judge Chinese readiness to wage war against Vietnam.

A related question arises: Are all these satellites worthwhile? They certainly are worth a good deal to the companies that make them. At TRW, a rather diversified company, its defense contracts—mostly in the field of DoD and CIA intelligence-satellite technology—accounted for one quarter of their entire sales in the second quarter of 1983. And TRW stands to receive roughly $3 billion in defense contracts over the next few years. To decide whether or not these satellites are worth it to the people who use them, we must first figure out how much they cost. Victor Marchetti put it this way: "Think how much it costs just to build an ICBM booster for the satellite [up to $30 million], and there is not only that one [estimated to be as much as $100 million each], and it also has research and development and overhead to support. Then there are the launches, which cost millions and millions of dollars per shot. And the satellite must be maintained and operated, and its material evaluated—all on special, expensive equipment." Then Marchetti added without a moment's thought: "It's well worth the cost."

On March 15, 1967, President Lyndon Johnson spoke to a small gathering in Nashville, Tennessee. In his speech on the space program he made some supposedly off-the-record remarks that reflect the importance accorded spy satellites. "I wouldn't want to be quoted on this, but we've spent $35-40 billion on the space program. [That, of course, included the manned missions. As of 1970 the space reconnaissance program had cost $10-12 billion; as of 1983, nearly $30 billion; the KH-11 alone over $1 billion. Spy satellites and their operation now cost over $2 billion per year.] And if nothing else had come out of it except the knowledge we've gained from space photography, it would be worth ten times what the whole program has cost. Because, tonight, we know how many missiles the enemy has."

Similarly, when pressed for an indication of the true ground-resolving power of satellites, former NPIC photo interpreter Dino Brugioni finally replied, "Let's put it this way—from 1950 to 1972 it was absolute, there couldn't be disarmament without on-site inspection. Then, in 1972, the President felt confident enough to sign SALT I. That's the bottom line."

SALT I and II

While satellite reconnaissance began solely as an intelligence operation, over the last decade it has gained the added responsibility of treaty verification. Article V of the SALT I agreement (signed May 26, 1972, in effect October 3, 1972) states in part that " . . . each party shall use national technical means of verification at its disposal" to verify the treaty. It wasn't until the debate over the much more comprehensive SALT II began in 1978 that those national technical means were officially identified, when, in his fight for ratification of SALT II, President Carter indicated his confidence in the capabilities of reconnaissance satellites to monitor and verify treaty compliance.

Another indication of the quality of the intelligence derived from satellites is that during the SALT II negotiations Soviet officials grew anxious when the Americans referred to facts and figures about Soviet weaponry that even some members of the Soviet negotiating team were not cleared to know.

Ultimately, of course, the treaty was never ratified (although both sides have, for the most part, abided by its provisions), in part because of the Soviet invasion of Afghanistan in 1979, which gave the opponents of the treaty in Washington all the fuel they needed to defeat it. But the main reason the treaty was never ratified was that many in the United States were not as confident as President Carter about America's ability to monitor and verify treaty compliance. Who was right, Carter or his opponents?

According to a United Nations study the highest ground resolution necessary for verification of a treaty would be two inches. That is the ground resolution required to describe artillery and rockets, the smallest strategically important objects mentioned in the study. In the UN report resolution requirements are given four gradations—detection, recognition, identification, and description. Detection of artillery and rockets requires only 35 inches; recognition, 24 inches; identification, 6 inches; and description, 2 inches. Larger objects, of course, require less resolution. Aircraft, for example, require 6 inches ground resolution to be fully described and only 35 inches to be identified. While complete description of artillery and rockets may be just beyond the KH-11's capacity, with its better than 6-inch ground resolution, it would be more than able to detect, recognize, identify, and describe an ICBM.

Another concern is whether or not the Soviets would have been able to cheat on SALT II and get away with it. There are restrictions in both SALT I and SALT II designed to ensure compliance: "Each party undertakes not to use deliberate concealment measures which impede verification of the other party." Treaty provisions notwithstanding, the question remains: Could the Soviets violate a treaty without the United States detecting it?

Dino Brugioni thought it unlikely. "A bomber requires a big airfield to land on. ICBM silos take months to dig. A 100-foot-long missile needs special roads and rail lines for transportation. Submarines need special bases. We can always readily recognize and identify their strategic forces." It might be possible to dig a silo underground, at night, camouflaged in such a way as to be undetectable, but such a buildup would be betrayed in other ways—by increased factory activity, housing construction, rail traffic, etc. To camouflage the entire infrastructure of the military would be impossible.

Some have pointed to the cruise missile as a destabilizing weapon, as it is only 21 feet long and can be hidden anywhere. It is likely, however, that the Soviet agents in the United States would soon ferret out their location, and Victor Marchetti is equally confident of U.S. intelligence resources if faced with a similar dilemma. "They could put missiles in a village, missiles in a barn, but they couldn't keep it secret forever."

A more serious problem lies in the area of determining whether or not a missile is MIRV (Multiple Impact Reentry Vehicles) equipped. It is very hard to tell what is under a missile's shroud, and this was a sticking point in SALT II. The Soviets said that they could tell the difference, so the Americans should be able to do so as well. The Americans, however, did not believe that the Soviets truly had such sophistication. This question has never been fully resolved.

A joint Soviet-American group, the Standing Consultative Commission, was established after SALL I to investigate each side's allegations of the other's impeding of their national technical means of verification. The SCC meets every six months, and so far each side has had little to complain about, although the Soviets once protested that silos in Montana were covered over. As it turned out, crews working in the winter had stretched tarpaulins across the silos' openings to keep out the cold. They had to take them down.

Undoubtedly, in any arms talks in the future, satellites will continue to play an important role. Perhaps as their sophistication increases, the negotiators for both superpowers will feel more comfortable about putting their nation's security in the hands of the spies in the sky.

The United States and the Soviet Union are not the only nations that are interested in spy satellites. France, long a nuclear power, has made noises to the effect that it might like to have its own reconnaissance capability. In 1975 China began lofting up its own 10,000-pound reconnaissance satellites from its launch site at Shuang-Cheng-Tzu Space Center, 1,000 miles west of Peking. There has also been a movement (begun by Valerie Giscard d'Estaing when he was President of France) to create a multinational reconnaissance satellite service. The UN has come up with a proposal for such an International Satellite Monitoring Agency, but so far the superpowers, jealously guarding their virtual monopoly in that arena, have responded negatively.

Secrecy and Spying from Space

There has been a great deal of discussion concerning the secrecy that surrounds spying from space. The official line is that the true capabilities of American satellites are of great interest to the Soviets, and if they were to gain access to this information, it would be seriously detrimental to America's national seccrity. The counterargument is that as the Soviets already have their own satellites, and as they obtained the KH-11 manual from Kampiles and the ELINT satellite information from Boyce and Lee, it is likely that they already know all there is to know about American capabilities. Therefore, the only people who are not being informed about the satellites are the American people. But, points out Victor Marchetti, long a critic of the cult of secrecy that pervades the American intelligence community, "I think the public gets enough information. They don't need to know how good the information is, or how often the satellites overfly. What would they do with such information?"

On the other hand, it has been pointed out that if the curtain were raised on satellite reconnaissance, there could be significant public benefit. The KH-11 could be used for search and rescue and, most of all, for LANDSAT-like resource work. The KH-11 is already used in some capacity for resource research in the analysis of other countries' agriculture and economy—we see evidence of this in those tiny newspaper articles that read, "Soviet Grain Production Down Ten Million Bushels"—and this capability of the KH-11 worries those who are already concerned about the use of LANDSAT information.

Third World countries fear that Americans, able to afford such high technology, will find oil or mineral sites in their countries from satellite photographs, then buy up the land cheaply. Such fears of a misuse of LANDSAT information are not ungrounded, and with the KH-11's awesome powers (100 times LANDSAT 4's) its use in such a manner would pose a grave economic threat to vulnerable, developing nations.

It seems likely that the secrecy surrounding spy satellites will continue at least through the rest of this century.

War in Space

Recently, spy satellites have become part of the larger question of the militarization of space. In March 1983 President Reagan made what is now known as his "Star Wars" speech, in which he envisioned a future where space-based lasers could provide the United States with an impenetrable defense, rendering nuclear weapons impotent and thus, in effect, eliminating the possibility of a nuclear war. Critics argue that even if such technology were feasible, the concept itself is destablizing.

In an article in *The New York Times* on November 15, 1983, Dr. Paul L. Chrzanowski, a key figure in the American development of the X-ray laser, was quoted as saying, "Anything this country is doing along these lines would be characterized as defensive. But I think that if the Soviets came up with the same technology, I would be a little bit nervous about possible offensive uses." Such possible offensive uses include knocking out enemy satellites as a prelude to war and, if only one country has the technology, using it to defend against a retaliatory attack after having already launched a first strike. But surely the Soviets must share Dr. Chrzanowski's worry that the other side is developing the X-ray laser for offense rather than defense. It was essentially such fear on both sides that led to the ABM treaty in the 1970s. Now, however, it seems that the only restrictions placed on this new ABM system in space will be one of cost—$1 trillion over the next 20 years, which is ten times what the space program cost over the last 20 years.

In a war in space reconnaissance satellites would be used to spot and track the rising missiles. More and more we see the evolution of the role of spy satellites from one of intelligence gathering to one that is integral to the plans for waging nuclear war. Some might even argue that spy satellites, once a key to world stablity because of their ability to prevent surprises and monitor treaties, are now a destabilizing factor because of their inextricable connection to plans for fighting and winning the unwinnable—nuclear war.

With Civil War balloons and World War I airplanes reconnaissance was initially strictly a matter for the military. It wasn't until the 1950s, when Eisenhower, Bissell, Kelly Johnson, and others saw the strategic importance of reconnaissance, that it became the province of the intelligence community. And now, it seems, after a relatively brief stint in the world of espionage, aerial reconnaissance—from the U-2 through the KH-11 to HALO of the 1990s—has become yet another cog in the war machinery. The spy is back in uniform.

PART II
THE SECRET AGENT'S TOOLS

Imagine some scenes:

There is a terrible security leak at the American embassy in Moscow, and it seems that it can only be coming from the ambassador's office. But the ambassador is above suspicion, and the room has been swept for bugs countless times to no avail: There is no electric or electronic listening device in the room. Finally, someone remembers that the great Seal of the United States above the ambassador's desk was a gift from the Soviets. A thorough search of it uncovers a small metal tube—no wires, no microphone, just a metal tube. Somehow, that tube, able to pick the vibrations of conversations out of the air without any electronic parts, has been responsible for grievous violations of U.S. security.

* * * *

In the basement of the largest, most expensive spy agency in the United States sits the fastest computer in the world. All it does, day in and day out, is crack codes, doing such complex work faster than it has ever been done before. This compact, 70-square-foot computer creates so much heat as it whirs that if its Freon cooling system failed for even a moment, the five-ton mass would melt in seconds.

* * * *

A PLO leader in Paris receives a phone call from the Italian journalist he met the day before. Strangely, the journalist asks the PLO leader to identify himself. He shrugs and says that yes, it is he. Then the phone blows up in his face.

* * * *

Unlike the spies we were concerned with in the first half of the book—satellites and airplanes that were invisible, ever vigilant, and performed their duties tirelessly—the spies we will deal with here are very much flesh and blood. They are the individual agents who use the techniques and technology of surveillance, cryptology, and "black-bag" work to gain their desired ends. They are the ones who sit up late at night, listening in on a wiretap or bug in a foreign embassy, who communicate in ciphers and codes; the ones who kill each other with poisonous dusts.

This is very much the other end of the spy spectrum. First, there is the simple matter of proximity: A spy satellite orbits 100 or so miles in space, while an agent may have to break into a building to steal a code book. Second, there is the cost factor: A spy satellite can cost $100 million, while even the most expensive radio-transmitting bug is no more than a few thousand dollars. Finally, while a system of spy satellites is espionage on the grand level of nations, involving thousands of employees, ground-based spying, and the techniques and technology it involves, is practiced bb individual agents, enforcement officials, criminals, terrorists, and even jilted lovers.

This last difference is important. In the first half of the book we were concerned with espionage technology that had global implications; that both instigated and abated crises; that was a paramount concern of the most prominent leaders of our time. Now, in the second half we will look at technology that is used to spy on corporate rivals as well as on foreign embassies. This is equipment made, not only by the Technical Services Division of the CIA and its counterparts in the secret agencies of other nations, but also by private companies both here and abroad, for use by private investigators, foreign governments, and "information brokers," who will spy for anyone willing to pay the price.

The examination of the secret agent's tools will be divided into three chapters. In the chapter on surveillance we shall take a look at how telephones are tapped, how rooms are bugged, how computers are invaded aad how people are spied on at night. This is the world of radio transmitters the size of a rice grain, of laser bugs that can pick up a conversation off a window half a mile away, of methods for deciphering what a computer is doing by noting the minute fluctuations in its power consumption. Also included will be a look at the countermeasures—from nonlinear junction detectors to time domain reflectometers—that can help prevent such intrusion. We shall also take a look at the future and what can be expected in the science of surveillance and countersurveillance in the next ten years.

The chapter on secret communications will examine secret inks, microdots, voice scramblers, and cipher machines. Also included will be a profile of the closely guarded National Security Agency which is responsible both for making U.S. national security codes and for intercepting the communications of other nations and breaking their ciphers and codes.

The black-bag chapter will cover how spies pick locks, bypass alarms, steal secrets, sabotage, and even kill. This is the truly nasty world of spy tech—a world in many ways the most exciting and the most deadly, for it is the arena in which silencers, lethal drugs, dart guns in the tips of umbrellas, blowgun pens, and other deadly dirty tricks can be found.

* * * *

The world of ground-based spying is a strange world: A world that most of us will never come in contact with; a world of spies and ex-spies, waging major and minor wars between countries and between companies, a world that is based firmly on technology—technology in which, after decades of spy fact and fiction, the public is understandably very interested.

4 SURVEILLANCE

Telephone Surveillance and Countersurveillance

Since Alexander Graham Bell patented it in 1868, the telephone has grown from a gadget that was at first deemed to have limited practical value into the most widely used medium of electronic information transfer in the world today. It has, understandably, become a prime target for those who wish to invade the privacy of others. What makes telephones even more desirable to eavesdropping spies is that, with the proper equipment, one can hear not only conversations over the wire but whatever is being said in the room as well.

Each individual telephone represents the end of a tendril of the vast electronic network known as the telephone system. In many countries (and in the United States until the breakup of AT&T in January 1984) the telephone network is owned and operated by one, generally state-owned company. This company provides the equipment that connects the telephones to each other. It also sends out over the wires the electrical current on which the system operates.

Bell's invention consisted of a tiny diaphragm attached to a metal coil that surrounded a magnet. When the diaphragm was vibrated by speech, it moved the coil back and forth over the magnet. Because of the principles of electromagnetism, this motion of coil over magnet created a small electrical current, which could then be sent over wires to a speaker that essentially operated in reverse—electricity moved a coil that vibrated a diaphragm that reproduced the original sound.

Bell's original invention was cumbersome and limited by range because of the small amount of power that a coil and magnet can produce. The next model worked a bit differently. Instead of the microphone (or diaphragm) itself producing the electricity the system used a carbon microphone with a small cavity filled with carbon granules that had a small amount of electric current running through them. When someone spoke into a carbon mike, the air vibrated a diaphragm that, in turn, compressed and decompressed the carbon granule cavity. It was this compression and decompression that affected the flow of electricity through the mike. At the other end of the line these fluctuations in current could be used to vibrate a diaphragm in a speaker. This is essentially the system in use today.

The four main components of a standard telephone are: the microphone, which is in the mouthpiece of the handset; the speaker, in the earpiece of the handset, the dial (rotary or push-button); and the "hook switch," the device in the cradle of most phones that keeps the mike, speaker, and dial disconnected from the phone system when the instrument is not in use.

"Off hook" means that the telephone is in operation—the handset has been lifted off the cradle; "on hook" means that the telephone is not in use—the handset is still resting on the cradle. On hook, the line current is 48 volts. When the telephone is lifted off hook, however, the voltage drops to between 6 and 12 volts. Approximately 60-100 milliamperes of current run through the telephone instrument when it is off hook and in use. It is this current that the carbon microphone modulates according to speech and that is then retranslated back into speech at the other end of the line.

This running current is important to eavesdroppers, for to listen in on a conversation, one merely has to intercept the current. To use the phone as a means of listening in on a room conversation, the agent has to bypass the hook switch in some way so that the phone, although appearing to be on hook and disconnected, is technically off hook and is transmitting over the telephone wires what it can hear of the room conversation through its own microphone.

Tapping

There are two types of taps—direct and wireless. Direct taps, as their name suggests, are intercepts that are attached directly to the phone line anywhere between the telephone and the exchange and then run off by wire to a listening post—which may be manned by either the stereotypical agent, sweating in the basement, or merely a tape recorder. A wireless telephone tap, although employing a direct intercept of the line current, uses a radio transmitter rather than a direct wire to send the intercepted call to the listening post.

If a spy wishes to tap a phone directly, he or she first locates the phone line that is to be invaded. This is obviously easier to do when it is just one overhead wire running from the suburban residence of a foreegn consul than when it is one line of thousands in a downtown building where the consul's office is located.

To tap a household in a suburban situation (the consul's or perhaps a suspected Bulgarian safehouse in a town near Silicon Valley), the wiretapper follows the "drop wire" that emerges from the house and goes to a nearby pole-mounted terminal, where it connects to a twenty-five-pair aerial distribution cable. The tapper then climbs the pole and notes the color of the pair to which the houses's drop wire is connected. He can either hook up a tap there or follow the aerial distribution cable a few blocks to another pole-mounted terminal, where it hooks up with an aerial branch feeder cable with 200 pairs (in eight binder groups). Again, he can either hook up the tap there or follow the line to the main feeder cable, which consists of 600 pairs in twenty-four binder groups. Agents consider it best to tap into the line at a terminal post because the cables between the terminals are pressurized, so that any break in their sheathing can be detected.

Tapping in an urban area poses problems. Whether the agent is after a consular office in an office building or the apartment home of a suspected terrorist, he must go to the basement where terminal boxes are usually located in apartment and office buildings. There are several ways the tapper can find the pair of lines he wishes to tap into if the subject is in an office or an apartment. If the person or persons he wishes to tap happen to be on the line while he is at the terminal box, he can simply hook up his headphones to each pair of lines until he finds the voice he is looking for.

He may also hook up a lineman's handset to any pair, then dial the number he wishes to tap, and let it ring. He then runs a wet finger or a coin down the terminal posts in the box until he feels either a small jolt or sees a spark from the 48 line volts being used to ring the person's phone. To avoid this minor shock, a small light bulb attached to a resistor can be touched to the posts, and it will light up when it touches the active line.

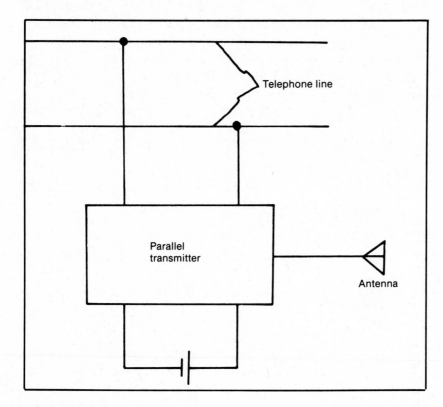

Diagram of the installation of series and parallel transmitters.

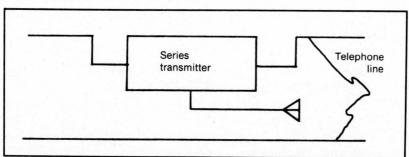

When the proper line has been determined, the wiretapper can then hook up a battery-powered high-impedance amplifier and some headphones to the line and listen in. This type of tap is hooked up in a parallel circuit, which does not use the phone system's power but requires batteries or some other form of power generation. If the spy must use the phone system's electricity, then the tap can be hooked up in series. These series taps create an extra draw on the line, causing a drop in the line voltage that is easily detected. In fact, any drop of over 20 milliamperes can be detected by the phone company itself, and if they do detect an extra draw, they will send out a repairman to investigate—something the agent does not want.

Another type of tap, the inductive tap, is also considered to be a direct tap even though it does not require any direct contact with either the telephone or the line. The inductive tap operates on the basic principle of electromagnetism, that a magnetic field surrounds

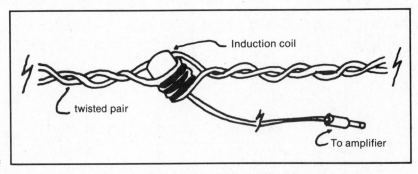

Installation of an induction tap.

any flow of electric current. Theoretically, therefore, by picking up the magnetic field surrounding the current in the phone line an agent can intercept a phone call without ever touching the line. But this is more than theory. The inductive tap actually works, using a metal coil wrapped around the phone lines, with wires from either end of the coil running off to an amplifier. One advantage of this method is that a properly installed inductive tap is virtually impossible to detect. There are, however, detractions. Because the magnetic field it taps is rather weak, the signal output from the sensing coil is somewhat low, and the coil is subject to interference and distortion from other magnetic sources as well.

Any tap can be made into a wireless tap. All that is necessary is to hook up a small radio transmitter to the tap itself, so that intercepted calls can be broadcast to a nearby receiver rather than run there by wire. The simplest of these is the drop-in telephone bug, a tap that is disguised to look exactly like a telephone microphone. The agent merely unscrews the microphone cap, takes out the old mike, and drops in the new one. Inside this otherwise normal-looking telephone mike is a small radio transmitter that broadcasts the intercepted conversation along the phone line to the eavesdroppers. Although easy to install, drop-in transmitters can be easily detected because they draw power from the phone lines.

Other radio-transmitting taps are usually hooked up somewhere along the line and are no larger than a grain of rice; tiny enough to be slipped inside the insulation cover on a telephone line. However, as will be discussed later, radio-frequency (RF) transmitters pose certain problems in operation, so that direct wiretaps are preferred by eavesdroppers.

There are a few devices that can make an eavesdropping agent's life easier. With a gadget called a dropout relay, a tap can be set to turn on only when the phone is in use (it detects the drop in line voltage when the handset is lifted off hook). Also useful are recorders, which will note when and to what number each call from the phone under surveillance was dialed. Of course, the numbers can also be recovered by taping the calls and playing them back at a slower speed in order to pick up either the number of rotary dial clicks or the tones from a push-button phone.

The Telephone as a Bug

Not only can a spy tap into a line to intercept phone calls; in addition, the telephone and its line also can be used to bug a room, and as the telephone is virtually omnipresent these days, such a prospect can be very attractive to the spy. Essentially, a phone used to bug a room must be actually off hook while appearing to be on hook. The hook switch must be bypassed so that some current gets through to operate the carbon microphone. Thus activated by the current, the mike can pick up the room conversation and then transmit it over the telephone lines as if it were a regular telephone conversation.

The notorious infinity transmitter is designed to do just that. This type of transmitter got its name from its original manufacturer who claimed that it could be operated from virtually an "infinite" distance—from anywhere in the world with direct dialing. It is a small device that is installed directly in the target's phone. When the spy wishes to listen in to the room conversation, he dials the target's number and immediately, before the phone rings, sends a tone along the line that activates the infinity transmitter, which bypasses the hook switch and cuts off the ring. The phone has, in effect, been answered: It is now off hook, even though it is still resting on the cradle and appears on hook, and the occupant of the room is none the wiser.

The infinity transmitters used by agents and other professional eavesdroppers have different levels of sophistication. The simplest is triggered by one tone sent over the line. The problem with this is that countersurveillance experts will "sweep" phone lines with a tone generator in an attempt to trigger such a device. However, the more sophisticated infinity transmitters are turned on by a coded sequence of up to five tones, which makes them virtually impossible to uncover with a tone sweep.

Infinity transmitters are not perfect eavesdropping tools. The telephone's microphone can only pick up conversation within about 30 feet of the phone (if that), and the sound quality is rather poor. Also, the switching systems in some countries may delay the triggering tone so that it does not reach the target telephone before it rings. The abbreviated ring may alert the person the agent is trying to bug that something is amiss.

Another problem is that the infinity transmitter only picks up room conversation and will shut itself off the instant the phone is put in use. It must do so, for if it remained in operation when the target picked up his phone, the target would have a direct line to the eavesdropper. Also, there is an attendant drop in line voltage with the use of one of these devices. It doesn't drop so much that the phone company thinks there is something wrong with the telephone; it only goes down to around 23 volts, the voltage used when one is on hold. But even this meager drop is easily detected by professional sweepers.

The biggest problem with the infinity transmitter is that while it is in use anyone else calling the target number will get a busy signal. People who are told by friends that their phone is busy all the time, even when they are not using it, would certainly get suspicious—if not of an infinity transmitter, then at least that the phone was malfunctioning.

The Listen-back, Keep-alive, and Direct Crosswire

The listen-back and the keep-alive, like the infinity transmitter, are tiny devices that are wired directly into the telephone instrument and that allow the eavesdropper to bypass the hook switch and listen in on the room conversation. But while the infinity transmitter is triggered by a tone, with a listen-back or keep-alive the target phone must be answered to trigger the circuitry. Then, when the target hangs up, the keep-alive or listen-back will continue to allow a small amount of current to trickle through the microphone and back down the line to the eavesdropper; this current is shut off when the eavesdropper hangs up. Of course, anyone calling in will activate keep-alives and listen-backs, which are also subject to the liabilities of an infinity transmitter (voltage drop, busy signal, etc.). Still, such devices are very small and may be harder to detect by visual inspection than an infinity transmitter.

The direct-crosswire technique can be used only with six-button

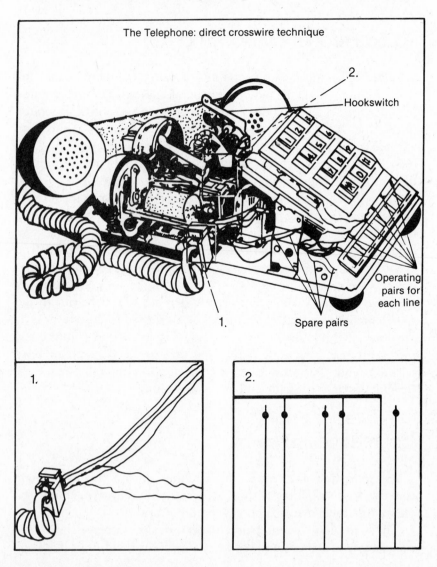

The Telephone: direct crosswire technique

2.

Hookswitch

Operating pairs for each line

1.

Spare pairs

The direct crosswire, listen-back and keep-alive techniques. In box one we see where the spare pair is hooked up to the lines coming from the curly cord. Box two shows the workings of the hookswitch. As shown, the phone is on hook; if the nodules were touching it would be off-hook. Listen-backs and keep-alives rig the switch so that it is always off-hook, whether the receiver is on the cradle and the buttons depressed or not.

1.

2.

phones (five lines and one hold button). In such phones there is usually one pair of lines to each button as well as a loose spare pair or two. One of these spare pairs can be hooked up directly to the lines coming in from the microphone through the curly cord that connects the handset to the phone. Then, outside on the line somewhere, this spare line can be tapped. In effect, hooking up the spare pair directly to the microphone bypasses the hook switch and keeps one line open at all times. In addition, as this is a spare line and not a number that one could dial, it does not cause anyone calling in to get a busy signal.

Radio Frequency Flooding

Perhaps the most exotic method of using the phone lines for eavesdropping involves radio-frequency flooding. The agent finds the telephone line to the target area, then hooks up an RF generator to the line. An RF generator can produce radio energy at different selected frequencies, so that the agent can turn the dial until he finds the frequency at which the line and telephone resonate—a process like tuning in a station on a radio. This is the operating frequency, and it will emanate from the phone's speaker into the room and will be picked up by the microphone. This RF energy will be altered by the vibraaions of any conversation in the target room. By demodulating the fluctuations in the resonating frequency, the agent is able to translate the modulations back into the original voices. One great advantage of such a bugging technique is that it is a passive system—it does not require that any device be put in the target premises—and it is impossible to detect when not in use. However, RF flooding is an extremely expensive and complicated method to use, for, while it isn't too hard to flood the phone lines with RF, interpreting it when it comes back, although technically possible, is very difficult and time-consuming.

Countermeasures

As spies are interested in listening in on the telephone conversations of others, they are naturally sensitive about the security of their own telephone communications.

The simplest countersurveillance device screws into the mouthpiece of a phone and has a little red light that blinks if anyone

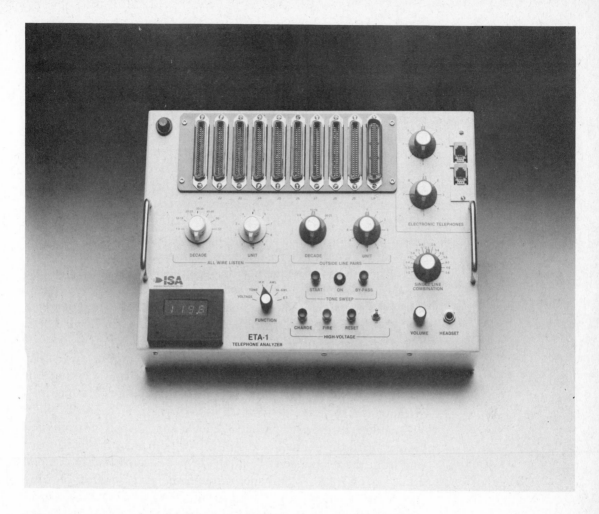

An ETA-1 countermeasures telephone analyzer. Courtesy of Information Security Associates (ISA).

is listening in on an extension—including most taps. Toward the other end of the scale in terms of sophistication is the ETA-1 Universal Telephone Analyzer, which can be used to test both on- and off-hook line voltages, to check the line for audio signals, and to do a tone sweep for infinity transmitters. The most sophisticated telephone-protection analyzers have microprocessors that memorize the conditions of the lines and can detect even the slightest change from one sweep to the next. Change is a crucial consideration and a key problem with any detection system. If one checks a line after it has been violated with a tap without any idea of what that line was like when it was "clean," then there is no way of judging the security of that line.

According to one debugging expert, no countermeasure available can conclusively determine the existence of a properly installed wiretap—in general, the only sure method to check for taps is to visually inspect the phone and its lines.

A time-saving aid in physical detection is the time-domain reflectometer. A TDR hooked up to a phone line will send an audio pulse along it. When the pulse comes back, it will have been altered by any joints, junctures, splices, kinks, or taps along the line. These "bumps" can be plotted and printed out in the form of a graph. Since there is no way to tell the difference between a simple kink in the line and an actual wiretap, however, every "bump" would have to be checked out visually. If the agent had a record of what the line was like when it was clean, he would need to check it only when a change appeared. If there is no trustworthy record of a clean line, the procedure in an office situation, where dozens of lines may follow the same route, would involve checking each parallel line individually, plotting with the TDR, and comparing their graphs. If all the lines show the same bumps, then it is likely that there is no tap present, but if the agent's line shows a major disturbance at the point where the other lines are clean, then there is a chance that the line has been tapped at that point.

If an agent believes a tap is present, he can remove it by visually following the line to the point of disturbance and yanking out whatever is causing it. One way to accomplish the same feat, without the spy having to crawl around in air ducts and between walls, involves the use of what is known as a "hi-pot" or insulation tester. With the phone line disconnected both from the instrument and from the telephone system, the hi-pot is connected to one end and a zap of 5,000 volts is shot through the lines, in effect blowing away any tap that might be present. It is vital that the agent disconnect the line at both ends before zapping, otherwise the spy will not only probably melt his own phone but will severely disrupt the phone company's lines as well.

Induction taps, it should be noted, are both undetectable with a TDR and immune to the blast of a hi-pot. Also, even the most thorough visual search may not turn up every tap. Some microminiaturized devices can be so cleverly concealed as proper parts of the telephone that they can be visually detected only with the aid of an X-ray machine. Nevertheless, even though all taps cannot be detected and removed, an agent can maintain security, by taking some simple preventive measures, such as not communicating sensitive information over the phone, or at least using some kind of ciphering or voice-scrambling device.

Also, as the phone not only can be tapped but also can be used as a bug itself, there are a few precautions for a spy to take:

1. On a six-button office phone the agent should make sure that all the buttons are up when the phone is not in use. This cuts in half the number of electrical connections in the phone, making it harder for the instrument to be used to pick up room conversation.

2. There are white-noise generators, which can put down a masking tone on the lines when it is not in use, and magnetic field generators, which will flood the telephone instrument (but not the lines) with a magnetic wash that will also disturb any bugging attempts.

3. The telephone should be disconnected when it is not being used, and if the agent suspects that it may contain a radio-transmitting bug, the phone should be removed from the room whenever valuable information is being discussed.

For the high-level agent afraid of telephone bugging by RF flooding, there are filters that can be put on the lines that will block out the RF frequencies while allowing audio to pass through.

Ultimately, detecting and defeating a tap depends on the level of sophistication of the device and of the people who installed it. Simple taps and poorly installed bugs can be detected because of voltage drops, because of a continuous busy signal, or because there is audio going over the lines that shouldn't be there. Well-installed, sophisticated taps are nearly undetectable and undefeatable, except with the use of equally expensive and sophisticated equipment. The trick for the agent is to evaluate his threat level realistically. For example, a junior analyst who works for the CIA cover company in Istanbul probably need not worry that his phone is being violated by RF flooding, in which case simple precautions, such as those already mentioned, may be all that is required. On the other hand, the KGB station chief in London can expect to have every conceivable sophisticated telephone-intrusion technique used against him.

The Future

Telephone surveillance may be on the verge of becoming a thing of the past. We are on the frontiers of a technology—fiber optics—that for all intents and purposes will spell the end of telephone tapping as we know it. With fiber optics telephone conversations are carried along as pulses of light inside tiny, hairlike fiber tubes. Although there have been some suggestions that it might be possible to make a laser holograph of the light pulses and then retranslate that holograph back into speech, for all practical purposes these communications would be untappable. Currently, fiber optics communications are in use by the DoD and in the internal-communications systems of some large companies.

There is also the possibility of untappable millimeter-wave communications, in which messages would be sent via superhigh-frequency waves in deeply buried tubes—deeply buried of necessity, because waves at such frequencies are in effect extremely dangerous radiation.

Phones may continue to be both tappable and buggable for only another five to ten years. When telephone surveillance as we know it comes to an end, the only method remaining for spies to eavesdrop on one another will be bugging.

Bugging and Debugging

In bugging we encounter the most exotic devices in the field of surveillance. There are the tiny bugs disguised as martini olives (the waterproof bug concealed in the olive, the toothpick acting as the radio antenna) that were popular in spy fiction of the 1960s; there are listening devices that contain a microphone, battery, and radio transmitter and are as small as the eraser on the end of a pencil; there is the laser bug, a "passive" listening device that can pick up the vibrations of a conversation off a windowpane, up to a half-mile away; then translate them back into speech; and there is the microwave resonating tube, the nonelectronic, passive device that Soviets used to bug the U.S. embassy in Moscow.

Yet, even with all these exotic devices, the bug that is most durable, most reliable, and hardest to detect is also by far the cheapest and the simplest—a tiny hearing-aid microphone connected to a listening post by a thin strand of copper wire.

Microphones

At the heart of every bug is a microphone, and there are several different types of microphones available to the eavesdropping spy. The carbon microphone used in the telephone is one of the simplest. As described in the previous section, the carbon microphone has a small cavity that is filled with carbon granules and that compresses and decompresses when vibrated by sound. These compressions and decompressions affect the small flow of electricity that courses through the granules. These electrical fluctuations can be translated back into speech. However, since carbon microphones require a constant flow of electricity to operate, they are not ideally suited for espionage work because their battery power consumption limits their operational life. Another problem is that carbon mikes can be easily damaged by jarring or by extreme temperatures.

Both crystal and magnetic/dynamic mikes produce their own electricity —not enough to send their message over a wire, but it

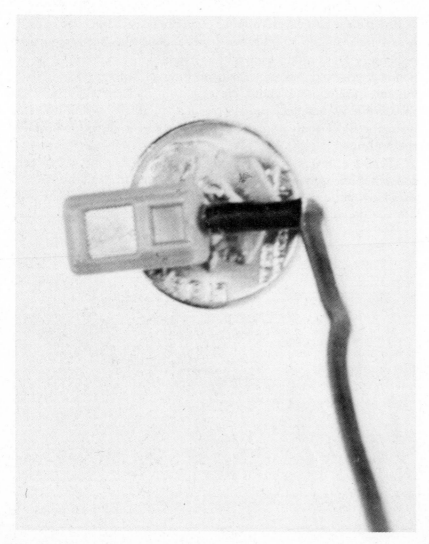

An ultra-miniature microphone. Courtesy of Law Enforcement Associates (LEA).

does lessen the overall power consumption, prolonging a bug's life. In the crystal mike, sound causes crystals inside the microphone to vibrate, which in turn creates a tiny fluctuating electric current. These are cheap, highly sensitive microphones, but they are very susceptible to temperature changes and must be handled carefully. The magnetic/dynamic mike is based upon Bell's initial design for the telephone. It contains a diaphragm attached to a coil that can move back and forth between the poles of a fixed magnet. Movement of the diaphragm (caused by sound vibrations) produces a weak, varying current in the coil. These are also small, very sensitive microphones, but their great liability is that they are susceptible to magnetic jamming.

Perhaps the best eavesdropping microphone is the electret, which is extremely small, is highly sensitive, and exhibits good frequency response. This mike cannot be magnetically jammed. It is nonmagnetic and has a permanent internal voltage charge that vibrates in response to audio, creating a small electrical output. As the output is very low, the electret has a built-in preamplifier to boost the signal (only a small amount of power is needed to operate the preamp).

There are several other microphones that can be used: the condenser microphone, which will pull in sound from all directions; the electrostatic mike, in which the diaphragm acts as one plate of a

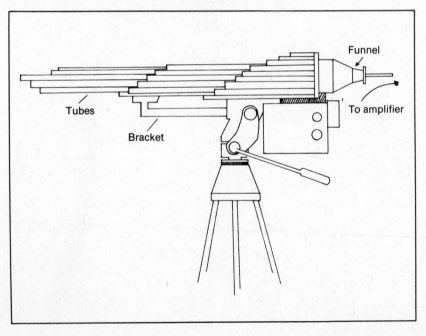

Diagram of a shotgun microphone.

capacitor; and the ribbon mike, a variation on the dynamic in which a ribbon, instead of a moving coil, vibrates in a magnetic field. Generally, the most commonly used bugging microphones are dynamic or magnetic. This is because of their size, ability to produce their own current, widespread availability, and durability.

If the spy wishes to listen in on a conversation on a street, in a park, or in any other large open space, there are two basic types of microphones available: the rifle, or shotgun, mike and the parabolic mike. The rifle mike uses an array of tubes of varying length as a waveguide for sound. One design employs thirty-seven tubes ranging in length from 1 to 36 inches, all bound together, feeding sound into a dynamic microphone. The parabolic mike focuses sound on a microphone at the center of a large parabolic dish (usually 1.5 to 3 or 4 feet in diameter).

The most common legitimate use of such microphones is at sporting events, to pick up the sound of soccer kicks, hockey slapshots, and colliding football players. Several factors make them less than ideal for clandestine work. First, although under ideal conditions (cool, clear, dry, still) a rifle mike might pick up a conversation up to 200 feet away, and a parabolic, up to 300 feet away, they are both susceptible to interference from thermal updrafts, wind, and ambient noise. Also, and perhaps most important, they are large devices that are easily visible, and it might be very hard for agents to explain just what they were doing pointing one at, say, a Soviet diplomat out on his balcony in Athens.

Bugging Configurations

The most common bugging configuration is the "mike and wire": A small microphone is simply concealed in a target room, and a wire is run off it to a listening post. This method is simple, cheap, and hard to detect.

To set up a mike and wire, the agent must first gain access to the premises and hide the bug in the target room. As the wire will both transmit conversations out and send power in, almost any kind of mike can be used. The best bet for the agent would probably be a tiny electret, which can be placed almost anywhere. Common places for spies to hide mikes are telephones, lampshades, potted plants, desk pen sets, and the like. If the device is small enough, it can be disguised as the head of a nail in the wall, or it can be slipped down the spine of a book. Once the bug is planted, a wire is run out of the room from the bug. The thinnest wire possible is used. Some resourceful agents have been known to unwind and use the thin copper wire that makes up the coil on a electric train-set transformer.

The wire is usually run along cracks in plaster or wood or under the baseboard. If at any point the wire must cross open floor space, special electrically conductive paint can be used in place of the wire for that stretch. To exit from the room the wire can be run out with the telephone line. If the wire is to run near AC-current wires for any stretch, it has to be shielded in some way from the effects of AC hum.

Once out of the room the wire is simply run to a listening post that can be up to a mile away, depending on the quality of the wire. The mike and wire can only be spotted through a visual search, and if well hidden, they will go undetected. The only other possible way to discover them would be with a metal detector, but with the bug so small and the wire so thin, they would not register on the metal detector as anything greater than a finishing nail, and thus would get lost amid all the various bits and pieces of metal in any room.

The big drawback of the mike-and-wire method is that its use requires that the agent gain access to the target premises for about five or six hours of uninterrupted installation time. Such a luxury is rarely available to the spy.

The Bug Next Door

If the agent cannot get into the room or is afraid to hide a device in it because it might be found, then bugging is often conducted from a room adjacent to the target room—to either side as well as above and below. Some technique must then be used to pick up the sound through the wall. For the spy in a hurry who must improvise, the simplest method is to cup a drinking glass against the adjacent wall and seal the rim to the wall with putty or tape. The agent then puts his ear up to the glass and, believe it or not, hears what is being said. The next step up in this vein is the electronic stethoscope, which is exactly what one might think it is—a medical stethoscope with a microphone inside that is wired up to an amplifier.

Beyond that, the spy can either drill into the adjacent room to make way for the entrance of a clandestine mike, or hook up a mike to the wall in such a way that it can pick up the conversations through the vibrations of the wall. Most microphones require that the sound striking them be transmitted through the air. To use such a mike, the spy has to drill right through a wall into the other room,

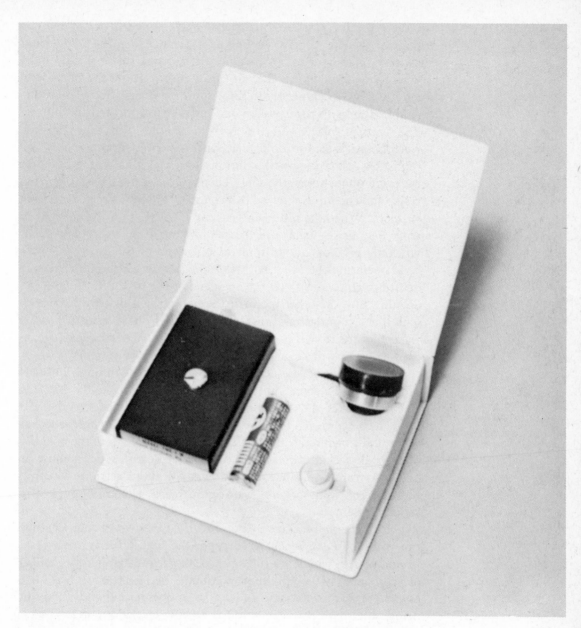

to allow the air to come through to the mike. Such drilling is usually
done slowly with a hand drill at the baseboard level, so that the drill
bit emerges through wood into the target room. If it came through
plaster or wallboard, it might cause chipping. The hole only needs
to be 1/8 or 1/16 inch in diameter.

   The mike used in a through-the-wall drill operation is most often
a tube mike, either rigid or flexible. As its name suggests, a tube

*An electronic stethoscope.
Courtesy of Private
Protection Inc.*

mike is a microphone—usually dynamic—sealed in at the end of a plastic tube that conducts sound to it. An agent in the field, bereft of ready-made surveillance equipment, could make a tube mike with a small dynamic mike, an empty 35mm film can, a foot-long length of 1/4-inch plastic tubing, some cork, and fiberglass resin.

The film can's top is taken off, and a hole is drilled through it. The cork is placed on the bottom of the film can, and the microphone is set on top of that, with its wires running out of the can. Next, the tube is stuck into the can and glued into place over the microphone set on the cork. Then the can is filled with fiberglass resin, and the top is screwed back on with the tube protruding from the hole. When the resin hardens, the agent runs off the wires to an amplifier, and—voila!—he has a working tube microphone that will only pick up sound from the open end of the tube.

In operation the agent will stick the tube mike through the hole drilled in the wall so that the open end of the tube is flush with the opening into the other room. If the hole is well placed (perhaps to look like a countersunk finishing nail hole in the baseboard), and if the end of the tube is painted a dark color to make it inconspicuous, then the bug will go undetected in most cursory searches.

Often it may not be necessary actually to drill through into the other room. In some buildings (especially poorly built ones) an electrical socket in one room will match up with a socket on the wall of the next room. All the eavesdropper need do is take off the socket cover in his own room and stick a tube mike through to the opening of the wall socket of the target room. Needless to say this must be done very carefully, since there is a good deal of electricity coursing through the wall sockets, waiting to teach a clumsy spy a very serious lesson.

Even if the wall sockets are not directly opposite one another, they can still be used as a port of entry for the spy. What is needed is a keyhole mike, which is a tube mike that uses a flexible tube instead of a rigid one. Although the sound quality derived from its use is not as good as that from a rigid-tube mike, it does have the advantage of being able to be threaded through narrow cracks, around corners, and through keyholes.

Nevertheless, no matter how small the hole into the other room, and even if the agent uses an existing entry—such as a wall socket, a crack, or a keyhole—if a thorough and detailed search is conducted, the device can be uncovered by sight. Therefore, contact and spike mikes are often used, since they do not require an opening into the target room. Contact mikes are most commonly used to amplify

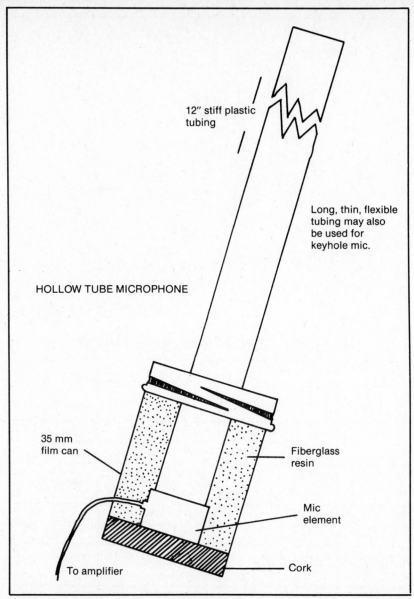

12" stiff plastic tubing

Long, thin, flexible tubing may also be used for keyhole mic.

HOLLOW TUBE MICROPHONE

35 mm film can

Fiberglass resin

Mic element

To amplifier

Cork

Diagram of a tube microphone.

acoustic musical instruments. They pick up the sound vibrations not from the air but from their contact with the vibrating surface of the instrument. Just as a contact mike can be attached to the wood of an acoustic guitar, it can be hooked up to a wall in order to pick up the sound of conversations bouncing off the other side of that wall.

In its simplest configuration a contact mike is placed up against a wall in common with the target room, ideally at a point where a structural stud joins the two walls, for the stud will conduct the

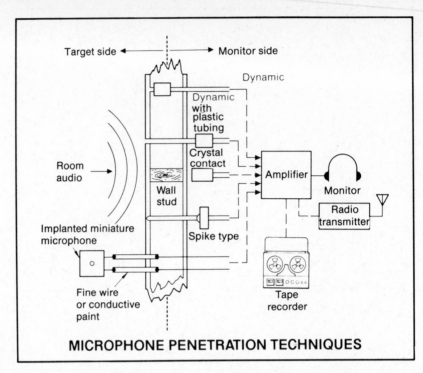

MICROPHONE PENETRATION TECHNIQUES

Diagram showing various next-door bugging techniques.

TYPE	USE	OPERATING PRINCIPLE	NOMINAL CHARACTERISTICS
CARBON	TELEPHONE MOUTHPIECE, AUDIO SECURITY SYSTEMS	VARIES CURRENT FLOW ACCORDING TO AUDIO RECEIVED	1" TO 3" DIAMETER
DYNAMIC	GENERAL WIDE USE	GENERATES ELECTRICAL SIGNALS ACCORDING TO AUDIO RECEIVED	½" TO 2" DIAMETER
ELECTRET	GENERAL WIDE USE	GENERATES ELECTRICAL SIGNALS ACCORDING TO AUDIO RECEIVED	¼" TO ½" DIAMETER
CRYSTAL, SPIKE AND CONTACT	SENSE WINDOW AND WALL VIBRATIONS	CONVERTS VIBRATIONS INTO ELECTRICAL SIGNALS	VARIOUS
PNEUMATIC CAVITY	SENSE WINDOW AND WALL VIBRATIONS	CONVERTS VIBRATIONS INTO ELECTRICAL SIGNALS	3" – 7" DIAMETER
SHOT GUN AND PARABOLIC	DIRECTIONAL SENSING OF SOUND, SPORTS, ENTERTAINMENT	FOCUSES SOUND VIBRATIONS COMING FROM ONE DIRECTION	18" – 36" DIAMETER OR 3' TO 6' IN LENGTH RANGE –60–300 FEET
CAPACITOR OR CONDENSER	GENERAL WIDE USE	CONVERTS AUDIO INTO CORRESPONDING VARIATIONS CIRCUIT FREQUENCY	½" TO 2" DIAMETER

Microphone devices summary.

MICROPHONE DEVICES SUMMARY

room's sound much better than will the airspace between the two walls.

A more sophisticated configuration employs the spike mike. A hole is drilled toward the adjacent room but is stopped short of puncturing the target wall. Then a metal spike is stuck all the way into the hole, until it presses slightly against the wall of the room to be bugged. A contact mike or even a crystal mike (in fact, even the stylus from an old record player would do in a pinch) is then attached to the end of the spike. Any conversations in the next room will vibrate against the wall, through the metal spike, and into the mike. The hole that is drilled through the first wall must be wide enough so that the spike does not touch the sides of the hole at any point, for if it does, the sound quality will be deadened. Also, the eavesdroppers must be very quiet, as any sounds they make will also be picked up by the spike.

Tape Recorders

Tape recorders are a critical part of any agent's eavesdropping operation, especially if the listening post cannot be manned at all times. The type of tape recorder to be used depends on the type of job to be done. If the spy is going to leave the recorder on the target premises, connected to the bug, then size is the main restriction. Some clandestine recorders are smaller than a box of wooden matches. Of course, the smaller the tape recorder, the smaller its tape spools and the shorter its running time. One way to get around this is to use extremely thin recording tape, but that can easily jam in the machine. Another answer is to slow down the speed of the recorder. This crams in more information per inch of tape, though it lowers the audio quality.

If the tape recorder is to be left just off premises—perhaps in an adjacent room—and the size, while still a consideration, does not have to be too small, then there are many tape recorders—of the Sony Walkman size and smaller—that will provide running times of twelve hours or more. In such cases, though, it is not the tape recorder size but its power draw that limits its running time. If the tape recorder can simply be plugged into a wall socket, that is not a worry, but if it has to run off a battery, then the battery's life (eight hours, on average) will determine the recorder's longevity.

One way for the eavesdropping agent to partially get around the constraints of battery power and tape supply is to use a voice-activation control—commonly known as VOX—which can be plugged into the remote jack of a tape recorder. When its own microphone hears a voice, it turns on the tape recorder, and then, when the voices stop for a certain length of time—longer than a conversational pause—shuts it off. The use of a VOX does not entirely circumvent the problem of battery life. Although the VOX will keep the tape recorder shut off while it is not needed, the VOX itself must run all the time, listening for sounds. However, the power consumption of a VOX is much lower than that of a tape recorder.

If the tape recorder does not have to be concealed (if the listening post is secure and well removed from the target area) and if power is not a consideration, then open-reel recorders are used, as they are of much higher quality and can record days of conversation on a single reel.

Wireless Bugs

All the technology described thus far in this section has had one major drawback: The eavesdropper must gain access to the target premises, or at least an adjacent room, for an extended period of time in order to install the listening device. To make matters worse, in many instances the eavesdropper may have to return to the scene, perhaps again and again, to change the recording tape or the bug's batteries. Naturally, this increases the possibility of the spy's detection and capture.

Ideally, the agent would make only one brief, initial sortie onto the premises, plant the bug, and then walk out, never having to return again. If there was not enough time to lay a wire, or if the listening post were too far removed from the target premises to permit the use of a wire, then a radio-transmitting bug could be used.

Basically, such a device is akin to a singer's cordless microphone. It is a miniature radio-broadcasting station that takes the sound picked up by the microphone and sends it out on the air in the form of radio waves. It is then picked up at a distance by a radio receiver, which amplifies it for other people to hear. In the case of a singer, this involves an audience of hundreds or thousands; in the case of a spy, one person in a basement with earphones.

Principles of Radio

Radio waves are but one part of the vast electromagnetic spectrum of waves, which ranges from the very long, very low-frequency waves of electricity to the extremely short, extremely high-frequency waves of light and beyond. Electromagnetic wavelength is calculated with electricity at 10-7 meters per wave and visible light at 10-7 meters per wave. Frequency is calculated in number of cycles per second (one cycle is called a hertz, after Heinrich Rudolf Hertz, a German physicist of the 1800s, with domestic electricity at 50-60 Hz and visible light at 10^{15} Hz. Other major signposts in the spectrum are: sound 90-7,000 Hz (or 7 kiloHertz [kHz]); AM radio, 550-1,600 kHz; FM radio, 88-108 megaHertz (mHz); and VHF and UHF TV channels, where channels 2-6 are from 50-88 mHz, and channels 7-83 are from 174-1,000 mHz, or 1 gigaHertz (gHz)). Above 1,000 gHz (1 trillion cycles per second) come infrared, visible light, ultraviolet light, and beyond, into X-ray and gamma waves.

In between and around the most commonly used frequency bands are other bandwidths used for both civilian and government communications purposes. Some of these are: shortwave (actually, relatively long waves at 2-25 mHz); citizens band, 25-31 mHz; government and public service, 31-50 mHz; aircraft voice communications, 116-135 mHz; business band and police, 150-174 mHz, microwave and satellite communications, 1-10 gHz. For the military the high-frequency, extremely shortwave bandwidths are the most attractive, as they can carry more information per second and are harder to jam. For the spy with a bug there are four general band ranges that are used.

The first spy band is 25-50 mHz, which is used for citizens band and government and public-service communications. This bandwidth is attractive to the eavesdropper because of the ready availability and low cost of both transmitters and receivers. But there are several drawbacks. Because of the high use of the bandwidth, there is the possibility of accidental detection by others listening to the CB band and finding that for some reason they are getting someone's private bedroom conversation. Also, harmonics in this band tend to pop up in the 88-108 mHz FM broadcasting range, where they can also be detected accidentally. Finally, the antennas for this bandwidth are conspicuously long.

A second bandwidth used by eavesdroppers is the FM range, 88-

The electromagnetic spectrum of frequencies and their use.

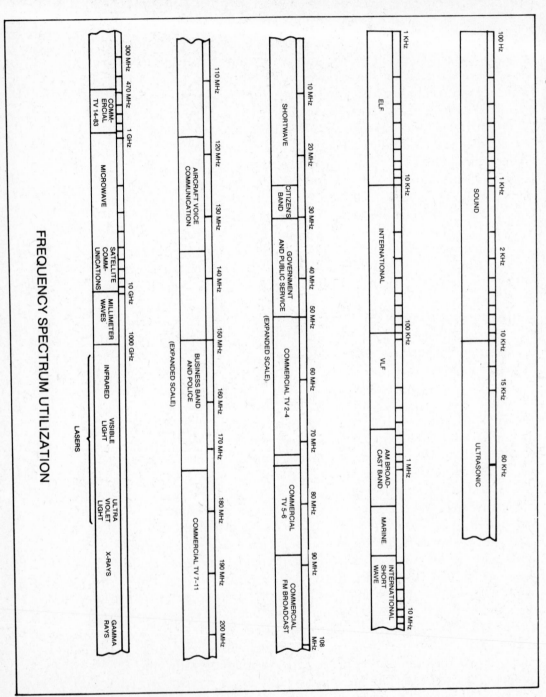

FREQUENCY SPECTRUM UTILIZATION

120 mHz. Again, the attraction for spies is the wide availability of receivers (any FM radio) and the ability of some of those receivers to be tuned to receive in the 108-120 mHz range, which are those frequencies in the bandwidth not used by commercial radio stations. However, if the FM bands are used, there is again the strong possibility of accidental detection. Furthermore, if the 108-120 mHz range is used, there can actually be dangerous consequences, as those bands are used by air traffic controllers. By transmitting in those frequencies one could fatally interfere with a landing approach. Also, the readily available receivers are designed to receive all stations, and so they tend to drift away from the transmitting frequency and require constant retuning, unlike those controlled by fixed crystals to receive just one or two stations.

The third band is the 150-174 mHz range, the business and police band. The more sophisticated agent might prefer this band, for although the equipment needed is relatively hard to come by and somewhat expensive, it is highly advanced and is precise in operation. Also, this band is relatively unpopulated, decreasing the possibility of accidental detection.

The fourth bandwidth popular with clandestine operators is the 40-512 mHz range, which straddles the gap between channel 13 on VHF and channel 14 on UHF. This range has all the advantages (infrequency of use, sophisticated equipment) and disadvantages (scarcity, cost) of the 150-174 mHz band, only more so (more sophistication, more expensive, etc.). In addition, this range is more susceptible to signal blocking by buildings or other physical obstructions, a problem that increases the shorter the wave and the higher its frequency. In fact, the very short microwaves can only travel on a line-of-sight path. However, this range does have one added attraction: All it requires for broadcasting is an antenna a quarter of a wavelength in length, which would only be an inch or so long. That's short enough for an agent to hide it in a cigarette butt.

Radio Bugs

Central to a radio bug's performance are its operating lifetime and its broadcast range. Both factors are primarily a function of the power used. Some bugs are designed to be hooked up to a wall outlet and run off regular current (some will even broadcast along the power lines—more on this later), but for the most part batteries are used. The two most popular batteries for surveillance work are alkaline and mercury primary batteries. Both nickel-cadmium (rechargeable) and carbon-zinc (flashlight) batteries cannot sustain a high drain as well as the alkaline and mercury types. The alkaline is the most widely available, while the mercury shows a slower decay of power. These batteries can be made very, very small, although such reductions in size limit the battery's lifetime and its power.

The main variables in determining a bug's range are the power output, the gains of the transmitting and receiving antennas, the sensitivity of the receiver, and the local conditions of weather, conductivity and dielectric constant of the Earth, physical obstructions, and the height of the antennas. All of these must be taken into account by the spy, and the range computed conservatively. If the agent thinks that the maximum range of the bug is 100 feet, then the receiver or repeater is set around 50 feet away.

Range is also a function of power—10 to 20 milliwatts will usually give a few city blocks of range, while 1 to 2 watts, under ideal conditions, may provide a few miles of range. Range can be boosted by boosting power, but it must be remembered that while the broadcast range increases, so does the field strength of the bug, making it easier to detect. Boosting power also increases the drain on the battery, shortening the life of the bug (and in most instances the agent would not want to make another surreptitious entry just to replace batteries.)

Another important characteristic of a radio bug is how its transmission is controlled. There are basically two types of RF transmitter—crystal-controlled and non-crystal-controlled. A crystal-controlled transmitter will put out a signal only on the band to which that particular crystal is tuned. To change the operating frequency, one has to change the crystal. This exactitude is important—and expensive. A non-crystal-controlled device can be tuned to any operating frequency within its range and is less than half the cost of a crystal device, but its transmissions are liable to slip all over the place.

Also, as has been mentioned, for optimum broadcasting the length of the bug's antenna should be one-quarter of a wavelength. With the use of some of the lower frequencies the antenna would have to be very long—several feet at least. A shorter antenna could be used, but it would severely cut down on the bug's range.

There are an enormous number of radio bugs in various configurations available to spies around the world. In Europe there is a transmitter the size of a rice grain (without battery) that can transmit up to 100 meters. From Japan there is a 1-by-1-by-1-inch cube transmitter that has very good performance characteristics and can operate in either the 100-250 mHz or 400-475 mHz ranges for anywhere from ten hours to ten days, depending on the range required and the power output. There are also battery-operated devices, 2.5 by 1.5 by 1-inch in size, that are able to transmit over half a mile. One of the best pieces to come out of the United States is an integrated system (microphone, transmitter, and battery) that is the size of the eraser on the end of a pencil and has a range of just under 100 feet.

Installation of Radio Bugs

Some manufacturers—the CIA and KGB included—produce bugs already built into certain office and home fixtures. They might come disguised as a potted plant, a wall switch (these can run off domestic current and usually have a range of 700-1,200 feet), chair legs, desk pen sets, ashtrays, and wastepaper baskets. Usually, these ready-made concealed bugs are not the agent's best bet, unless they happen to fit exactly into the surroundings: What if the light switch is not quite the same type as the others? How does one explain the presence of a new painting or chair? The bug can, however, be

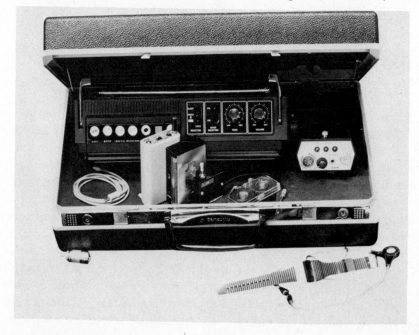

A surveillance broadcast receiver kit, with a microphone hidden in a wristwatch and another on its own, with antenna. Courtesy CCS Communications Control.

custom-designed for the target premises (a new chair leg is built to exact specifications, or a replacement book for one already on the bookshelf can be procured), or an everyday concealment package, such as a pen, pencil, or cigarette, can be used.

A typical scenario for the installation of such a device would begin with an ostensibly routine visit to the target premises. Perhaps it is the office of a spy's opposite number in Bogota. At some point in the meeting the agent pulls out a pen, only to discover that it is out of ink (or the lead in a pencil is broken, or he pulls the last cigarette out of a pack). The spy casually throws the pen, pencil, or cigarette pack into the trash. When the meeting is over, he gets up and leaves. But he has left something behind, for inside the wastepaper basket, hidden in the pen, pencil, or empty cigarette pack, a radio bug begins operation. In an outer office or somewhere nearby the agent must plant a repeater that will boost the signal along to the receiver. Then, outside or in a nearby office, the spy can wait with a receiver to hear whatever goes on in the rival's office. Ideally, the receiver should not be in a car, as steel can act as an insulator against radio waves.

One of the greatest bonuses of this scenario is that when the contents of the wastepaper basket are removed at night by the cleaning staff, the bug can be recovered later from the refuse. In the case of a spy on a budget using a $2,000 bug, this can be a very important consideration.

Body Bugs

Rather than planting a bug, spies can themselves be the bug, carrying a device that will transmit the conversation to a nearby accomplice. In most cases body transmitters are larger and more powerful than regular radio bugs, using up to between 100-1,000 milliwatts (1 watt) of power, so that the signal can be received several city blocks away. Again, though, the more power one uses, the easier the bug is to detect. The best of these small transmitters have crystal-controlled frequencies and are about the size of a cigarette pack.

The big problem with the use of body bugs the size of a cigarette pack is that they are easily discovered when the agent is frisked. The alternative is to use a smaller bug, but then the range is drastically reduced and the accomplice has to remain close by, perhaps suspiciously close. The other problem with this type of bug is that the human body is an excellent absorber of radio energy, which means that either a longer antenna or more power must be used, both of which increase the chance of detection.

Directional Beepers

Radio-direction-finding (RDF) devices are used by agents to track cars. Essentially, an RDF device is a small box, usually about the size of a thick paperback book, that acts as a radio beacon, sending out a radio signal that a receiver (or receivers) can home in on. Most often the device is fitted with magnets so that it can be slapped under a car in a few seconds. The most common place to stick the device is under the bumper, giving rise to their common name in surveillance argot—bumper beepers. A bumper beeper is usually battery-powered and will operate for ten to 100 hours depending, as with all bugs, on the battery capacity and the amount of power being used to boost the range of the device.

As with bugs, range is the key characteristic of a bumper beeper. With a lot of power they can be tracked in the city over a few blocks, in open country for several miles, and at sea for over 50 miles. Ideally, the spy would wire the beeper into the car's electrical system through the cigarette lighter—but this is a job that requires precious time for installation. Another key to the beeper's performance is the antenna, but as with most bugs, the problems of concealment tend to compromise its length. Again, ideally, if the agent has a good deal of time, he can wire the bug into the car's own radio antenna. While bumper beepers operate on almost any operating frequency, the AM and FM bands are generally avoided, as the bug could cause strong feedback in the car's radio.

The receiver in the trailing car detects the distance of the beeper by gauging the strength of the signal. It can tell which direction the target car turns by noting any changes in the polarity of the beeper's antenna. However, bumper beepers don't always work as well as agents might hope. The problem is multipath signal propagation—the beeper's radio signal may bounce off so many buildings that the following car will get sixteen different readings for the location of the target car.

The spy's best bet is to use a commercial radio-direction coordinate system already set in place such as LORAN—LOng range RAdio Navigation—which uses fixed high-powered radio beacons to help ships and planes to navigate. In using LORAN the beeper on the car would actually be a receiver for the pulses from the LORAN beacons. By measuring the time the various signals take to reach it, the beeper can gauge its own position and then transmit coordinates to the chase vehicle. This system can also suffer from multipath propagation, but with the aid of a computer the various paths can be averaged out to give a good idea of where the beeper is. The preeminent technology is a LORAN system that displays color maps of the area, with a little glowing dot to represent the position of the tracked vehicle. This sophistication has its price though—$10 million or more.

Frequency Modulation

There are two basic ways to send information out over the airwaves. The first is amplitude modulation (AM), in which the intensity of the signal is varied by the transmitter to correspond to the information being transmitted (music or voice); the receiver translates this modulated amplitude back into sound. The second method, frequency modulation (FM), is the most widespread and the method most often used by spies. In FM the frequency is varied slightly, again corresponding to the information that is being transmitted. For example, if a radio station's operating frequency were 104.5, then the signal that it broadcasts would warble back and forth a bit on either side of 104.5, and that warbling of frequency would represent sound or music.

As we will see in the section on countersurveillance, the detection of radio bugs involves the use of highly sensitive receivers to scan the various frequencies, searching for transmitters. The key to protecting the security of a radio bug from such sweeps is in some way to hide the radio signal so that it is undetectable.

One way is to use subcarrier frequencies. Basically, instead of modulating the frequency in a high range (such as 150-174 mHz), the information is first modulated on a very low frequency, perhaps 80 kHz, and then that signal is remodulated at a higher frequency, perhaps 160 mHz. In effect, the transmission has been modulated twice to achieve a type of coding. If a countersurveillance team sweeping for the bug comes across 160 mHz, they will hear an undecipherable babble, no different from static, and if they tune in on 80 kHz, they will get the same thing. Decoding the transmission requires two receivers, one to demodulate the higher frequency, the second to demodulate the lower, subcarrier frequency.

Another method for hiding the signal is the spread-spectrum technique. With spread spectrum the modulated frequency is made so wide, perhaps 10-20 mHz, that any countermeasures receiver tuning in on it will be too narrow in its field of reception and will only get a small part of the signal, which will sound like babble or static. There is also a concealment technique known as frequency hopping, in which the transmitting device hops around from one frequency to another, so again, a receiver tuning in on one frequency will only get one part of the message.

We've mentioned that the FM radio band (80-108 mHz) is often avoided for spying purposes because of the likelihood of accidental detection. However, the heavy use and popularity of the FM band can be used to the eavesdropping agent's advantage. If the spy puts the bug's frequency close to that of a nearby commercial radio station (a technique known as "snuggling"), then the automatic frequency control (AFC) on most receivers will zero in on the big radio station, missing the bug completely. Of course, the eavesdropper's own receiver must have its AFC disconnected and must be very sensitive and precise in order to pick up the bug's signal.

One last method for transmitting information by radio involves the use of carrier-current devices, in which the radio waves are sent, not over the air, but along telephone or power lines. Power lines are preferred, as they are less likely to be monitored than telephone lines. A carrier-current device will modulate information on a very low frequency—between 100-550 kHz. Very little RF will be radiated at these frequencies, but it is enough to travel along power lines.

Carrier-current devices are available commercially as wireless intercoms. Hooked up in one room, an intercom will connect with another in another room over the power lines—no separate line has to be run. Although very appealing to the spy for these reasons, the one major problem with carrier-current devices is that their transmission is usually blocked by the first transformer they run into. Any attempt to bypass a transformer is very dangerous and potentially deadly because of the high voltages involved.

Another possible means for transmitting information involves the use of light rather than radio waves. A mike can be hooked up to a light-emitting diode (LED) either set in a window or up on the roof of the target premises. The information from the bug is transformed into pulses of light, which are picked up by a telescope across the street or even several blocks away. Lasers and microwave beams can be used in a similar fashion to transmit information as well. Such links are attractive because they offer greater range than a radio link. But they would be relatively easy for the counterspy to discover in a physical search, and unlike radio links, they can only operate on a line-of-sight basis.

Passive Devices

For the agent, all the bugs mentioned so far have two big drawbacks: First, their use requires that something be installed in or near the target premises, and second, their transmissions can be detected. The ideal bug would be one that requires no presence at the target scene and that operates without batteries, so that even if it had to be installed, it would not have to be serviced. In addition, the ideal bug would transmit information in a way that would be undetectable. Such wonder bugs do exist. They are called passive devices.

The most famous of the passive devices in eavesdropping lore—because its very existence and plausibility were so long both highly touted and hotly denied—is the laser bug. In such a bug a laser beam (used instead of normal light because the laser beam is so much tighter and more coherent) is directed at a target window, where it is modulated by the vibrations of the window caused by the conversation inside. The beam then bounces off the window and returns to the receiver, which demodulates the beam and turns the resulting information back into conversation. This is the theory; in practice, it is not so easy.

First, there are the logistics of setting up such a device. The wider the angle between the beam going to the window and the beam bouncing back, the better the reception. But this means that one has to find not only a place to set up the rather conspicuous laser but also a place to set up the large receiver. In addition, any other noise in the area can cause the window to vibrate, essentially wiping out the conversation from within the room. For this last problem the only solution is to plant some kind of reflective surface, such as a mirror or a plaque inside the room so that it can be used as a sounding surface for the laser to bounce off of, immune to the extraneous noise outside. Of course, as soon as someone closed off the window with curtains or some other covering, the laser's path would be cut off. Finally, the laser itself has to be kept absolutely stable. Any

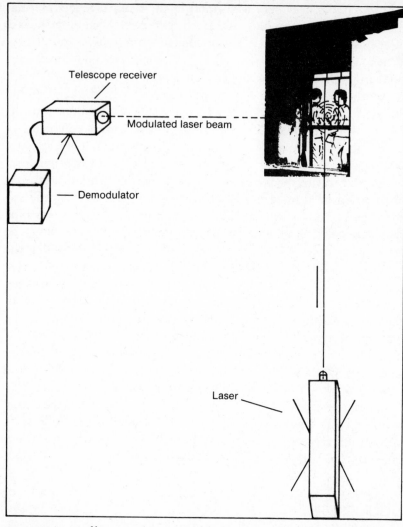

Telescope receiver

Modulated laser beam

Demodulator

Laser

movement at all, even that caused by a passing truck, could disturb the beam.

The most infamous passive device is the microwave resonating cavity bug, which had its first publicly acknowledged use in 1952, when the Soviets gave the Americans a giant engraved Seal of the United States, to be hung in the U.S. embassy in Moscow. Little did anyone know that inside the seal was a small metallic capsule, 3 inches in diameter, with a 9-inch antenna. The capsule was very carefully milled, so that if a particular radio frequency were beamed at it, it would resonate, creating an inaudible frequency—330 mHz—that could be picked up by a receiver. At one end of the capsule was a thin metallic membrane, which acted as a diaphragm that vibrated when there was sound in the room. These vibrations moved the diaphragm back and forth, effectively changing the size of the capsule, which in turn modulated its resonating frequency. When the frequency was picked up and demodulated, the eavesdroppers could hear the conversation.

Another passive method was first conceived of by the late Bernard Spindel, the recognized king of the electronic eavesdroppers in the 1960s. Spindel theorized that as water was a great conductor of sound, it could be used as part of a bugging system. Theoretically, an agent could put a bug in a room and then transmit the sound out of there by way of the water pipes, on the notion that all extraneous noise could be filtered out. Taking this one step further, the spy could go up to the roof of a building and locate the air-access pipe that is used to operate the toilet in the target premises (there must be air coming down from the top of the building in order for the suction process of the flush toilet to work). If an agent put a microphone inside that pipe and then sealed off the top, a vapor lock would be created between the sealed end of the pipe and the water in the toilet. Then the surface of the water in the toilet would act as a diaphragm to pick up any nearby conversation. Of course, the agent would have to unseal the pipe whenever he suspected that the toilet was about to be used, or it would not flush because the suction of the vapor lock would hold the water where it was.

Passive devices are the most sought after and the most exotic eavesdropping equipment. They are also generally very difficult to operate and very expensive. If someone is being bugged, the toilet is probably the last place they are being bugged from.

Debugging

Finding a bug is usually a great deal harder than placing it. In fact, it is virtually impossible to find a well-concealed mike and wire, as both the metal of the mike and the wire will usually be lost to a metal detector in the general hum of metal present everywhere. Virtually the only way to uncover a mike and wire is through an extensive physical search.

If there is a transistor diode or an integrated circuit element anywhere within the bug, then a boomerang nonlinear junction detector can be used. This device generates a low-level microwave beam that will bounce off any transistor diode or integrated circuit,

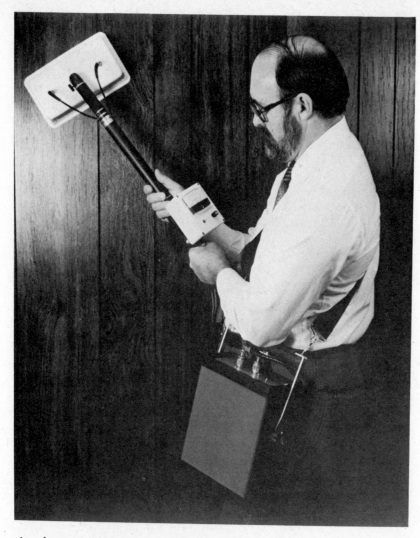

Operation of a boomerang non-linear junction detector. Courtesy ISA.

thus betraying its presence. Powered by batteries and weighing only 9 pounds, one of these little gadgets costs about $15,000. However, any shielding of the bug—with copper or lead—will render the boomerang useless.

To find a carrier-current device, the counterspy will usually have to hook up to the line to see if there is any radio transmission traveling over it, as the RF transmitted by the bug will most likely be too low to turn up on a simple RF scan of the room. Other equipment that might be useful in the search for bugs includes metal detectors, X-ray machines, and photo equipment to check for optical links.

Radio Frequency Detection

Most countersurveillance equipment is designed to detect RF transmitting bugs. The equipment available ranges from small $300 bug detectors, which agents can carry in their pockets, to $500,000 computerized pulse-interval processors used in full-scale sweeps of classified premises. All of this equipment for RF field detection breaks down into two areas: field-strength detection, and frequency detection.

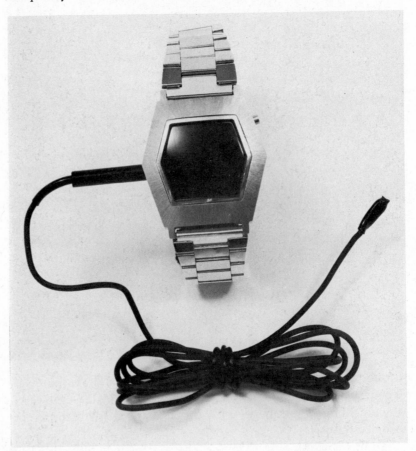

Wristwatch bug/recorder alert. Courtesy ISA.

The pocket bug detector is basically a field-strength meter. It flashes a light or activates a little buzzer when there is a strong radio transmitter nearby, no matter what the frequency. The trouble is that any local radio station could set off a field-strength meter, so the detectors must be altered to disregard any very strong signals. Also, they need to be equipped with two antennas, so that if there is a bug in a room, one antenna will be closer to the device and will register a slightly different field strength than does the other antenna. However, eavesdroppers may use one high-power, easy-to-spot bug as a decoy, or they may snuggle their operating frequency up close to a major commercial band (so that if the meter has been altered to ignore strong signals, it will miss the bug as well). Thus, for the most part, the field-strength meter can be used only as a secondary, confirmation device.

Basically, frequency detection involves intercepting the bug's transmission. To do so, of course, it is necessary to find out what frequency it is on. For an agent in the field who needs to check the security of a room and who does not have the proper equipment, an improvised frequency-detection system could be fashioned using a simple transistor radio. The agent walks around the room, slowly tuning in the various frequencies while singing to himself. If he hits upon the operating frequency of the bug, he will either hear his own voice or the squeal of feedback from the radio's speaker.

For frequencies outside of the AM and FM range, the agent could walk around the room with a small TV, trying all the channels from 2 to 83. If he hits on the right frequency, then a pattern will appear on the screen, not unlike a wave pattern on an oscilloscope. In truth, though, such scanning is hopelessly inadequate, as the operating frequency might be out of the range of the radio or snuggled near a major frequency so that automatic frequency control would skip over it, or it might be between the channels on the TV or off that range altogether. If the bug is a professional bug that has been set up by a professional, then the counterspy will need professional detecting equipment.

A $9,000 countermeasures receiver will scan the frequencies from 20 kHz (just above human hearing) to 1 gHz (the end of TV, the beginning of microwave). It can do this slowly or quickly—too quickly, however, and it may miss things—and it will display its findings on a screen or on a chart recorder. This recorder or screen is a very important accessory. The counterspy will need a panoramic printed display of the signals in order to detect snuggling or subcarrier techniques. The snuggling would show up on a chart as a minor peak next to the major peak of the radio station, while a subcarrier signal could be detected because the peaks at the two frequencies used would be similar. Chart records are also necessary in the detection of spread spectrum, which would appear as a long, low plateau rather than a peak, and frequency hopping, which would show a series of similar peaks. The chart record is also

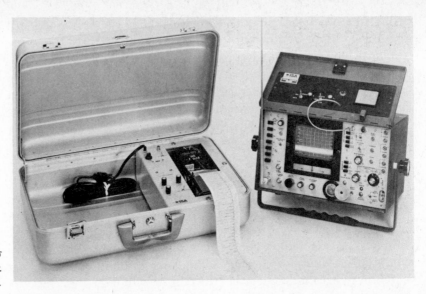

Electronic countermeasures
receiver and chart recorder.
Courtesy ISA.

important so that the room can be checked over time to see if any new radio peaks are in evidence from one time to the next. It is technology at this level that could be issued to agents overseas for their security checks of embassy, consular, and home living areas.

The most elaborate RF countermeasures device is the pulse-interval processor, which costs $500,000. This piece of equipment is fully computerized, with a memory that automatically compares peaks and valleys, from all over the spectrum and over time, in a search for patterns, changes, and discrepancies. However, when one speaks of spending $500,000 on a detection device, or, as previously mentioned, $10 million on a LORAN tracking device then one is really getting out of the realm of the individual agent and into major government spending on electronic warfare, electronic countermeasures, and electronic countercountermeasures.

Preventive Medicine

For the highest security the affluent spy could build an acoustically secure, "floating" room with space in the walls, ceiling, and floor flooded with a wash of white noise. But such a room is very expensive, and there is little need for one outside of the highest levels of government. At the other end of the expense scale, the old spy-movie trick of simply turning on a radio very loud in a room that is suspected of being bugged will generally be ineffective, as a good eavesdropper can tune into the same radio station and electronically subtract it from the conversation he is overhearing. However, a recording of party noise or specially produced tapes of human babble may work to disguise a conversation, since they cause garble in the human speech frequencies, mixing everything up.

Acoustic noise generators can be hooked up to walls if the agent suspects that there is a spike or contact microphone somewhere on the wall. However, these generators only work on some surfaces; they are excellent on drywall, but on concrete, where the acoustic noise travels but a few inches, one is virtually useless. To combat the use of laser bugs, the agent could simply tape a small radio, vibrator, or buzzer to the window; the vibrations it causes will wash out the conversation vibrations. In high-security government installations there often are no windows, or, as is the case with NPIC, they have been bricked over.

It would be possible to build a room that is shielded from either receiving or transmitting radio waves, but again, this is so sophisticated and expensive as to be out of the question in most situations. There is always the possibility of jamming radio signals, but it requires an enormous amount of energy to jam even a small part of the spectrum with static. And besides being illegal and easily detectable, it is also very dangerous (it would play havoc with air traffic control, for one thing). Ultimately, spies who want to be sure that their communications are safe and secure should never say anything out loud that they don't want others to know.

The Future of Bugging

There has been talk of a bug that one could swallow and that would use the body's skeleton as a resonating structure. There are also reports of a trailing beeper that could be surgically implanted under the skin and would be powered by the body's nervous system. While such devices may be possible several decades in the future, they are now little more than science fiction. The real outlook for the immediate future of bugging is not so exotic.

Passive microwave devices will become more and more attractive as technology for working with higher microwave frequencies advances and becomes more accessible. With higher frequencies the resonating cavities could be much smaller, and it is size that is currently the limiting factor in the use of microwave devices: The one the Soviets used in 1952 was 3 inches long, a size that is easily detectable under close physical scrutiny.

Size will always be a key issue in espionage technology. The smaller the bug, the harder it is to detect. In the past, if something was very, very small, its quality was also reduced. With new advances in micro-miniaturized computer technology, however, the quality of these tiny devices has improved significantly. While microphones are now about as small as they need to be, there will be continuing reductions in size for radio transmitters. They will be the width of a pencil lead and only 2-3 inches long; best of all, they will be cheap and disposable. Batteries will be replaced by tiny nuclear cells, like the kind used for pacemakers, as well as solar cells where applicable.

We can also expect the addition of microprocessing chips that will process the signal before it is sent out. This processing will include noise filtering, directional focusing, and voice identification and separation. Smaller tape recorders with longer running times will become available, but tape recorders will eventually be replaced by digital information-storage equipment that will be smaller than the smallest tape recorder, while having much greater memory.

The greatest advances will probably come in the field of signal modulation for radio transmitters, enabling clandestine eavesdroppers to cipher and hide their broadcasts so that they will be virtually undetectable. Built-in microprocessors may store several hours worth of conversation and then transmit it all in one burst, which would probably go undetected unless the countersurveillance team happened to be scanning the right frequency at the exact moment the burst was sent.

For the foreseeable future, then, spies will maintain their slight advantage over counterspies.

Data Surveillance

Telephones and rooms aren't the only things that can be tapped. Any form of information transmission can be intercepted, including the micro-wave beams now used both by government and business for communications purposes. AT&T uses them as part of the intercity telephone network, while a business may use them between offices in one area.

In January 1977 the MITRE Corporation published a report, "Selected Examples of Possible Approaches to Electronic Communication Interception Operations," in which a possible operation for intercepting telephone calls between two cities was outlined. This system would be used for a large-scale espionage operation, such as the interception of communications between an embassy in Washington and its United Nations mission in New York. Calls between two cities are transported in one of three ways: coaxial cable, pressurized multipair cable, or microwave radio. The coaxial cable path must be disregarded because of the alarm systems and electrical hazards present, and the multipair carries too few calls to be of concern. The answer, then, is for the spy team to intercept the microwave link and be satisfied with whatever percentage of calls between the two targets they manage to catch.

As microwave beams can only be used on a line-of-sight basis—from tower to tower or hilltop to hilltop—MITRE suggested that the intercept team find out through FCC filings where the repeater towers are located, then "acquire the use of a small farm along the route with sufficient line-of-sight access to the radiated energy." The next step is to "set up radio interception equipment including a sufficiently large antenna in a barn to avoid being observed." Then, with the aid of a computer, the team would scan the various bands to find out which trunks are being carried on which frequencies. Finally and laboriously, the team would have to monitor all the calls, listening and taping the ones of interest. Micro-wave communications from building to building could also be intercepted in this manner simply by setting up shop on a nearby rooftop.

Intercepting computer communications involves basically the same procedures as phone tapping. If a target uses a phone link through a modem between a remote computer and a data bank or mainframe computer, then the agent finds the cable that the information is traveling over, and taps in. The trick is more in descrambling the information than in intercepting it. The spy may have to bug the premises to find out what type of scrambler and cipher system is being used.

The information gained from such an operation may be an end in itself. A KGB agent may simply want to know what type of data a software company's branch plant is sending to its mainframe at the headquarters in North Carolina. Or the agent may want to use his knowledge of codes and procedures to enter the mainframe itself. This is what most frightens those concerned with computer security. This type of information can be used not only by the "hackers" we have read about, who may interfere with companies' shipping and billing, but also by thieves, who may surreptitiously transfer funds or steal proprietary information, and by computer saboteurs, who may seek to disrupt or destroy a rival using the information stored in the computer. Vital to computer security are restricted access-to-entry codes and enciphering of data.

A spy need not tap a phone line to gain access to a company's data communications. Every electromechanical device emanates some level of magnetism, radio frequency, or electronic noise on power lines. These emanations, as well as the draw of power that the device uses, will fluctuate to some degree relative to the use of the device, and it is technically possible to intercept communications through the analysis of these fluctuations. Although this process would be extraordinarily expensive, the U.S. government was worried enough about it that the Pentagon initiated Tempest, a program to deal specifically with this threat. Equipment purchased by the government and defense contractors must meet certain Tempest restrictions, which include radio-frequency shielding and power filtering on the lines.

It would also be technically possible to bug an office and record the sound of the workings of a typewriter or teletype machine in order to reconstruct what was being typed. (The sounds of carriages moving, daisy wheels whirring, and characters striking are different from letter to letter.) Such a process would be monumentally tedious and time-consuming, of course, so that it might be better simply to recover used typewriter ribbons from the trash and reconstruct documents from them.

Visual Surveillance

In the past two decades there have been two major advancements in the field of visual surveillance: The development of night viewing devices for observing targets in low-light situations, and the pinhole lens, which has been used in concealed camera situations such as the Abscam and DeLorean cases.

There are essentially two types of night viewing devices, active and passive, and they both came out of the technology developed in the Vietnam War. With an active device, an invisible infrared (IR) light is shined onto the area to be viewed, which is then looked at through binoculars or a viewing scope sensitive to the IR spectrum. These devices are effective for up to 450 feet, but their drawback is that they are active: The agent has to shine a light on the subjects to see them, and the light can be seen by anyone who is looking through a similar IR-sensitive viewer. The cost of such a device is about $1,600.

The revolutionary passive night viewing device works on the principle that in most situations, no matter how pitch-dark it seems, there is never absolutely no light. These night viewers are sensitive to the very lowest levels of light unseen by the unaided eye. They use a photomultiplier to boost the light from 35,000 to 80,000 times, which takes it up to visible levels. These are often called "starlight" scopes (one of the most famous brands is the StarTron) because, as the name suggests, they can be used to see outside with only starlight for illumination.

These passive night viewing devices come in many different forms. There are monocular scopes that weigh from 1-4 pounds, operate on batteries for 40 hours, multiply light up to 55,000 times, and can be used to detect a man up to 600 feet away in the dead of night. One of these costs roughly $4,000. The next step up is night vision goggles, which strap onto a surveillant's head and

Night vision goggles. Courtesy Private Protection Inc.

M-802 Night Vision Goggles

ELECTRON TUBE DIVISION
Litton Electro-Optics Department

allow continuous night viewing. These goggles are absurdly funny looking, rather expensive ($7,000), and not in the least inconspicuous, but for the viewer they perform the invaluable task of turning night into day. Next, at $10,000, are night vision binoculars, which magnify the field of view as well as boost light intensity. The latest generations of these devices are designed to adjust quickly to higher light levels so that the person using them will not be momentarily blinded if a bright light comes on. There is larger, heavier night viewing equipment available that can be used to spot a man in starlight at up to 4,500 feet, under moonlight at up to 6,000 feet.

For video purposes there are small (6 inches long, 1.5 inches in diameter) color TV cameras sensitive to low light. They can be hooked up to videotape recorders and set to start recording when a microphone picks up a sound in the room or when the camera detects motion. Video surveillance cameras can be built into desktop intercoms, wall clocks, even clothes mannequins in department stores. What is important with these cameras is not so much the video technology as the size of the lens opening, for the smaller it is, the easier the camera is to conceal.

Pinhole lenses have front openings as small as 1/16th of an inch in diameter. They are revolutionary in that even with such a tiny aperture they still remain highly sensitive in low-light conditions.

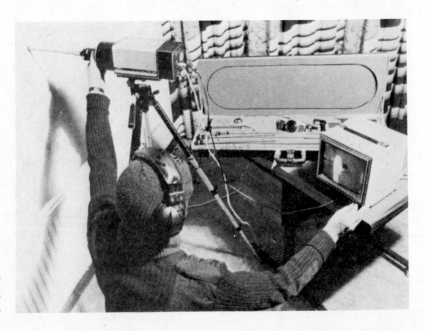

"Abscam" pinhole lens surveillance system. Courtesy LEA.

Flexible fiber optic pinhole lens with VCR and monitor. Courtesy LEA.

One lens can cost $500; an entire visual-surveillance outfit (including auto-iris pinhole lens, video camera, videotape recorder, cabling, and all cases) runs close to $9,000.

There are also fiber-optics lenses that can be used to gain access to where the confinements of space do not permit the use of a regular lens. A rigid fiber-optics lens perhaps a foot long can be used in many ways like a tube microphone to hear, but in this case to see, through a hole drilled in a wall. There is also a flexible fiber-optics lens that is 36 inches long and can be snaked into awkward places, such as through a keyhole.

Cameras have long been used in espionage to take pictures of secret documents. Soviet spy Christopher Boyce, while working for TRW in California, used a small Minox-B to take picture after picture of classified spy-satellite-related materials. Such a task is not as simple and straightforward as one might think. While a picture of a family pet can afford to be a little bit blurry, photographs of documents will be unreadable unless they are shot in perfect focus, and this may be hard to judge if the spy is hurriedly taking as many pictures as possible, as fast as possible. Even Boyce, who took the documents home and photographed them at his leisure, found that the Soviets would not buy some of his material because it was unusable.

Size of camera and image quality are the important considerations in this type of work. An agent could use a camera the size of a matchbox, but if the pictures are poor, then the mission will have been for naught. A simple, fairly small 35mm camera such as Boyce's Minox, with a chain measure for focusing and a small tripod stand for steadiness, is all that is needed. If concealment is the paramount concern, the spy can use a camera hidden in a briefcase, operating the shutter by pressing a tab on the case's handle. If size is the major worry, then a digital wristwatch camera that can take seven pictures without reloading can be used.

Wristwatch camera.
Courtesy LEA.

Perhaps the best bet for a spy who wants to photograph documents would be to wire a tiny camera into the target office's copier so that it takes a picture of every piece of paper that passes through it.

The future of spy cameras lies in areas pioneered by the spy-satellite program—infrared sensing technology and charged-coupled devices (CCD). As was demonstrated in the film *Blue Thunder*, there are IR cameras that can "see" through a wall by detecting the level of heat emanated by bodies on the other side of the wall. CCD technology created the digital camera (used in the KH-11 satellites), which utilizes an array of sensing elements, rather than a sheet of film, to sense light levels. On the Fairchild CCD 211 chip there are 244 by 244 sensing elements, each one picking up one part of the image that the lens focuses on it. The information can then be transmiited digitally, a distinct advantage in that data in this form can be manipulated by computer (enhanced, brightened, shifted, searched for patterns, etc.).

Summary

There are four basic ways a spy can spy. First, a spy can tap into the telephone system, either to eavesdrop on someone's calls or to use the phone as a means to bug the room. If properly hooked up, a tap can be next to impossible to detect. The second primary method of electronic spying is bugging. All bugs are composed of a microphone and a transmission system. The two primary transmission systems are the wire and the radio-frequency transmitter. A simple hearing aid microphone connected to a listening post with a length of transmitter wire is very hard to detect. Entire radio transmitters—a mike, transmitter, and battery—can be as small as a pencil eraser. Radio transmitters can be detected with the aid of field-strength meters and finely tuned receivers and spectrum analyzers. However, radio bugs resist detection if their frequencies are modulated by spread spectrum, hopping, subcarrier, or snuggling techniques.

Third, an agent can intercept another's data communications, tapping either a phone link between a computer terminal and a mainframe or a microwave link. As well, electromechanical printing devices emanate magnetic, electrical, and sound fluctuations that can be picked up, analyzed, and retranslated back into what was being printed.

Fourth, there is visual surveillance, a field in which there have been two relatively recent technological advancements—night-vision devices and pinhole lenses. Night-vision devices magnify all available light up to 80,000 times, allowing agents to see in what would otherwise appear to be absolute darkness. Unlike a normal lens, a pinhole lens has a very tiny opening, which makes it less prone to detection. There are also fiber-optics lenses, which can be sneaked into awkward places.

There are two areas in which surveillance equipment may significantly advance over the next few years. First, all equipment will probably continue to get smaller, even as its capabilities continue to improve. Second, microprocessing chips inside the devices will allow for greater exactness in the interception of information, especially in the area of bugging, for the bottom line in bugging is that with enough filtering and processing you can pick a voice out of almost any mess of sound.

5 SECRET COMMUNICATIONS

From Secret Inks To Cryptology

A fundamental rule of surveillance is that no matter how well the lines of communication are checked for interception, secret agents cannot be fully confident that their security has not been compromised. Indeed, the only way for an agent to be assured of the inviolability of communications is to disguise them in such a way that even if others do intercept them, they won't know what they have.

In Ancient Greece a military scientist, Philo of Byzantium, discovered that if one made an ink out of certain nut galls and wrote with it, the words would appear to be invisible, though they would become readable if heated. This is an organic invisible ink, and along with chemical and radioactive inks it is one of the three main types of secret inks that have been used by spies. Other organic inks include lemon juice, vinegar, and bodily fluids (saliva or urine). When these liquids are used as ink, the writing appears invisible, but when heated, the words appear as the liquids are charred into visibility. These secret inks provide the lowest level of security, since paper can be easily tested for their presence. Nevertheless, possible scenarios could arise where an agent might need to employ such archaic methods.

Chemical inks are invisible when dry but become visible when the paper they are used on is treated with another specific reagent. Most often these "sympathetic inks," as they are known, are colorless chemicals that suddenly become colorful when mixed with another chemical. An example is clear iron sulfate, which turns Prussian blue when mixed with potassium ferrocyanide and turns brown when mixed with sodium carbonate. Other chemical ink combinations in this group are colorless lead subacetate, which turns brown when mixed with sodium sulfhydrate, and copper sulfate, and phenolphthalein, which become colorful when exposed to ammonia fumes. For chemical secret inks to be secure they must be very reagent-specific. The most secure of these inks can only be read when they have been treated by a prescribed series of other chemicals, administered in precise amounts under controlled conditions.

The third type of secret inks are radioactive, and they can only be read with an X-ray device. There are medical tests that pump radioactive dyes into the bloodstream so that the internal system can be examined with an X-ray machine; similarly, messages can be written with such colorless dyes—on paper or any material that will carry the dye, even clothing—and then exposed to X-rays for decipherment.

Perhaps the simplest secret ink of all is plain tap water. If one writes a message on a blank piece of paper with water, then lets it dry, the writing can be recovered if the paper is exposed to iodine vapor. The water will have disturbed the paper fiber slightly during writing, and the iodine vapor will settle on the areas of disturbance, reproducing the message. In general, though, secret ink is something of an archaic tool that provides agents with a very low level of security, for if counterspies suspect that secret inks are being employed, even the most sophisticated inks can be betrayed, and the message recovered, rather easily.

Microfilm and Microdot

In spy fiction there always seems to be an agent transporting secrets out of a country, hidden on the ubiquitous microfilm or microdot. This has become such a cliche precisely because it has been used so often in real life. The most notorious case involving microfilm concerned Soviet spy Col. Rudolph Abel, who, in New York City in 1957, made a crucial error and inadvertently tried to pay for a newspaper with a fake, hollowed-out coin that had microfilm in it. When the coin popped open, the newsboy became suspicious, and that was the beginning of the end for Abel.

As it is really nothing more than a roll of regular film, albeit somewhat small, microfilm is used far more often by banks and libraries (which wish to condense documents in order to save space) than it is by spies.

Microdot technology was invented in Germany during World War II. Like microfilm, it uses lenses to reduce the size of documents to the smallest possible dimension. But microfilm uses film composed of silver-halide particles, embedded in a layer of cellulose, that react when exposed to light. The very size of those tiny silver halide particles limits the degree to which any document can be reduced. Microdot technology uses aniline-based photosensitive particles, which are so small that a document could be reduced to the size of the period at the end of this sentence. However, as is the case with secret inks, if one's adversaries are on the lookout for either microfilm or microdots, they can be discovered, and the message easily read on a viewing machine.

One method the British used in World War II to frustrate German spies using either secret inks or microdots was to photocopy all their mail and send the copies—from which the secret ink or microdot would be irretrievable—rather than the originals.

Cryptology

The best way to transport secret information is not simply to make it small and concealable but to mix up the apparent meaning of the message so that no one coming across it will understand what it means. This is the field of cryptology (the word comes from the Greek *kryptos*, "hidden," and *logos*, "word").

The science of cryptology is divided into two systems: ciphers and codes. In a cipher system a message (or plaintext), is transmuted through a certain set of rules into a form that is indecipherable except to those who know the rules. Coding, on the other hand, uses a series of symbols and words to represent the symbols and words in a plaintext, and unless one has access to the codebook or list, the message will be unintelligible, or it may even seem to say one thing while in fact meaning something quite else. The line between these two branches is not always clear, but in essence the difference is this: in a cipher the word "AIRPLANE" might appear as "PUEOKBW" (shifting one letter to the left on a typewriter keyboard), but in code, the word for airplane might be set down arbitrarily as "cabbage." These two systems can of course be used in conjunction with each other, as a message is first coded and then ciphered.

Codes are most often used by agents, as they can be designed so that a message may appear to say one thing when in fact it actually means something else entirely. A spy's cable home—AUNT AUDREY READY FOR SURGERY STOP SEND NO FLOWERS—might in fact mean "Sabotage operation canceled. Stay away." Codes require the use of codebooks and lists and cannot be mechanized, while ciphers are now created and interpreted almost solely by machines.

Encryption Machines

One of the first encryption machines was invented by Sir Charles Wheatstone of Great Britain in 1867. His device was composed of two concentric rings: On the outer ring were the twenty-six letters of the alphabet, A through Z, and a space; on the inner ring were the twenty-six letters arranged in random order, with no extra space. The device had two arms, like a clock, one long and one short. To encipher a message, one would point the long arm to the plaintext letter on the outer ring and then write down what letter the short arm was pointing to on the inner ring. Then, one would move the long hand onto the next letter (always moving in the same direction) and so on.

The trick was that because of the extra space on the outer ring, every time one made a full revolution with the long hand, the inner hand would move one letter more. This meant that a letter would not receive the same substitute until twenty-six revolutions were made, and the speed at which those twenty-six revolutions were made depended on the nature of the plaintext being enciphered. (For example, ciphering BACON, one would start at B, go a full revolution to A, then to C and O, and then another full revolution back to N, whereas FIRST would not take up even one full revolution.)

One of the first of the more modern machines was invented in 1924 by Alexander von Kryha of Germany. It employed two spring-operated sets of concentric disks. Using one set, one would find the plaintext on the outer wheel of the disk, the cipher text on the inner wheel. Then, one would take that cipher text and encipher it a second time with the other set of disks, thus mixing up the message still further. The key difference between Kryha's machine and the Wheatstone device was the effect of the springs, which caused the displacement between the outer and inner disks to be irregular.

The only man ever to make a great deal of money from building cipher machines was Boris Hagelin of Sweden, whose M-209 cipher machine was the major device used by the United States in the 1930s and throughout World War II. It consisted of six wheels, each of the same diameter but each requiring a different number of movements before completing one full revolution—26, 25, 23, 21, 19, 17 (selected because they do not have any factors in common)—with a corresponding number of letters on the outside of the wheel. As a further complication there was a drum with horizontal bars and lugs in place behind the wheels that was used to displace the wheels a certain amount—these displacements could be easily changed from day to day. Because of all these variables the machine would have had to be used to type 101,405,850 letters before all the wheels would return to the same position.

Enigma and Purple

Enigma and Purple, the cipher machines the Germans and Japanese, respectively, used in World War II, were both electric rotor cipher machines. Such machines are composed of a series of disks. On each side of the disk, around the circumference, is a series of bumps, each bump corresponding to a letter of the alphabet. A letter's bump on one side of the disk is connected by wire, through the disk, to a bump on the other side of the disk that corresponds to a different cipher letter. The disks are mounted side by side, the bumps of one disk touching the bumps of the adjacent disk.

The disks are hooked up to a keyboard so that when the cipher clerk depresses a letter key, an electrical signal is sent to the corresponding bump on the first disk—let's say, "a." The signal then passes through the disk to the cipher letter on the other side of the disk—say, "e." The signal then jumps to the bump on the adjacent disk—say, "t"—then through that disk to another bump—say, "x"—and so on throughout the machine's sequence. When the signal comes out the other end, the resulting letter is different from the one that went in. To crack this system would be a simple matter of solving a substitution cipher (a = h, b = q, c = m, etc.) if it were not for the fact that the disk rotors move a certain irregular amount each time a letter is typed. Thus, while the first "a" in the message may be ciphered as "h," the second one might come out "f," the third one "w," and so on. This system makes the ciphers created by these machines extremely difficult to crack.

The Enigma machine used by the Nazis throughout World War II was invented by Arthur Scherbius of Germany in the 1920s. His machine had an added feature: It would send the signal back through the rotor disks once it had got to the end, in effect doubling the number of disks. But this also gave rise to some reciprocal substitutions—if Z became P, P would become Z—something that cryptanalysts love to discover. Although the gearing made the rotors move irregularly, they would repeat their position every 53,295 letters. The Enigma did not print the letters but, rather, lit up lights behind them. Thus, two people had to operate the machine—one typed in the message, and one recorded the ciphered text.

Purple (the name the Americans gave to the Japanese machine) was adapted from Enigma. It employed two Underwood typewriters with a black box hooked up between them. There were plugboards on either side of the black box, each with twenty-six sockets. Each typewriter was connected to the box by twenty-six cords, and, each cord was connected to a letter in the machine. Inside the black box were four rotor disks, each revolving a certain amount after a letter was typed. To operate the machine, a cipher clerk would consult the codebook to see how to plug in the cords that day, for this was part of the key, as was the position of the disks in the black box. The clerk would type up the message on the plaintext typewriter, it would go through the black box, and it would be printed on the second typewriter.

The only way to crack such a cipher system is to get a copy of the machine—a difficult if not impossible assignment—or to recreate the machine mathematically. Both Enigma and Purple were broken in this manner by cryptanalysts. Enigma was cracked by British and Polish cryptanalysts; the American attack on Purple was led by one of the giants of modern cryptology, William Friedman.

He and his team pored over reams and reams of ciphered messages produced by the Japanese machine in the 1930s. By searching for patterns and pouncing on any errors that a Japanese cipher clerk may have made (using the same key twice, repeating a message, or—glory of glories—sending a plaintext version of a message and then a ciphered one), and by evaluating those patterns statistically, they eventually created a mathematical model of the machine. They then took that to their engineers, who built a model of the machine.

Rather eloquently, the product of their interception and decipherment was called MAGIC (when the British cracked the German machine, they called the product ULTRA).

Machines for the Individual Agent

The simplest ciphering machines that agents use are the voice scramblers for use on telephone lines. These may simply invert the high and the low tones of the human voice, or they may perform

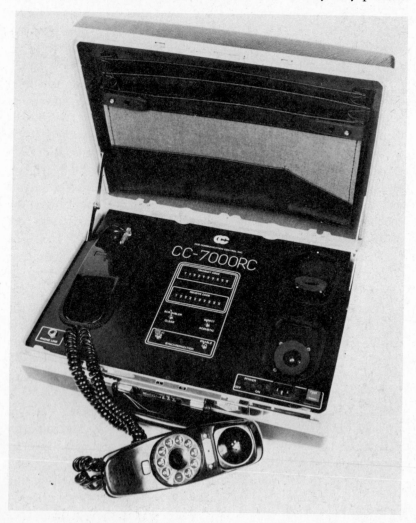

Telephone coded scrambler. Courtesy CCS.

more complicated tasks, such as spreading the spectrum of the voice or hiding it in a wash of seemingly indecipherable white noise. Although devices offer an obstacle to anyone trying to listen in, they do not offer long-term security because they are commercially available. Anyone wanting to listen in need only purchase a similar machine, hook it up, and flip through the various coding selections to find the one used by the agent and the person to whom he is talking. The simple ciphering machines have a similar liability in that they are widely available. Also, both voice scramblers and ciphering devices such as these can only be used between two people who have purchased the same machine. If the agent wants to secure the communications between himself and someone who does not have the same machine, he would be unable to do so.

Public-Key Cryptology

This last problem—that the person the agent wishes to communicate with must have access to the same cipher system and key—was solved, at least to a certain extent, by two groups of mathematicians and engineers at M.I.T. and Stanford. Independently, the two groups devised what is know as public-key cryptology.

In most cryptologic systems one uses the same key for enciphering as deciphering. In public key, however, there are two different keys, one for enciphering, the other for deciphering. With this system, if Agent A wished to communicate secretly with Agent B, he would look up Agent B's enciphering key, published in a directory. The key would be a long series of number groups. Agent A would then convert his message into binary digits (a equals 00001, b equals 00010, c equals 00100, etc.), multiply them by the key, and then transmit this jumble of numbers to Agent B. Agent B would then be able to recover the message using his own secret deciphering key. The trick to all of this is that if counterspies were to intercept this jumble of numbers, they would be unable to decipher it even if they knew the "public" enciphering key.

This seems strange and somewhat counter to common sense. Logically, if an equation is used to change a into b, it can be used to change b into a. This does not hold true for public key, however, for public key operates in a region of higher mathematics that involves what are known as nondeterministic polynomial time problems—or

NP problems. Basically, these are called trap door equations—easy to fall into, almost impossible to get out of.

NP problems involve very large numbers, often more than fifty digits long—more than the number of all the atoms in the known universe. One NP problem involves taking two fifty-digit prime numbers and multiplying them together to produce one very large number. Now, if one were presented with this number and told to figure out what the two numbers that produced it were—its factors—the only way to do so would be by trial and error, and that could take years—(millions of years with 100-digit numbers), even with the fastest computers. Another NP problem is to solve for a and n in the equation $x = a^n$, when x is fifty digits or larger. In public-key cryptology the huge product number is used as the enciphering key—the one that is publicly available—while the two numbers that produced it are kept secret and are used to decipher messages.

Three points should be made about public-key cryptology. First, mathematicians have found flaws in some of the NP problems that allow shortcuts to their solution. As well, with the use of a superfast Cray computer, a group at the Sandia Corporation in New Mexico found the factors of a sixty-seven-digit number. They have also been able to cut the time needed to factor a fifty-five-digit number from fifty hours to four hours, and they expect to be able to crack the primes of a 100-digit number by the 1990s. Second, this type of cryptologic system is unlikely to be used by individual agents, although anyone with a home computer able to perform the math could use the public key.

Public-key cryptology was once touted to be unbreakable (this has since been disproven), and the appearance of such a system in the private sector did not please some people in the American government, and so there was an effort made to suppress public key. The effort came from the agency entrusted with making U.S. national security ciphers and codes and with the responsibility for cracking the similar efforts of other nations—the National Security Agency.

The Technology of the National Security Agency

Outside Washington, D.C., on 1,000 acres of Maryland countryside, stands Fort George G. Meade. It is encircled by a double set of 10-foot-high Cyclone fences topped by barbed wire, between which runs a high voltage electric fence. Armed guards with attack dogs patrol the grounds. Cameras survey the scene. On the outside fence there are warnings that no photographs may be taken and no sketches drawn. Inside the perimeter are several large, anonymous-looking buildings and one nine-story tower. The roofs of many of the buildings are cluttered with satellite-signal reception dishes, microwave dishes, wire antennas, and a couple of huge, ball-like radomes, one smooth, the other pockmarked like a golf ball. Inside the buildings are the men and women whose responsibility it is to secure the communications of the government of the United States and to pick apart the communications security of other nations. They work for what was for a long time the most secret of American secret agencies—the National Security Agency (NSA), the free world's largest intelligence agency.

They are the spy's spies, although they do not operate with cloak and dagger but use pencils, graph paper, and computer terminals in an all-out effort to uncover whatever it is that anyone doesn't want them to know. The NSA has the biggest budget and the most employees of any agency in the U.S. intelligence community, and its technology—from the dishes that intercept communications to the superfast computers that bust ciphers by "brute force"—is the most advanced of its kind in the world.

The NSA was established in 1952 by a still-secret directive from President Truman in an effort to unify and centralize the cryptologic efforts of the armed services, which at that time were not only poorly coordinated but often uncooperative and counterproductive. The NSA's true predecessor in spirit was the so-called Black Chamber of the 1920s, founded by Herbert O. Yardley, the patriarch of American cryptology. The Black Chamber, which made a name for itself intercepting and reading ciphered Japanese telegrams in the 1920s, paving the way for the cracking of Purple and the mother lode of MAGIC in the 1930s and thoughout the war, was eventually shut down in 1929 by Secretary of State Henry Stimson, with the words, "Gentlemen do not read each other's mail." It would pale in comparison to the size and scope of the NSA's operations today. As James Bamford writes in *The Puzzle Palace*, his excellent history and exploration of the workings of the NSA, "What started out as a Black Chamber . . . [has become] a Black City."

It is indeed a small city, for 3,500 people live at the headquarters full time, while another 45,000 commute there daily. There is a barbershop, a bank, a travel agency, a library, a cosmetics store, medical facilities, a bus service, police and fire departments, a college (with 18,000 students), a television station and studio, a post office, and a power station. Just like any small American city of 50,000, except that, in Bamford's words, there's "no Chamber of Commerce and no Grayline tours."

The sheer physical size of the operation is stupendous. The Operations Building (actually, two buildings linked together) is the size of the CIA Headquarters at Langley, Virginia, and the Capitol in Washington, D.C., put together. Other figures Bamford uncovered: There are 7,560,000 feet of telephone wire, 70,000 square feet of sealed windows, and 16,000 light fixtures in the place. As well, it can boast the nation's longest unobstructed corridor—980 feet (over three football fields in length). Furthermore, if all goes according to plan, a second nine-story tower will be added to the Operations Building, bringing in an additional million square feet. The size of the headquarters will then be second only to the Pentagon in Washington area government buildings.

In addition to the Operations Building there are also dormitories for those who live there, a recreation building, a printing plant, an administration building, a Sensitive Materials Center that houses the millions of miles of stored audio tape at the correct temperature and humidity, and a logistics building to store and handle all the paper and supplies. As if that were not enough, there is an annex located 20 miles away near the Baltimore Washington (Friendship) Airport, as well as the numerous NSA facilities around the world.

The long corridor that runs down the center of the Operations Building serves as Main Street, housing the shops and services and providing access to the various sections within the complex. Everything is highly compartmentalized, operating on the basis of the old military dictum of "need-to-know." Employees are required to wear identity badges, which limit where they can go. Each badge is magnetically coded, so that those who wander into a restricted area for which they do not have clearance will cause an alarm to sound, and they will have to explain their presence to an overhead camera.

Like its Operations Building, the NSA is itself highly compartmentalized, divided into ten key components, including operational divisions, five staff and support sections, and one training group. At the head of the NSA is the director (DIRNSA—pronounced "durn-sah"), currently Lieutenant General Lincoln D. Faurer.

The Office of Signals Intelligence Operations (OSIO) is the largest single organization in the NSA. It is headed by the deputy director of operations (DDO), under whose responsibility falls the entire spectrum of signals intelligence, including interception, code breaking, and analysis of both high and low priority. OSIO's work is broken down into three geopolitical groups: (1) Asia (especially Communist Asia), (2) the Soviet Union and satellites, (3) all others. In addition, there are two support sections: C Group for computers and telecommunications, W Group for the coordination and operation of intercept operations.

Their opposite at NSA is the Office of Communications Security. Known as COMSEC, it is responsible, as its name implies, for the methods, principles, and equipment used to secure all classified U.S. communications. COMSEC creates America's national security ciphers and codes, and Signals Intelligence tests each one as it comes along.

At NSA, scientific research to push forward the frontiers of eavesdropping science is conducted by the Office of Research and Engineering. This group works both with all kinds of equipment, from electronic components so small that they can be seen only by a scanning electron microscope, to mammoth antennas the size of two football fields. R & E is also known for the occasionally bizarre and arcane idea—like the notion in the 1960s of pumping tons of barium salts into the atmosphere to be used as a reflective element for the interception of directional microwave transmissions.

Within the Office of R & E are the Mathematical Research Techniques Division, which conducts research into obscure branches of statistics and the higher reaches of mathematics; the Intercept Equipment Division, on the lookout for new and better methods of signal interception and storage; the Cryptological Equipment Division, which builds sophisticated cryptanalysis machines; and the Computer Techniques Division, which searches for better ways for computers to build and break ciphers.

Computers are the heart of NSA today. While most companies and government agencies measure their computer space in square feet or, at most, square yards, the NSA measures in acres. The agency has been a silent partner in the development of computer technology from its inception. The very first cipher machines were primitive computers of a kind, and from the early 1940s on, cryptologists knew that the future of their field lay with computing machines. Throughout the 1950s the NSA judiciously supported the burgeoning computer industry, and they were always, and still are, the first to have the newest, fastest computers available.

In the basement of the Operations building is the largest and most advanced computer setup in the world. It is divided into two halves, Carillon and Loadstone. Carillon is composed of four enormous IBM 3033s linked together and attached to three IBM 22,000-lines-per minute printers. Loadstone contains just one computer, a Cray-1.

At first glance the Cray-1 seems almost decorative, with a long, curved, benchlike design, green and gold walls, and little to betray its true nature. Inside, however, there are 200,000 integrated circuits and 3,400 printed circuit boards connected by 60 miles of wire. Although taking up only 70 square feet, the Cray-1 weighs 5 tons and is so compact that the amount of heat it generates would be enough to melt the machine within seconds if not for the special Freon cooling system that keeps the temperature down.

This remarkable computer was the invention of Seymour Cray, who built code-breaking machines for Engineering Research Associates in the 1950s, and always dreamed of fashioning a computer that could perform 150 to 200 million operations per second—20 to 100 times faster than the fastest IBM. Cray fulfilled his dream and sold the first of his computers to a production plant in Chippewa Falls, Minnesota, in 1976. The second went to the Institute for Defense Analysis, an NSA think tank at Princeton, New Jersey.

The Cray-1 and its successors are used in "brute-force" code breaking, in which every possible combination of a cryptogram is tried in rapid succession. Speed is the thing, and the Cray is capable of transferring 320 million words (2,500 books of this size) per second.

The NSA, of course, will never be satisfied. They want faster computers with greater memory, and so they continue to pursue digital applications of Josephson junction technology, magnetic bubble memory, optical logic elements, and lasers. They are now stepping into analog optical computing, light/sound interaction devices, and charge transfer devices, all in an effort to achieve their current goal—a computer capable of performing one quadrillion (1,000,000,000,000,000) operations per second. With such a machine they would be able to crack a public-key system in a little over a minute.

NSA computers are built not only for speed but for other applications as well. For plaintext material that goes through the computers there are programs that will automatically look up and define foreign words, and others that will flag and key any words that are put on a watch list. As well, there is speculation that the

NSA computers are able, or soon will be able, to perform voice identification and transcription from audio tapes.

Information to keep these computers busy comes in from all over the world on DIN/DSSCS, the DIgital Network/Defense Special Security Communications Network, which bounces the signals off a geosynchronous satellite down to dishes hidden in the woods behind the NSA. The signals are then channeled along a 3-mile cable into the communications center, where the information is made available to linguists, analysts, and code breakers.

The NSA Network

The NSA intercepts communications all around the world, using either its own equipment and personnel or those of the armed services. Its main targets are the Soviet Union's radio and radar signals. Because of this there are listening posts flanking all sides of Russia—in the arctic, Japan, Turkey, Germany—wherever a base can be put close to the border. A listening post can be anything from a receiver in the back of a van in Berlin to a mammoth Wullenweber antenna sprawling across the Scottish highlands.

The Wullenwebber facility in Edzel, Scotland, looks like something out of a science-fiction movie—a 20th-century Stonehenge. Designed to pick up everything from low-band submarine communication to high-frequency radiotelephones, it is composed of four concentric rings of poles, ranging in height from 8 to 100 feet, with the outer ring having a diameter of 1,000 feet. The outer ring, which picks up high-frequency transmissions, is a series of 120 poles, one for each 3 degrees of the circle. The next ring coming inward, or second ring, is a reflector screen that protects the outer ring from unwanted signals. It is made up of wires dangling down from horizontal braces suspended between tall poles. The third ring picks up low-frequency signals with a series of very tall poles, and the fourth ring—the inner ring—acts as the third ring's reflector screen.

In the middle of the Wullenwebber antenna are two boxlike operations buildings. Cables, all exactly the same length, run from the poles to the buildings. By noting which pole receives a signal first, operators get the direction of the transmitter, and by cross-referencing with other listening posts, they can figure out exactly where the signal is coming from by using a process of triangulation.

Two of the major listening posts in the United States are at Vint

Hill Farms in Virginia (30 miles south of Washington) and Two Rock Ranch in California (north of San Francisco). Vint Hill uses rhombic arrays to pick up communications to and from the embassies in Washington. A rhombic array is a wire strung a few feet off the ground around a set of four posts arranged in a diamond shape, with no more than 10 feet separating any two posts. Unlike a Wullenweber antenna, a rhombic array will only receive in a very specific direction, and so there are thirty or forty of these arrays scattered over several hundred acres at Vint Hill, all connected to an operations facility by coaxial cable.

The NSA's biggest station, and their biggest failure, is the antenna at Sugar Grove, West Virginia. Sugar Grove is in the middle of a 100-square-mile radio-quiet zone, initially established in the 1950s for the purposes of radio astronomy. In 1959 the NSA decided that it would be an ideal place for the ultimate listening post. The grand scheme was to build an antenna that could pick up Soviet communications as they bounced off the Moon. Originally priced at $60 million, the antenna was to be the largest movable structure ever created. It was to take 36,000 tons of steel to make the dish, which was to be 66 stories tall and 600 feet wide, and was to rest on mammoth drives capable of angling it up and down and moving it 360 degrees around a 1,500-foot track. Unfortunately, the mathematics needed to build such a structure was so complex that at that time there wasn't a computer in the world that could handle it. As well, the costs of the project skyrocketed—it was estimated that it would have cost $200 million or more to complete—and eventually it was canceled.

Even though the big dish was abandoned, to this day an intense secrecy still surrounds Sugar Grove, perhaps because only 60 miles away, in Etam, West Virginia, are the COMSAT dishes, used to carry half of the commercial international communications that go in and out of the United States. Etam is only one of the COMSAT's four ground stations. Conveniently, the NSA has a station nearby the three other COMSAT facilities in Maine, Washington, and California.

Not all international communications go via satellite. How is the NSA to tap the transatlantic cable? It would be possible to lay a second cable down nearby and pick up the conversations by induction, but that would be very expensive and complicated. As it happens, at the U.S. end of the cable, in Rhode Island, the signals are converted to microwaves and beamed to the AT&T station in Montville, Connecticut. It is a simple matter for the NSA to intercept that link (as we saw in the earlier section on data surveillance) as well as any other microwave links in the country—especially those used by foreign governments between New York and Washington.

Intelligence From Above

As was mentioned in the first half of this book, in order to gain information on how the air defenses of an enemy operate, the United States flies quick-penetration border sorties to trigger radar and radio alerts, while nearby (or actually flying the penetrations themselves) are reconnaissance planes such as an EC-47 or an EC-121, waiting to pick up this RADINT (RADar INTelligence) and ELINT (ELectronic INTelligence). The NSA is responsible for analyzing much of this data, much of which also comes from satellites.

The most important satellites to the NSA are the Rhyolite series, all of which are designed to monitor Soviet missile test launches (picking up TELINT, or TELemetry INTelligence) as well as to intercept whatever microwave transmissions they can. It is believed that Rhyolite, although a successful satellite, is nevertheless no replacement for the loss of the ground station in Iran, which was only a few hundred miles away from the Soviet test site at Tyuratam, instead of over 20,000 miles up in space. The only possible replacements for Kabkan may be a combination of the new Aquacade ELINT satellite (if it ever gets up in the shuttle) and a listening post in the Xinjiang Uighur Autonomous Region, a remote mountain area in China. (At this point the Chinese are willing to cooperate with the United States if it means getting information on the activities of the Soviets.)

While the National Reconnaissance Office operates the satellites, the NSA maintains its own ground stations to receive the data the satellites pick up. There are stations in Australia (at Pine Gap), England (Menwith Hill Station in Harrogate), and the United States (Buckley Air National Guard Base near Denver).

Listening From the Sea

In the early 1960s, while the NSA had the Soviet Union and China well covered, they lacked an extensive listening-post network for the rest of the world—there were only two posts in all of Africa—so a decision was made to copy the Soviets and outfit trawlers with listening gear and send them along the coasts of the world. The NSA used big, old boats that could creep along the shore without creating suspicion, for they moved so slowly. They patrolled the coasts of Africa, South America, and throughout the Indian Ocean, the South Seas, and the Pacific. However, after what many refer to as the "accidental" destruction of one such ship, the *Liberty*, by Israeli jets and torpedo boats during the 1967 war, and after the capture of the *Pueblo* by the North Koreans in 1968, the sea venture, as a clandestine eavesdropping activity, was dropped. Military ships, however, continue to listen in to whatever they can pick up as they patrol.

The Targets of the NSA

The main target of the NSA is of course the communications of the Soviet Union. That is what makes the computers whir and the cryptanalysts sweat over their blackboards and graph paper, as they consult their foreign language dictionaries. But it also appears that there have been times when the NSA has done some eavesdropping at home.

It began in 1945, when AT&T, ITT, and RCA were approached by the U.S. government to turn over all international cables sent or received by foreign governmental representatives in this country. Although the companies were at first reluctant, afraid they would be breaking the law, they were assured that all was legal, as the government was only interested in the activities of foreign nationals. Operation Shamrock, as it was known, did indeed begin its career as a foreign intelligence operation, but over the years it grew increasingly domestic, and by the 1960s the system was being used to gather information on drug traffickers, criminals, and even peace groups, in a direct contravention of the U.S. Constitution. When Shamrock was exposed in the mid-'70s, it was quickly dismantled.

Some suspect that the NSA is still secretly conducting domestic surveillance. It has been estimated however, that even with its vast facilities the NSA is at best only capable of monitoring one tenth of one percent of the nationcs communications, primarily because listening in requires so much time and manpower. Still, one tenth of one percent of the American population is roughly 250,000 people, a not insignificant amount. In the future, voice identification and transcription computers may drastically cut down the amount of effort required to mount such an operation.

How Good Is the NSA?

According to its own estimates, the NSA codemaking and -breaking techniques are from five to ten years ahead of the competition. Unquestionably, the NSA is the undisputed leader in its field in the world today. Because of its supercomputers and high technology, it does more with 50,000 employees than the Soviet Union does with its 300,000 cryptologists. Yet, some have questioned the NSA's boasts. They point to reports about the NSA supposedly recording and storing thousands of miles of tapes with recorded information that it has no idea how to crack. Some feel that the NSA is highly overrated, doubt it can do all that it says it can, and point out that it is the nature of any such ever-expanding bureaucracy to protect itself and to ensure its own continued high level of financing by continually touting its own crucial importance and exceptional abilities.

We may never know the truth about the NSA. Like all those in the intelligence community whose business it is to dig up the secrets of others, the NSA chiefs jealously guard their own.

Summary

We have examined various types of secret communications. There are invisible inks, ranging from rudimentary onion juice to highly complex chemical and radioactive mixtures. There are microfilm and microdots, the old mainstay of spies in both fact and fiction. Above all there is cryptology, which hides messages in codes and ciphers. We examined the cipher machines—Hagelin, Enigma, and Purple—that were so crucial to the outcome of World War II, and we introduced the cipher machine of today, the computer, the fastest of which, the Cray-1, can perform over 200 million operations per second. Perhaps the most advanced ciphers are those based on problems in higher mathematics that, when one doesn't know the key, can take years, if not centuries, to solve.

Finally, we looked at the NSA itself. With a vast network that covers and even orbits the Earth, the NSA intercepts and tries to decipher all the communications it can, as well as designing systems that will allow the United States to keep its own communications secure. In these tasks the NSA employs the fastest computers in the world, not to mention some of the most fluent linguists, adept cryptanalysts, and imaginative higher mathematicians. Nevertheless, the NSA may not be able to do all that it says it can.

The future is hard to predict, but as one by one the public keys fall, and as the NSA gets ever-faster computers, it seems that the codebreakers will continue to be right on the heels of the codemakers.

6 BLACK BAG WORK

This chapter deals with the stuff of James Bond—the technology of espionage that we have come to know through spy fiction. It is the technology that we often find the most fascinating. When the investigations into the CIA in the 1970s revealed serious wrongdoing, both at home and around the world, it was expected that such adverse publicity would be a detriment to the agency. However, over the next three years applications to work for the CIA skyrocketed rather than plummeted. The reason? For many years the public had been told that the gadgets used in James Bond books and films bore no relation to the real world of spying. But some of the revelations in the CIA investigations brought to light poison pens, exploding clamshells, depilatory-laden cigars (this latter invention was intended to deprive Castro of his beard). When such information became public, many of those people who had fantasized about the life of a spy only to be assured that it is mostly bureaucratic drudgery, were emboldened by suggestions that maybe one really could live like 007.

Granted, so-called black-bag technology is employed far less often than spy fiction would have us believe, but it does have its place. It is used in a gray world, a world in which the lines between terrorist and freedom-fighter, spy and traitor, are often very hazy.

Black-bag work involves three areas of activity that would probably top any man-on-the-street opinion poll of the most antisocial acts one could commit: burglary, destruction of property through the use of explosives, and assassination.

Spies often go to their black bags simply as a matter of expediency—it can be easier to steal a codebook than to crack a difficult code. The black bag may also be resorted to out of a kind of desperation—the final option, so to speak. Then too, many spies are big fans of spy fiction, and they are more than willing to play the role of master "spy" wherever and whenever possible. It's like the adage that the big trouble with politicians is that they want to be politicians. So it is with spies.

As many black-bag operations begin with surreptitious entry (to steal codes, plant bugs or explosives, etc.), we will look at the basic principles of burglary—picking locks, bypassing alarms, and cracking safes. Under the heading of sabotage we will examine how some types of explosives are made, where they are placed, and how they are detonated. Finally, we will look at the so-called "wet work" of spies—killing. Covered will be the conventional and not-so conventional weaponry, ranging from pistols and silencers to bolos and garrotes, as well as the truly "dirty tricks"—the gadgets of clandestine murder, from pistols in pens to poisons that kill on contact.

Again, this is not a how-to book. Although the ingredients and general procedures for the making of TNT are included here, no one will be able actually to make it simply by following the information presented in this book. The reader should be cautioned against any book that purports to offer recipes and instructions; even testing or playing with such formulas can cost a limb or, more likely, a life.

Burglary

A proper evaluation of threat level is essential both for those who wish to protect their premises from surreptitious entry and for those who wish to bypass such protection. When an agent has to gain access to a building, whether to steal something or to plant a listening device or an explosive, he is nothing more than a burglar, and as such, his overriding concern is to get in and out without being caught. The premises will have been protected to a degree deemed sufficient by those who evaluated the threat level: A common suburban house may have nothing more than locks on the windows and doors, while a sensitive foreign embassy might have ultraviolet-light alarms, armed guards, attack dogs, and extensive camera surveillance.

The general rule of a burglar looting a house or, for example, an agent on a mission to steal codebooks, is to follow the path of least resistance. Agents don't want to spend an hour trying to pick a difficult lock mounted in a heavy steel door when in a few minutes they could break through the wall on either side of the door.

Alarms

There are four basic components in an alarm system: sensing (how the alarm is set off), signal transmission (how the alarm signal is sent), signal reception (how the alarm signal is received), and action (what is done in response to the alarm).

The most common form of alarm sensing is contact sensing, which sets off the alarm either when a circuit is broken or when a circuit is closed, depending on the configuration of the alarm. The type that sets off the alarm when a circuit is closed is used infrequently because such sensors are the easiest to bypass. One need only tape over the contact points to ensure that the circuit never closes. Most common are the contact break variety, which are often seen in shop windows—the metal foil strip connected to wires. When this strip is broken, the alarm is set off.

To bypass such a sensor, the intruder could connect a long wire to both sides of the circuit, thus keeping it closed, and then break the strip without disrupting the current. However, sophisticated contact-sensing systems may be able to detect a change in impedance if such bypass wiring is used, setting off the alarm. In window-strip alarms the burglar will often follow the path of least resistance and just cut through the glass where the alarm strip doesn't run. Contact sensors can also be hooked up so that an alarm is sounded when a desk drawer or cabinet door is opened, or when a light is turned on or an object is moved.

One of the weaknesses of contact sensing systems is that they are generally easy to spot (telltale metal strips, wires, or contacts), but this can also be used to lull careless agents into a false sense of security. Thinking that all they have to do is bypass a simple metal strip alarm, they may forget about the possibility of a pressure-sensitive alarm in the flower bed or a touch pad under the rug by the window just inside the room.

Alarms can be hooked up to microphones so that they will be triggered by the slightest sound. Contact or spike mikes can be hooked up to windows, walls, doors, and floors to detect the smallest vibration.

Light beams are often used as sensors in alarm systems. Such sensors consist of a light beam directed across an access way to a photoelectric cell on the other side. If for any reason the light beam is broken, the alarm will sound. (An everyday use of such technology is in modern automatic elevator doors, which will not close if the beam is broken.) Although a light beam itself is invisible, an agent can detect it by spraying something reflective, such as water vapor, into the air. If there are ultraviolet and infrared beams, which remain invisible even when sprayed with water or smoke, the burglar can use specially filtered glasses that will make the beams visible.

Exotic alarm systems may employ ultrasound waves or radar to detect any motion in a room, or antennas that can detect the proximity of objects by their capacitance, sounding the alarm if the capacitance changes. There are also thermal IR alarms, which are triggered by even the most minute change of temperature in a room.

There are weaknesses in every alarm system, generally because of the need to build in a workable false-alarm threshold. For instance, an alarm that goes off at the presence of a mosquito is unusable, so it will be set to have a certain level of tolerance. In some instances this can be exploited by a burglar who moves quietly, avoids vibration-sensitive surfaces, dodges light beams, and takes other evasive action. For the most part, however, a spy breaking into a building will attempt to disconnect an alarm.

Signal Transmission

An alarm sensor may be hooked up either to an on-premises system of lights and bells or to the phone lines to notify the police or an alarm company of an intrusion. The on-premises type of alarm will only frighten off the nervous novice, for the experienced burglar will know how long it will take the police to get there and will ignore the sirens and flashing lights. The more sophisticated systems have silent alarms, so that the burglar is not warned if and when he triggers it, and so may be caught unaware by the police. Experienced agents are often able to plug into the alarm system with a meter that will provide them with a warning when they have tripped the alarm.

Some burglars may try to disconnect the alarm in the link between sensor and receiver, in which case they will try to duplicate the signal to the alarm company or police. Thus, even if the circuit is broken, there will be no disruption of the signal. As a further complication, however, burglars may have to contend with a coded signal, and if they don't match it exactly, the alarm will sound.

The other point at which the alarm can be disconnected is between the sensing device and the transmission of the alarm signal. If the agent can in some way cut off the flow of information from the sensor to the signal transmitter without disrupting the alarm, then the alarm signal will continue to be transmitted as usual.

Lock Picking

Lock picking is used by agents when a job has to be done quietly or when they want to gain access to premises without leaving any indication that they were there. Good lock pickers have an extensive knowledge of all of the locks they might encounter—who builds them, how they work, the tricks and traps that might be employed, how long it should take to pick one, and so on. They own several of each type of lock so that they can practice their picking technique, which may require the delicate touch of a surgeon. Above all, good lock pickers are patient, for they can't just pop open a lock as the actors do in the movies. Even a simple lock may take half a minute or more.

The simplest lock is the warded lock. The key is a metal rod with a flat piece on the end. When the key is inserted into the keyhole and is turned, the flat piece on the end of the key engages the bolt and slides it free, unlocking the lock. To complicate matters, the old locksmiths would put wards, or obstructions, at the mouth of the keyhole, so that only a key with the proper cuts could pass into the lock. Inside the lock further wards were set to stop the key from turning and sliding the bolt unless, again, the key had the necessary corresponding cuts. In making these locks ever more complicated, the locksmiths produced keys with so many cuts in them that they began to look like skeletons—hence the term "skeleton" key, which is a key that has so many cuts in it that it can open many different locks.

To bypass a warded lock the agent needs to have the appropriate key blank with the proper cuts in its sides to pass the warding at the keyhole entrance. The agent will cover such a blank key with lighter or candle soot, then stick it in the lock and jiggle it back and forth. Upon removing the key, he will see where the wards have rubbed off the soot. Key cutting and grinding tools are then used to cut out the sections that correspond to the wards. As warded locks offer such low security, they are infrequently used today, though they still may be found in old houses, desk drawers, and old handcuffs.

Pin Tumblers

Pin-tumbler locks are found everywhere—in cars, homes, and offices. These locks have a shell pierced by a cylindrical hole, with a core, that fits inside the shell. The key is inserted in the core, and if

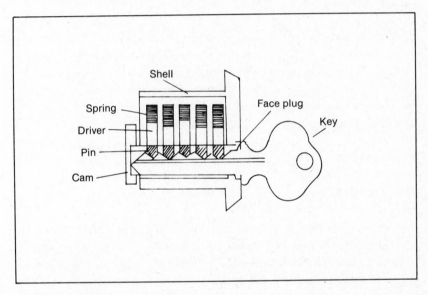

Diagram of a pin tumbler lock.

the key is the proper one, the core can be turned inside the shell, which will in turn slide the bolt in or out of the locking position. What usually stops the core from turning is a series of spring-driven pins that descend from holes in the shell into the core. The pins that stop the core from being rotated are cut in half—the top is called the driver, and the bottom, the pin—so that when all the breaks between the driver and pin match the shear line—the division between the shell and the core—the core can be rotated.

However, the breaks between the pins and the drivers are not all in the same place. This is why the key to a pin tumbler lock will have a series of V-like cuts in it. Each cut corresponds to a pin, and when the key is slid into the lock, the key will raise each pin to the point where the break between it and the driver matches the shear line.

To pick such a lock requires the use of a tension tool and a pick. The tension tool is usually an L-shaped piece of hard metal wire. It is slid into the back of the lock and turned in the direction that the lock opens (the picker will know this from research into the various types and makes of lock). It is turned hard enough so that the pins will stick when lifted up, but not so hard that they jam.

The pick is also a length of hard wire. It may have any one of a number of different head configurations (diamond, ball, square,

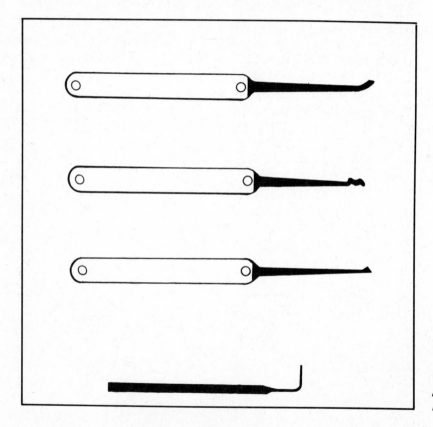

Various pick configurations and tension tool (at bottom).

curved, etc.). While applying tension, the picker slides the pick in and carefully lifts each pin up to its shear point. He will feel the slightest jump on the tension tool as each pin goes into place. Once all pins have been picked, the core should turn with the tension tool.

A faster method is raking the pins. Again, tension is applied, but instead of picking each individual pin, the picker inserts a raking tool (one with a circle or triangle on the end) and slides it in and out rapidly. This should pop all the pins up to the shear line, where they should hold as the tension increases. If, after ten or more rakes, the picker has not succeeded, he must start from scratch. The so-called automatic pick is really just an instant raking pick. It is a gun with a long, spring-loaded straight pick extending from it. The pick is slid into the lock, the trigger is pulled, and the straight pick snaps up against all of the pins, knocking them up to their shear lines.

One problem with pin-tumbler locks is that the pins may not all be of the same diameter. The picker can distinguish the fat pins from the thin ones by doing a quick pick of each one to see how they hold in their cylinders—the fat ones will hold with little tension, while the thin ones will require more. Then the picker will proceed to pick the fat pins first, because when they are picked, the tension will increase enough to hold the thinner pins. (If the thin pins were first, the fat ones would jam.)

Another obstacle the lock picker may face is the mushroom pin. These pins have notches in the driver, so that when a pin is picked and the notch in the driver meets the shear line, the core will turn

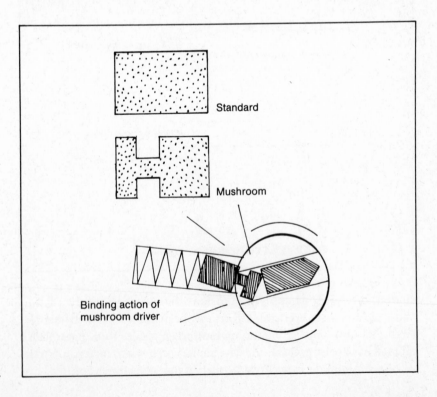

Standard

Mushroom

Binding action of mushroom driver

The mushroom pin.

second number, and so on. Eventually, when all the slots in all the wheels have been aligned, a bar, known as the fence, will drop into place in the aligned slots, releasing the bolt that locks the safe. It can then be opened.

With safes made before the mid-1960s it may still be possible for the spy to use the cliche method of opening a safe by holding his ear or a stethoscope up to the safe and listening for the tumblers as they fall into place. Even with those safes, however, such a method is enormously time-consuming. Safecrackers find that it is much simpler just to drill.

To drill, the safecracker needs to know what the safe looks like inside, so that he knows where to drill for the bolt. High-speed drills with inch-wide hardened carbide or diamond bits are used. A safecracker who encounters hardened plate might heat the plate, then rapidly cool it. This makes the plate more brittle and easier to drill. Safes can also be punched out: The dial is ripped off with a crowbar, and the spindle of the locking mechanism is punched out with a hammer. Some safes, however, have spindles designed to lock if they are tampered with in any way.

Safes can also be cut open with a high-speed grinder (the kind used to cut up pavement) or a torch. The grinder can cut open either the safe or the wall around the safe. The latter method will give the safecracker access to the sides and back of the safe, which are generally weaker than the door. An acetylene torch can be used to cut out the dial mechanism so that the tumblers can be manipulated by hand. To counteract torching, safes often have layers of copper sheeting, which act to conduct away the heat of the torch. Some safes have been booby-trapped to release tear gas if drilled, cut, or burned.

While safes can also be dynamited, it is not a matter of simply taping a stick of dynamite to the safe door and then igniting it. For the most part this would leave the safe untouched, since the explosion would simply reflect off the door. Holes have to be drilled into the safe at strategic points (near the lock mechanism, by the hinges, etc.), and the explosive inserted in the holes.

The most exotic method for cracking a safe uses a burning bar, or thermic lance. With extremely high-temperature incendiaries, a safecracker can burn through the safe, hardened or heat-conducting panels and all, very quickly and quietly. A thermic lance is composed of an ignition material such as barium oxide or magnesium, which in turn ignites a burning rod composed of a combination of aluminum and iron oxide, which burns at a temperature of 2,500 degrees C (4,500 degrees F). The lance will burn a hole through the metal as if it were a hot poker being stuck in the snow. Safecrackers wear filtered goggles, to protect their eyes from the searing light, and a gas mask, in case there is a tear gas booby trap.

The techniques of surreptitious entry are central to many black-bag operations. An agent may break into a building for a variety of reasons—to steal something, to photograph a document, or to plant explosives.

Sabotage and Explosives

We are accustomed to the use of sabotage in wartime, when agents make their way behind enemy lines and plant explosives that wipe out a fuel depot, a railway line, or a squadron of airplanes. These days we are becoming more and more accustomed to the use of sabotage in what we consider peacetime—the CIA mining the harbors of Nicaragua; Soviet-backed terrorists taking out trains in Europe; car and bus bombs set off by terrorist organizations around the world. All of these efforts are designed to undermine the effective operations of the other side.

The term *sabotage* comes from the French word for wooden shoe, for in World War II resistance fighters were supposed to have disabled machinery by tossing wooden shoes into the works. The principle remains the same—disablement by whatever means available, whether it's epoxy glue squirted into a lock to make a door unopenable, or sugar put in a gas tank to ruin a car's engine. In covert action, however, sabotage usually means blowing something up with explosives.

Types of Explosives

There are both high explosives and low explosives. High explosives are materials that create a tremendous explosion when ignited, whether or not they are confined. On the other hand, low explosives are materials that, when ignited, burn so rapidly that if the reaction is confined, the force of the expanding gases will cause the confining container to explode. High explosives include TNT, nitroglycerine, dynamite, and plastique, among others. Gasoline, saltpeter, picric acid, acetone peroxide, and urea nitrate are among the low explosives.

Explosives are obtained in one of three ways. First, agents and terrorists obtain explosives from their own or a sponsor government. (In the United States individuals purchasing explosives must be licensed and have a legitimate use for them, such as blasting away a landslide on a ranch or setting off an avalanche before it becomes dangerous.) Second, explosives are stolen from government depots, mining companies, or explosive manufacturers. (In Europe batches of explosives are now laced with colored thread or chemicals, so that when a bomb goes off the explosives used can be traced.) Third, explosives are made by the bomb makers themselves, since it's easy to buy basic ingredients such as gasoline, paraffin, naphtha, acetone, swimming-pool cleaner, and high-nitrogen fertilizer.

Edwin Wilson, an ex-CIA man, was recently convicted on charges of conspiracy to murder, and of selling explosives to the Libyans. When he first began dealing with Qaddafi's men in Tripoli, he could bring them only low explosives—ingredients purchased from agricultural and chemical supply houses in Europe. His big coup, however, was supplying Libya with 40,000 pounds of C-4 plastic high explosive. He bought the explosive from manufacturers in the United States and Canada and then smuggled it to Libya in drums of drilling mud. Many believe that much of that American and Canadian C-4 ended up in the hands of terrorists throughout Europe.

Field-Expedient Explosives

Agents may be required to make explosives in the field out of relatively easy-to-obtain materials. The equipment needed to make such explosives may range from little more than a pail with holes cut in the bottom to a fully equipped laboratory. The ingredients are available from pharmacies, lawn-care stores, and chemical and medical supply houses, among other places. The procedures for making them can often seem straightforward and simple, but in truth they are not, and nowhere is the old adage, "A little knowledge is a dangerous thing," truer than in making explosives. In the past few decades we have heard countless reports of homemade-bomb makers going up with their own devices. So common an occurrence is this that in the lingo of terrorists there is even a term for blowing oneself to bits—"scored an own goal."

High Explosives

One of the basic ingredients for many high explosives is nitroglycerin. It is based on the nitrating principle—creating a nitrate out of almost any substance by combining it with nitric acid. Other explosive nitrates include nitrated mercury (mercury fulminate), which is used in detonating caps, and nitrated sawdust, which produces nitrocellulose, a smokeless powder. Nitroglycerin (NG) is made by a chemical procedure combining nitric acid (made by mixing saltpeter and sulfuric acid, then heating them and condensing the fumes), pure sulfuric acid, and glycerin.

The chemical procedure for making nitroglycerin is complicated and dangerous. If an agent makes even the slightest error, the solution will literally blow up in his face. The result of the process, the nitroglycerin itself, is no more stable. Its portrayal in many films has been reasonably accurate—the slightest jar can set it off.

Alfred Nobel (of the Nobel Prize) invented a way of stabilizing nitroglycerin so that it could be transported safely and used as an effective explosive without fear of premature detonation. Nobel's creation is known as the straight dynamite series. There are hundreds of recipes for straight dynamite, and they all involve mixing NG with a secondary, less volatile explosive and with various amounts of incendiaries, binding agents, and filler. One can mix NG with potassium nitrate, woodmeal, gun cotton, petroleum jelly, and powdered charcoal. Another recipe consists of NG, sodium nitrate, woodmeal, potassium chloride, and chalk. Although for the most part stable, such dynamite can degenerate and the NG can separate over time, again making it very dangerous to handle.

A far more stable high explosive is trinitrotoluene (TNT). It combines high power—2.25 million pounds of explosive force per inch—with great flexibility—it melts at 85 degrees F and can be poured into whatever shape is required. When commercially manufactured, it comes in the shape of a dry-cell battery, with the connections already in place for electrical detonation. It is made with a nitric acid, sulfuric acid, and toluene in a process that involves careful regulation of both temperature and measure.

Plastique (plastic explosive) is the explosive of choice for terrorists and covert agents everywhere, for it combines the stability of TNT with the pliability of children's plasticine. The plastique known as C-4 in the United States is composed primarily of cyclotrimethylene trinitramine, isomethylene, and motor oil. The explosive can be handled rather roughly and transported within a fairly wide temperature range. When ready to use, it can be molded into shape in and around the object to be destroyed, making for a much more effective blast. A hunk of C-4 the size of a potato will level a bungalow.

Another high explosive, RDX, can be either extracted from C-4 or made with a mixture of hexamethylenetetramine and nitric acid purified with acetone. RDX is a very versatile explosive. It can be moistened and used like plastic explosive, or it can be mixed with flour and stored without arousing suspicion. In fact, the combination of RDX and flour can be mixed with eggs and milk and made into pancakes and biscuits. Although not for eating, these pancakes can be easily transported, then moistened with water to remove the air pockets, and used as a high explosive. An improvised plastique can also be made by mixing high explosive with potassium chlorate and petroleum jelly, making what amounts to an explosive paste.

Low Explosives

Saltpeter (potassium nitrate) is extracted from any soil with old, decayed animal or vegetable matter—an old compost heap, farmer's field, barn floor, graveyard, etc. The process involves pouring boiling water through such earth, then filtering the water through wood ash. Finally, the solution is boiled, the salt crystals removed, and the remaining solution left to evaporate until only the potassium nitrate crystals are left. Saltpeter can be used as a primary explosive if contained in a pipe, or it is used as an explosive extender in other charges. When mixed with sulfur, lampblack, and sawdust, potassium nitrate becomes one of the many black powders (there are hundreds) that are used both to make bullets and as an explosive charge.

Another such "salt-of-the-earth" recipe produces urea nitrate. It involves boiling a large quantity of urine (human or animal) down to one-tenth its volume, then mixing that with nitric acid and filtering for the urea nitrate crystals. Like saltpeter, these crystals are used in pipe bombs.

Picric acid is used on its own, as a low explosive, or as a booster for high explosives. It is made from common, over-the-counter aspirin, which is crushed, purified with alcohol, then mixed with sulfuric acid and saltpeter.

Mercury fulminate is made either with a combination of mercury, nitric acid, and ethyl alcohol, or with mercury oxide and ammonia. It is used in pipe bombs, or in blasting caps. Its special attribute, and liability, is that it is very susceptible to shock and friction and can detonate with the least provocation.

One of the most dangeeous and unstable of the low explosive is nitrogen tri-iodide, a substance that most kids in chemistry class discover at one time or another because it is so simple to make. Essentially all one does is filter ammonia through iodine crystals. When the resulting brown sludge dries, it will explode on contact, easily taking off a finger or a hand.

Some of the most volatile low explosives begin with ingredients found at almost any hardware and household supply store. Fertilizer with not less than 32 percent nitrogen is ground up, mixed with fuel oil (or a mixture of motor oil and gasoline), and stuck in a pipe as a bomb. A 5-pound bag of household flour is used with a small amount of low explosive and an incendiary such as aluminum powder to create a dust explosion big enough to demolish a 10-by-20-by-10-foot room. HTH granulated swimming pool cleaner mixed with petroleum naphtha has been used in pipe charges. Hair bleach, acetone, and sulfuric acid combine to form a primary explosive.

The explosive from the center of commercial detonating cord can be removed and mixed with acetone and some mineral oil. Paper—a book or a newspaper—is soaked in the solution, then set out to dry for twenty-four hours. Once dry, the paper or book will appear normal, but it will actually be a powerful explosive that can be detonated with a blasting cap.

Many other low-explosive charges are made by combining almost any oxidizer—an agent that creates a great deal of expanding gas when ignited—such as nitric acid, with a combustible—to ignite the oxidizing agent—such as resin.

Incendiaries

Incendiaries are firebombs. The infamous Molotov cocktail is made out of a mixture of gasoline and oil that is contained in a corked bottle. As a fuse, a strip of gasoline-soaked rag is affixed to the bottle. The strip is ignited just before the bottle is thrown. When it lands and breaks, the flaming rag ignites the fuel.

A similar incendiary device is the chemical fire bottle, which contains a mixture of gasoline and sulfuric acid. On the outside the bottle is wrapped in paper that has been soaked in a mixture of potassium chlorate, sugar, and water. The bottle is thrown with the paper wet or dry (when dry, however, the paper is liable to ignite under the slightest friction). When the bottle breaks, the sulfuric acid comes in contact with the chemically soaked paper, and the reaction between sulfuric acid and potassium chlorate/sugar causes an explosion that ignites the gasoline.

Gelled flame fuels stick (not unlike napalm) to most surfaces, burn extremely hot, and are almost impossible to put out. They are made by mixing gasoline with lye and tallow, rosin, egg whites, soap, rubber cement, wax, or animal blood. Other common incendiaries are mixtures of saltpeter and sawdust or paraffin and sawdust, both of which burn very hot and are hard to extinguish.

Materials like aluminum powder, although very hard to ignite, offer advantages to the saboteur as incendiary components precisely because of their high ignition point. They can be mixed with plaster of paris and disguised as anything from a statuette to an ashtray. An incendiary brick can be made with black aluminum powder, red iron oxide, and plaster of paris. The brick is soaked in linseed oil to inhibit burning on the outside, and then a hole is drilled into the brick for the ignition charge. When ignited, the brick spouts a hot flame out of the ignition hole that can be directed to cut through metal, such as a fuel tank. The brick must be anchored, though, or the force of the flame will act as a jet and drive it away.

Setting Charges

In the demolition of buildings and bridges saboteurs plant their explosives at points that are structurally crucial. But, as such points are usually the strongest in the structure, a great deal of explosive may be needed. If a sufficient amount is not available, then the saboteur may opt for attacking points that are structurally weak and easier to demolish, although less permanently disabling.

The effectiveness of explosives depends on how the blast is contained and directed. A stick of dynamite exploded on a road surface may create a crater less than a foot deep, as most of the explosive force will reflect off the road. If, however, the charge is tamped—covered with sandbags or heavy rocks—the charge will be directed downward, creating a much bigger hole. Tamping is used to direct charges to cut cables and rail lines, to blast through walls, steel plating, etc.

The explosive charge itself can be shaped to increase its directional force. A champagne-bottle charge uses the bottom half of a false-bottomed champagne or wine bottle. By filling that part of the bottle with plastique or melted TNT, the saboteur gets a charge with a cone-shaped indentation in it. The charge is then set 3-4 inches above the target surface and is tamped from above with sandbags. When detonated, the charge implodes on itself, directing the explosive force to concentrate on the surface below. A Coke bottle sealed in a cylinder has been used the same way. The space around the top of the bottle is filled with explosive. The bottom of the bottle acts as the stand-off distance for the explosive when detonated. Indeed, any funnel or cone can be used to shape such charges. Charges can also be shaped linearly (a V-like trough down the center of a bar of explosive) if the saboteur wishes to cut a line through something, such as a cable or a bridge support.

Not all charges are designed for sabotage—some are designed to kill. The infamous nail bomb is little more than a charge wrapped with two layers of nails that become devastating shrapnel when the charge is detonated. The pipe bomb—or Bangalore torpedo—is essentially a grenade, an antipersonnel fragmentation bomb that consists of a length of pipe capped at both ends and filled with explosive. One of the deadliest charges uses a concave metal disk placed at the bottom of a coffee can filled with explosive. When the charge goes off, the concave disk is propelled out the bottom of the can. The force of the explosion causes the disk to turn inside out in a split second, an action that causes so much friction heat in the metal that it becomes instantly white hot. This flying disk of metal can be used either to cut into fuel tanks or as a lethal antipersonnel weapon.

Detonating Charges

Most explosives require the use of a blasting cap to set them off. A blasting cap is composed of a flash charge, a priming charge, and a base charge. Each successive charge raises temperatures high enough to ignite the charge following it, until the base charge sets off the primary explosive. There are two kinds of blasting cap: nonelectric and electric. Nonelectric caps can be set off by a fuse, inserted into the end of the cap, with the edges of the cap crimped around it. This must be done carefully by the saboteur with special crimping tools, as the flash charge can be set off by friction, and a blasting cap packs enough explosive to blow off a hand. A nonelectric cap can also be set off if the flash charge is struck hard and sharp enough—just as the explosive in a bullet is ignited. With electric blasting caps an electric charge is used to ignite the flash powder. Both blasting caps and fuses can be made with field expedients—a fuse can be made with string, glue, and black powder, and blasting caps can be made with empty .22 caliber shells—but such concoctions are not as reliable as those that are ready-made and commercially available.

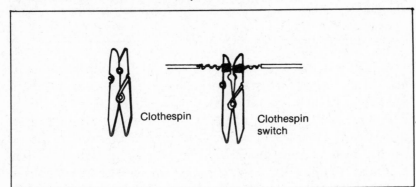

Illustrations of clothespin and mousetrap detonation switches.

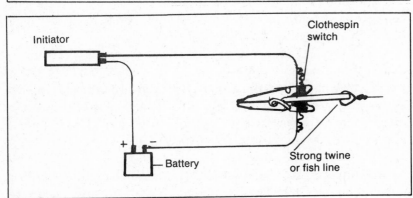

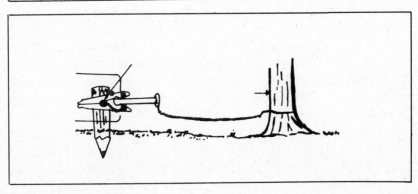

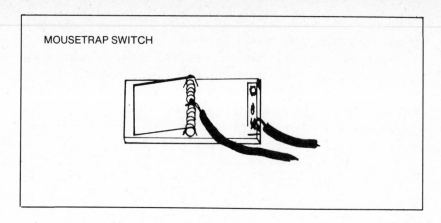

MOUSETRAP SWITCH

A charge is set off in many different ways. In a tension-release mechanism, when a trip wire is broken, a spring-loaded spike is freed to drive into a blasting cap, setting off the charge. Or a trip wire, when pulled, could bring two contacts together, closing an electric circuit that would also detonate the explosive. Other tripped charges include land mines like the "Bouncing Betty" used in Vietnam, the mine that would shoot up 3 or 4 feet and then explode. The sea mines used by the CIA to mine the harbors of Nicaragua consist of a section of sewer pipe filled with explosive and a contact detonator provided by the Navy.

Explosives are triggered by virtually any activity: turning a doorknob, opening a drawer, sitting in a chair, starting a car, turning on a light—anything. Explosives can also be hooked up to a barometric-pressure gauge, to go off if there is a change in altitude, or they can be hooked up to a thermometer to detonate upon a temperature change. In many cases they are set to go off at a certain time.

The simplest time delays are fuses, which are designed to burn at a certain number of inches per minute. Clocks with wires hooked up to the alarm bell are often used as time delays. The timer pens Ed Wilson sold the Libyans were digital and could be set to go at any time from a minute to a year in the future. Other time delays are used to set off bombs at an unspecified time in the future. These often use chemicals—such as sulfuric acid and a potassium chlorate/sugar mixture—which explode when they come in contact with one another. A charge of TNT could be set with a layer of potassium chlorate on top, connected by fuse to a blasting cap. On top of the potassium chlorate could be set pharmaceutical capsules filled with sulfuric acid. When the acid had eaten through the capsule and contacted the potassium chlorate, the bomb would go off.

Another such combination uses metallic sodium in one set of capsules and calcium carbide in another set. Both sets are put into a small jar of water, which is then poured into a vehicle's gas tank. When the water dissolves the capsules, the sodium comes in contact with the water, creating hydrogen gas. As the bottle is sealed, the heat of this reaction ignites the hydrogen. Meanwhile, the calcium carbide creates acetylene gas when it meets the water. The hydrogen flame ignites the acetylene gas, exploding the container and detonating the gas tank.

Anything that exhibits changes that can be measured over a short period of time—even the expansion of dried seeds in water or the opening of a flower—can be used as a time delay.

The detonation method of choice for most terrorists and agents is the radio transmitter. Just as a room is bugged from a distance with the aid of a tiny radio tramsmitter, so a bomb can be set off with a small radio receiver attached. The killers assigned by the Chilean secret police to assassinate Chilean exile Orlando Letelier in 1975 put a radio-controlled bomb in his car, then triggered it as he drove through the streets of Washington, D.C. The Mossad hit team that was involved in the reprisals for the massacre of Israeli athletes at the 1976 Olympics put a bomb in the telephone of Mohmoud Hamshari, telephoned him, and when he identified himself, set the bomb off from across the street, fatally wounding him.

The chief problem with radio-controlled bombs is that any transmission that is made in the bomb's frequency can set it off. In their fight against the IRA, the British exploited this liability by running high-powered radio transmitters up and down the frequencies, in an attempt to trigger bombs before they were set. This worked for a time, with several IRA bomb makers apparently scoring their own goals, until the IRA responded by fixing the bombs on safety timers that would only allow detonation after a certain time had passed.

Booby Traps

Booby traps are essentially activity-activated bombs that are small and inconspicuous. The refill cartridge of a pen could be removed and replaced with high explosive that would be detonated when a friction-sensitive blasting cap was triggered by depressing the button at the end of the pen. Similarly, a cigarette lighter can be filled with high explosive, and the wick replaced with a fast-burning

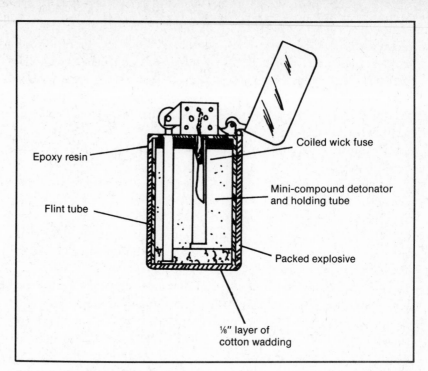

Epoxy resin

Flint tube

Coiled wick fuse

Mini-compound detonator
and holding tube

Packed explosive

⅛" layer of
cotton wadding

*Illustration of a cigarette
lighter booby-trap bomb.*

fuse. Cigars and cigarettes can be emptied of tobacco, then filled with an explosive and fuse. Bombs of even this small size can kill.

A kerosene lamp filled with a mixture of gasoline and fuel oil, its wick replaced with a fuse, is a devastating antipersonnel incendiary. So is the light-bulb bomb, which is made by drilling a tiny hole in the metal screw section of a light bulb, then filling the bulb with either explosive powder or gasoline. The bulb is screwed into place, and when someone turns on the light, the instantly hot filament ignites the explosive.

Friction-sensitive explosives have been used in many deadly traps. The inside of a whistle is coated with such material so that when the whistle is blown, the ball in the whistle strikes the explosive, setting it off. A wine bottle filled with high-octane gasoline, then plugged by a cork coated with a friction-sensitive igniter, would explode when the cork was pulled.

Letter and parcel bombs, usually made out of plastique or a thin cake of TNT, are triggered in several different ways. Some are simply set on a delay fuse, in the hope that the bomb will be in the target premises when it goes off. Others have friction-sensitive tabs that set the explosive off when the letter is opened—sometimes this occurs when the letter is merely being handled. In some letter bombs there are two separate capsules of chemicals—perhaps sulfuric acid in one, potassium chlorate and sugar in the other. When the letter is opened, the capsules are broken, the chemicals come into contact with one another, and an explosion occurs. This type of bomb can also go off prematurely. The simplest method employs a mousetrap, held open, that snaps shut, setting off the explosive when the package is opened.

Letter bombs are usually 1/4 to 1/2 inch thick, resembling a report, a pamphlet, or a thin book. However, they weigh more than would a sheaf of papers of that thickness, and they are either more rigid than a pamphlet would be (if it is a hard explosive like TNT) or much too pliable (if it is plastique), feeling more like putty or clay than paper. They may also "sweat," leaving grease stains on the outside of the package, and there may also be a slightly sweet, almondy smell of marzipan. The smart victim will get bomb-disposal experts in to deal with a letter bomb. Those who try to defuse it without help are just as likely fulfill the bomb maker's intentions and blow themselves to bits.

In general, agents use explosives in paramilitary operations such as mining harbors or blowing up trains, both in peacetime and while at war. With the use of antipersonnel letter bombs, however, the agent is no longer either a spy or a soldier—he is an assassin. Such "wet operations" are the subject of the next section.

Weaponry and Dirty Tricks

The cold war is a war of information, contacts, theft, subterfuge, and trickery, but usually not one of murder. Nevertheless, people are occasionally killed: Agents vanish, or collapse of a surprise "heart attack," or wind up floating in a river somewhere. While we began to look at the technology of death-dealing in discussing antipersonnel explosives such as letter bombs and land mines, the "dirty tricks" of espionage usually involve techniques that are less distant than setting off a charge by radio; technology that is, because of its secretive nature, far more insidious. This is the equipment used by the agents with ipso facto licenses to kill.

Weaponry

Almost anything can be used as a weapon in an emergency. Anything small and weighty held in the hand gives added weight to a punch. A watch can be strapped over the knuckles, a glass broken and used to give lacerating punches, a set of keys stuck through the fingers of a fist. A shoe with a hard heel makes a decent club; a belt with a heavy buckle, a whip. Bottles, rocks, books (the spine edge of a book is hard and can be used as a club), pens, pencils, umbrellas, canes, shoelaces (as a garrote), a sock partially filled with wet sand—almost anything can be used in a tough situation.

Of the weapons ready-made for hand-to-hand fighting, the most common is the knife, which comes in many different shapes, sizes, and designs. There are switchblade, flick, and gravity knives, all designed to provide instant extension of a concealed blade. There are trench knives, with built-in finger grips; balanced flat knives, for throwing; pin-prick poisoned knives; knives hidden in belt buckles—and many more. Venturing into the more arcane, there are hatchets, clubs, boomerangs, the dreaded Nunchaku sticks (two lengths of hardwood joined by a metal chain), the silent garrote, South American bolos, sword canes and umbrellas—the list is endless. But the trouble with all these hand-to-hand weapons, especially the knife, is that unless the agent is an expert in their use, he is just as likely to hurt himself as his opponent.

If an agent is in a situation where he has to fight, he is probably in a situation where he has to kill, and in that case the best weapon for hand-to-hand fighting is a gun.

Guns

Rifles, because of their size, would only be used by an agent performing a long-range sniping assassination. In that case almost any rifle could be used—the Soviet AK-47, the American M-16 or M-18, or any number of hunting rifles with a range of 300 yards or more. Accuracy would be a function of the assassin's skill, the trueness of the barrel, and the power of the scope, which is essentially a telescope mounted on the gun, with sights that are synchronized with the trajectory of the bullet. A new development in this area is the laser scope, which projects a tiny, ruby-red laser beam that points directly at the spot where the bullet will land. One need only point the beam at a target and pull the trigger.

For defense and assault an agent needs something that is small, lightweight, readily concealable, and automatic. Machine guns are too big, even the small Israeli Uzi. Between the machine gun and the pistol, though, is the machine pistol. The most famous of these are the Ingram M-10 and M-11. They were developed by Gordon

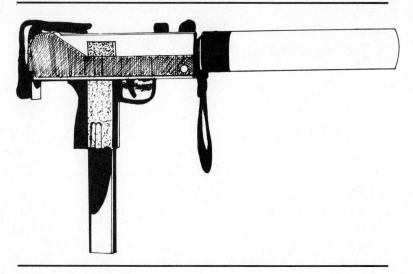

An Ingram M-10 machine pistol with silencer.

Ingram in the 1960s, while he was working for Mitch WerBell III's SIONICS—Studies in the Operational Negation of Insurgents and Counter-Subversion—Corporation (since submerged into the Military Armaments Corporation). Both the U.S. M-10 and the M-11 weigh less than 4 pounds and are less than 10 inches long. The M-10 can fire 700 rounds (.45 and 9mm caliber) per minute, while the newer M-11 puts out 850 rounds (.38 caliber) per minute. The muzzle velocity on both is subsonic, so they can be fitted with silencers. The Eastern-bloc counterpart is the Czech Skorpion VZ

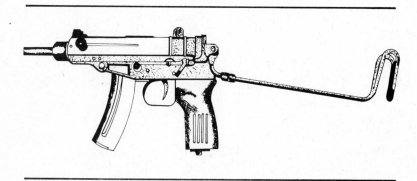

A Czech Skorpion machine pistol.

61, which has similar characteristics. As all these machine pistols cannot carry much more than a thirty-round clip, however, they expend their ammunition very quickly, allowing for nothing more than a two-second burst; this is one reason agents prefer pistols.

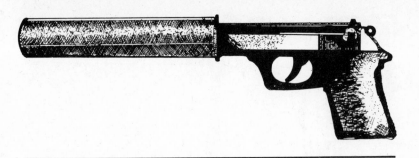

Illustration of a pistol with silencer attached.

A pistol is chosen for its reliability, size, and stopping power. Many feel that an agent's gun must be powerful and have a large caliber, preferably a magnum, to be effective, but the Mossad (Israel's espionage agency), for one, provides its agents with .22-caliber pistols. They are small, lightweight, easy to conceal, easy to use, and can be quiet enough that silencers aren't necessary. And for their intended use—within 10 yards—they are more than accurate enough.

The only defense against guns is body armor. At one time made out of heavy metal mesh, armor today is made out of fiberglass or (better) Kevlar, a very strong yet lightweight fiberglass. Notwithstanding the sense of security it provides, full body armor is bulky and very hot. An alternative is bullet-resistant clothing, which appears to be regular clothing but has Kevlar woven throughout it. However, such clothing might not withstand a direct shot at close quarters. There are also bulletproof briefcases, briefcase liners, and clipboards that one can use as a shield in an emergency. Two things should be remembered regarding agents' defense from bullets. First, the movie practice of turning over a table and hiding behind it won't work. A .22 slug can go through 7 inches of soft wood, and a .45 can go through an automobile lengthwise, stopping only at the engine block. Second, wearing body armor does not mean the spy won't get hurt. A piece of metal traveling 2,000 feet per second will knock a person to the ground, probably breaking a rib or two if it hits the chest armor.

Ammunition

Ammunition is often modified to make it even more deadly. Dumdum bullets (banned by the Geneva Convention) are bullets with hollow tips or cuts in the tip that cause the lead to fragment upon impact. A dumdum bullet will create a regular entry hole, but its exit hole, because of the lead fragmenting and splitting apart, will be huge. Bullets similar to these are used by the air marshals who ride U.S. planes to thwart hijackers. These bullets spread out so much upon impact that they don't make it through a body, and even if the shot misses, they will not pierce the airplane's skin.

So-called exploding bullets usually do not carry explosives—if they did, they would probably explode on firing. Instead, they are bullets with a drop of mercury in a hollow tip. When the bullet is shot out of the gun, the mercury is pressed to the back of the cavity, and when it hits the target it vaporizes and explodes from the tip of the bullet. This explosion has an effect that is similar to, but even more devastating than, the fragmenting of a dumdum bullet.

Three other exotic rounds are poison, uranium, and Teflon-jacketed bullets. The Soviets were accused of using poison bullets (also banned by the Geneva Convention) against the Germans in World War II. Coated with arsenic or cyanide, a poison bullet will kill those who are even just slightly wounded. Uranium bullets use depleted, nonradioactive uranium, instead of lead, as the projectile. As a bullet's power is limited by the size of its slug and the amount of explosive powder in the shell, and as uranium is much heavier than lead, it can be used to make a bullet with a smaller slug and a larger portion of explosive, thus sending the bullet out faster, with increasing range and throw weight. Because of the antifriction characteristics of Teflon, bullets jacketed with this substance can pierce body armor: They literally slip through between the fiberglass or Kevlar fibers.

Silencers

A gun may make three sounds when it is fired: the sound of the mechanism, the bang of the exploding gases escaping from the muzzle, and a small sonic boom if the bullet travels faster than the speed of sound. If a gun is loud mechanically, or if its bullets travel at supersonic speeds, it cannot be silenced, unless the gun is retooled to be quieter and the ammunition is loaded with less explosive. Silencers, or "sound suppressors" as their makers prefer to call them, attempt to contain the second sound, the loudest one—the bang of the exploding gases.

The inventor of the silencer was Hiram P. Maxim, a part-time screenwriter who came from a family of ordnance entrepreneurs: His father invented the first true machine gun, and his brother came up with smokeless powder and the self-propelled torpedo. Maxim started work on a silencer in 1906 and patented it in 1910. As the bang we hear when a gun goes off is caused by the rapid expansion of the gas that escapes from the muzzle, Maxim realized that if that gas could be slowed and contained, then there would be little or no noise.

A silencer works much the same way a muffler does on a car engine, but whereas a muffler employs circuitous routing of the exhaust gases, a silencer must obviously leave a clear path for the bullet. There are basically two types of silencer design used today. One uses a series of baffles and chambers to catch and slow the gases; the other uses layers of absorbent materials, usually wire mesh.

After Maxim, the recognized king of silencers is Mitch WerBell III, the man who was also behind Ingram's M-10 and M-11 machine pistols. WerBell developed a silencer that employs a series of wire mesh doughnuts encased in a metal tube that screws onto the end of the rifle or pistol. His silencer not only suppressed the sound down to about the level of a BB gun, it also contained the muzzle flash and, some say, even improved the aim of rifles and pistols by reducing the recoil.

Silencers are perfectly suited for clandestine work, which is why they are illegal to own, make, or sell in most parts of the world.

Improvised Guns and Silencers

If an agent is in the field and the enemy is closing in to kill him, he could make a workable pistol or rifle out of a length of metal tubing, a rubber plug, a nail, a piece of wood, and some elastic bands. The big problem with such improvised guns is that they pose as much, if not more, of a hazard to the person who fires one than to the person being fired at, as they are just as likely to explode as to fire a bullet. A pistol, rifle, or shotgun made out of metal pipe, especially if used with muzzled-loaded improvised ammunition, could turn out to be a pipe bomb in the maker's hands.

There are several designs for homemade silencers. One involves simply drilling a series of twelve holes in the barrel of a pistol, covering the holes with several layers of wire mesh and absorbent material, then encasing all that in a tube. Other methods include building a screw-on extension tube filled with wire mesh or bottle

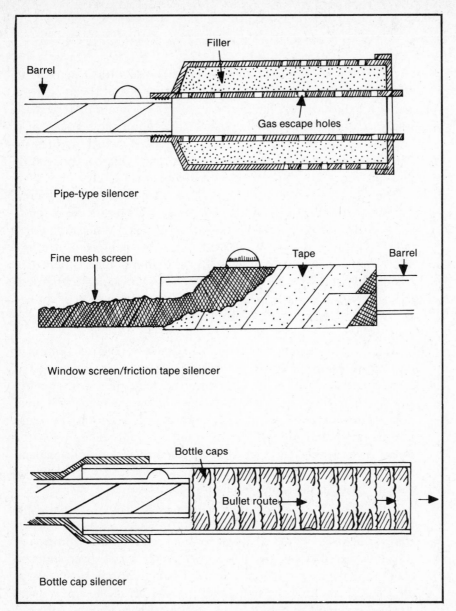

Filler

Barrel

Gas escape holes

Pipe-type silencer

Fine mesh screen

Tape

Barrel

Window screen/friction tape silencer

Bottle caps

Bullet route

Bottle cap silencer

Assorted improvised silencers.

caps, with a path for the bullet cut through them. The trouble with such homemade silencers is that they have the potential of getting in the bullet's way if the bullet path is at all askew.

One-time silencers have been made out of baby bottle nipples; out of balloons stretched over the muzzle; by shooting through a pillow (it will not slow the bullet much, but will greatly reduce the noise); or by wrapping a towel around the muzzle of the gun.

Exotic Weaponry

An improvised flamethrower can be fashioned with an aerosol can of auto-start fluid. A grip, trigger, and firing assembly can be made out of a length of coat-hanger wire, a battery, and a battery spark igniter. When the trigger is pushed, the top of the aerosol can is depressed, and fluid jets out over the spark, which ignites it. Although makers of such flamethrowers claim an arc of fire can be sent 50 feet, a 10-20-foot range would be more likely.

The Taser is an electric gun that fires two barbed prongs connected to the gun by wires. (Of course, this limits the range of the gun to the length of the wires—about 15 feet.) When the prongs lodge in a victim's body, 2,000 volts are pumped down the wires—supposedly not so much to kill as to immobilize. Tasers, like tranquilizer guns, were initially designed as weapons that would incapacitate but not kill. It is difficult to judge what level of voltage or drug will kill a person and what won't, and so tasers and tranquilizer guns are highly restricted weapons.

Sound can be used as a weapon. Sounds above the pitch of human hearing, transmitted at a high decibel level—100 db or more—can cause headaches, nausea, and confusion without the victims having any idea why they feel that way. Sounds below the range of human hearing transmitted at a similarly high decibel level can also cause disorientation and distress. If the volume is high enough and the sound low enough, the sound can be used to shake buildings and even rupture internal organs. The problem with such weaponry is that it can have the same effect on those using it.

The crossbow, a tool of war with a long history, is an exotic weapon of sorts today. With recent improvements such as reflex and compound bows, which are easier to shoot, and with the addition of a scope, the crossbow can be as effective as a rifle over short to medium distances. It has the virtue of being entirely silent except for the dull twang of the string and the whisper of the arrow shaft. Arrows, it should be noted, because of their sharp pointed tips, can often pierce body armor that would deflect a bullet. Other exotic silent weapons include spear guns, slingshots, and blowguns.

The exotic weapon of the future might include some sort of portable laser gun or pistol, along the lines seen in science-fiction films. Today's small lasers could only be used to instantly blind an opponent, and the technology necessary to make a laser gun seems a good distance off.

The Dirtiest Tricks

On September 7, 1978, on the Waterloo Bridge in London, Bulgarian defector George Markov felt a sharp stab of pain in his leg. He turned to see a man stooping to pick up an umbrella, apologizing profusely for having accidentally jabbed Markov. Then the man got into a cab and drove off. Markov shrugged it off, but four days later he died.

Markov was killed by the man on the bridge, for the umbrella contained a miniature air gun that drove a pellet containing potassium cyanide into his leg. The tiny pellet, less than one-tenth of an inch in diameter, worked its way into his bloodstream, where it eventually killed him. (An autopsy revealed the poison the day after his death, but the pellet was not found until September 29.) This killing was only one in a series of reprisals by the Bulgarian secret police against defectors to the West—they also stabbed Vladimir Kostov in Paris around the same time, but the pellet did not kill him.

The method chosen for Markov's assassination is a perfect example of the dirtiest of tricks—cynical in its ingeniousness, and deceptive. It was also designed more for psychological impact than for efficiency—after all, they could have just shot him late at night. But the Bulgarians were sending a message to other defectors and exiles by killing in such a way, a message that said, "You will never be safe. We can get you anytime, anywhere."

Dirty Weaponry

Guns have been built into books, the soles of shoes, pens, musical instruments, cameras, casts, and, like the "Secret Sam" toy of the 1960s, in briefcases. Of course, such weapons are not always easy to use. When a gun is in a shoe, the agent must be in the exact correct position—on his back on the floor with his toe pointed up at his attacker—or else end up shooting himself, or someone else, in the foot.

To disguise the true cause of death, bullets made out of fiberglass or plastic can be used, since they will often not show up in X-rays. Similarly, the shot can be removed from a shotgun shell and replaced with water, rock salt, or ice. Fired at close range, such a shell would be lethal yet would leave little evidence.

Other insidious weapons include Frisbees with razor blades

sticking out of the side, an arm cast made out of reinforced concrete to be used as a bludgeon, radio-controlled model airplanes loaded with explosives, yo-yos with wire for a string to be used as a garrote, and dart guns of all shapes, sizes, and disguises.

Weapons can be used in booby traps. Doors, drawers, and objects can be rigged up to fire bullets instead of detonating bombs. With a length of rubber tubing fastened securely at both ends to the outside of a windowsill, a knife can be set with its tip in the closed window so that it launches into the midriff of anyone who opens the window. A gun can be booby-trapped by blocking the barrel so that it it will explode in the hand of anyone who tries to fire it.

Poisons

Poisons are either organic or inorganic. The organic poisons include those derived from the over 2,000 toxic plants, such as wolfsbane, hemlock, oleander, poinsettia, rhubarb leaves, potato sprouts, and nicotine from tobacco leaves. They can also be extracted from poisonous animals such as rattlesnake, cobra, stonefish, and Japanese puffer fish. The inorganic poisons of chemicals and metals include arsenic, thalium, and the cyanide series, as well as poison gases such as phosgene.

Poisons can be administered in several ways. They can be ground up and mixed in with food, they can be injected, or they can be set into some kind of booby trap. One such method is to place slivers of Teflon in a cigarette. Smoking the cigarette will burn the Teflon, releasing deadly methane gas. Or commonly available carbon tetrachloride is boiled or burned so that it gives off lethal phosgene gas, which has the relatively innocuous smell of musty hay.

In early days of the Cold War the Soviets developed a method for administering prussic acid (one of the cyanides), which provokes what appears to be an instant heart attack. KGB agents would "take out" an adversary by blowing prussic acid dust through a rolled-up newspaper into his face. Now there is a gun, the MVD gas pistol, to do the job. Shortly before such an assassination, the agent using the prussic acid would have to inhale amyl nitrate, which acts as a counteragent, in order to avoid suffering instant cardiac arrest himself.

Perhaps the nastiest method for poisoning involves smearing a surface that the target is likely to touch with a poison, such as concentrated nicotine, that can enter the body through the skin. Or, any poison can be simply mixed with DMSO (dimethyl sulfoxide), a readily available chemical that can enter the body through the skin, and can take anything with it, (if one mixes DMSO with lemon juice and rubs it on one's thigh, a few moments later that person will taste lemon in his or her mouth).

Drugs

In its search for a "truth drug" the Office of Strategic Services (OSS), the CIA's predecessor, tried alcohol, barbiturates, caffeine—whatever they could find, including scopolamine and peyote. What they settled on was an extract of cannibis (marijuana), which they called TD—Truth Drug. But even TD was eventually judged to be inadequate: Some subjects would laugh uncontrollably after a dose, while others would become intensely paranoid.

When the CIA took over in the late 1940s, they ventured into narcohypnosis, in which the subject was given a mild sedative, followed by hypnosis. Then they tried a two-drug combination—a heavy barbiturate such as Seconal or sodium pentothal, followed by a strong amphetamine such as Dexedrine or Desoxyn. The idea was to keep the subject in the twilight world between consciousness and unconsciousness. They would even hook up intravenous-feeding bottles with the drugs in them, one to each arm, with valves to control the flow so that the interrogator/clinician could keep the person in the desired state. Their research into behavior control led them to experiment with heroin, morphine, methadone, cocaine, and LSD (lysergic acid).

MK-ULTRA was the name given to the LSD research project conducted by the CIA's technical services staff. The TSS employees all tried the drug and for a while were surprising each other with it—slipping it into colleagues' coffee or soup—to check their reactions. One aborted plan called for putting it in the punch at a CIA Christmas party, to see how unsuspecting people behaved when hit with the drug.

It was eventually realized that LSD was not going to be the mind control wonder drug that everyone hoped it would be. There is, as of yet, no "truth drug," although there are drugs that will lower a person's defenses to a degree. When these drugs are combined with hypnosis and/or coercion, any secret the person has will likely not remain a secret for long.

It might seem strange, even comical, that a government agency should spend so much time, effort, and money researching the clandestine applications of drugs. However, military and paramilitary organizations such as the CIA are always interested in anything that might give them an edge. This is why the Air Force researches UFOs and the Soviets study parapsychology. Currently, there is renewed interest in truth drugs, based on recent research that shows that the brain manufactures its own stimulants, depressants, euphorics, and even hallucinogens.

Summary

We have examined the three main areas in the field of black-bag work: burglary, sabotage and explosives, weaponry and dirty tricks. Of the three, burglary is the most commonly used, for it can be fruitful and efficient, and it is really no more illegal than tapping a phone or bugging a room. With sabotage, the lines of distinction between military and espionage activity begin to blur, for while the tactics seem military in nature, they are carried out by secret agents, not soldiers.

Although agents do not kill each other as often as they did in the early part of the Cold War, every now and again something like the Markov incident will remind everyone that the violence still does go on.

It is hard to say where black-bag work will progress to in the future. As alarm systems grow more complex, locks more unpickable, and safes more uncrackable, there will most likely be an accompanying escalation in the sophistication of the techniques set against them. Sabotage will probably only advance in the area of radio-controlled detonations, with greater range and security being the goals. Spy weaponry is likely to remain the same for the next decade except for the development of smaller, quieter pistols. As always, dirty tricks such as the Markov umbrella will continue to be more the fruit of twisted minds than of technological advance.

THE WORLD OF SPY TECHNOLOGY: CONCLUSION

This book has examined the two worlds of spy technology: the spying done by satellites and airplanes, and the espionage carried out by individual agents. In the first half of the book we saw how spy planes and satellites developed out of military reconnaissance efforts, and how the tactical intelligence need to know what is going on over the hill evolved into the post-World-War-II strategic intelligence need to know what was going on deep behind a country's borders.

There is an interesting irony in all of this: The technology of such large-scale espionage is inextricably linked to, and continues to grow out of, the technology that it is designed to monitor. The U-2 airplane closed the "bomber gap," missile-launched Discoverer and SAMOS satellites closed the "missile gap," and perhaps in the future Teal Ruby and HALO will be used to close a "space-based laser gap."

A further irony is that spying technology is often guarded with greater secrecy than weapons systems themselves. The public knows a good deal about the MX missile and the B-1 bomber but next to nothing about the KH-11, HALO, or Teal Ruby. The reason for this seems to be that people whose job it is to uncover the secrets of others become somewhat pathological about protecting their own.

The technology of spying from space and the skies continues to be vital in world affairs, primarily by aiding in the monitoring of treaties and thus reducing tension by eliminating the possibility of surprise attack. However, while these machines were first designed solely for the purpose of intelligence gathering, they are becoming increasingly important in military plans for the contingencies of both conventional and nuclear wars, and all indications are that in the future this trend will continue. In a sense, while initially part of the solution for dealing with the threat of nuclear annihilation, this technology is now becoming part of the problem.

There are a few safe predictions that can be made about developments in spy technology over the next decade. The future of surveillance equipment promises greater ease in bugging with sophisticated radio-frequency transmitting equipment. Conversely, there will be greater communications security with the use of fiber optics. Cipher technology offers a highly secure means of exchanging information, and with the growing abundance of computers, its use will become more widespread. The National Security Agency already has a number of superfast computers and is currently after one that will be able to make one quadrillion operations per second. It seems that black-bag technology will not change much over the next ten years.

This book began with a description of a toy sold in the 1960s called Secret Sam, which was a plastic rifle that could be fired out a briefcase. Technology similar to this, and to the devices we have encountered in books and in movies, actually does exist. While some of it may not be quite as outlandish as its fictional counterpart, much of it—like the spy satellite that can see through clouds and the laser bug that can pick up conversations off a windowpane—is, as the saying goes, stranger than fiction.

ACRONYMS AND BIBLIOGRAPHY

Acronyms

ABM—antiballistic missile
AC—alternating current
AFB—Air Force Base
AFSATCOM—Air Force satellite communications
AI—artificial intelligence
AM—amplitude modification
ASAT—antisatellite weapon
AT&T—American Telephone & Telegraph Company
BMEWS—ballistic missile early warning system
CCD—charged-coupled device
CIA—Central Intelligence Agency
COMSEC—Office of Communications Security (NSA)
CSOC—Consolidated Space Operations Center
DARPA—Defense Advanced Research Projects Agency
DCI—Director, Central Intelligence
DDO—Deputy Director of Operations, NSA
DES—Data Encryption Standard
DEW—Distant Early Warning

DIA—Defense Intelligence Agency
DIN/DSSCS—Digital Network/Defense Special Security Communications Network
DMSO—dimethyl sulfoxide
DoD—Department of Defense
DSCS—Defense Communications Satellite
DSP—Defense Support Program
ECCM—electronic countercountermeasures
ECM—electronic countermeasures
ELINT—electronic intelligence
EMP—electromagnetic pulse
ERTS—Earth Resources Technology Satellite
FBI—Federal Bureau of Investigation
FCC—Federal Communications Commission
FLTSATCOM—Fleet Satellite Communications
FM—frequency modulation
FOB—fractional orbital bombardment
gHz—gigahertz
GPS—Global Positioning System
HALO—High-Altitude Large Optics
HICAMP—Highly Calibrated Airborne Measurement Program
HUMINT—human intelligence
Hz—hertz
IC—integrated circuit
ICBM—intercontinental ballistic missile
IEEE—Institute of Electrical and Electronics Engineers
IGY—International Geophysical Year
IONDS—Integrated Operational Nuclear Detection System
IR—infrared
IRA—Irish Republican Army
IRBM—intermediate-range missile
ISMA—International Satellite Monitoring Agency
ITSS-Integrated Tactical Surveillance System
JPL—Jet Propulsion Laboratory
kHz—kilohertz
LED—light-emitting diode
LORAN—long-range radio navigation
LSD—lysergic acid
LTTAT—Long Tank Thrust-Augmented Thor

mHz—megahertz
MIDAS—Missile Detection and Surveillance
MILSATCOM—Military Satellite Comunications
M.I.T.—Massachusetts Institute of Technology
MOL—Manned Orbiting Laboratory
MRBM—medium-range ballistic missile
mw—milliwatt
NACA—National Advisory Committee for Aeronautics
NASA—National Aeronautics and Space Administration
NG—nitroglycerin
NIE—National Intelligence Estimate
NPIC—National Photographic Interpretation Center
NRO—National Reconnaissance Office
NSA—National Security Agency
NSC—National Security Council
OSS—Office of Strategic Services
PHOTINT—photographic intelligence
PI—photo interpreter
PLO—Palestine Liberation Organization
PMALS—Prototype Miniature Air Launch System
POW—prisoner of war
PST—Pacific Standard Time
RAE—Royal Aircraft Establishment
RDF—radio direction finding
RF—radio frequency
RPV—remotely piloted vehicle
RSO—Reconnaissance Systems Operator
SAC—Strategic Air Command
SALT—Strategic Arms Limitation Talks
SAM—surface to air missile
SAMOS—Satellite and Missile Observation System
SBL—space-based laser
SCC—Standing Consultative Committee
SCF—Satellite Control Facility
SIONICS—Studies in the Operational Negation of Insurgents and
Counter-Subversion
SIRE—Satellite Infrared Experiment
SLAR—side-looking airborne radar
SLBM—submarine-launched ballistic missile

SLGS—Space Link Ground System
SNAP—Systems for Nuclear Auxiliary Power
STC—Satellite Test Center
TAT—Thrust-Augmented Thor
TD—truth drug
TDR—time-domain reflectometer
TDRSS—Tracking and Data Relay Satellite System
TELINT—telemetry intelligence
TIROS—Television and Infrared Observation System
TNT—trinitrotoluene
TV—television
UHF—ultrahigh frequency
USA—United States of America
USAF—United States Air Force
USIB—United States Intelligence Board
VHF—very high frequency
VHSIC—very high speed integrated circuit
VLSI—very large scale integration
VOX—voice activated

Bibliography
Part I, SPYING FROM ABOVE

Key Sources: *Secret Sentries in Space* by Philip J. Klass (Random House, New York, 1971) is *the* book on spy satellites, from Discoverer to Big Bird. Most subsequent work on spy satellites is based on Klass's book. *Red Star in Orbit*, by James Oberg, is *the* book on the Soviet space mission, including their spy satellites. The other primary sources were the trade magazines *Aviation Week and Space Technology* (which is nicknamed "Aviation Leak" in Washington because of the amount of classified information that ends up in its pages—so much so that as soon as an issue hits the stands a copy is jetted to Moscow, translated in flight), *IEEE Spectrum* (their single topic issue, "Technology in War and Peace", October, 1982, won a National Magazine Award) and *Military Electronics/Countermeasures*. Two excellent bibliographic sources are the *Scholar's Guide to Intelligence Literature*, a bibliography of the Russell J. Bowen Collection at Georgetown University, and the *Foreign Intelligence Literary Scene* (FILS), a bi-monthly newsletter about what has been written recently about intelligence.

Books:

Ambrose, Stephen E., with Immerman, Richard H. *Ike's Spies: Eisenhower and the Espionage Establishment*. Doubleday and Co., New York, 1981.

Angelo, Joseph A., Jr. *The Dictionary of Space Technology*. Facts On File, New York, 1982.

Baker, Wilfred H. *Elements of Photogrammetry*. Ronald Press Co., New York, 1960.

Bluth, B.J. and McNeal, S.R., eds. *Update on Space: Volume 1*. National Behaviour Systems, Granada Hills, California, 1981.

Brock, G.C. *Physical Aspects of Aerial Photography*. Dover Publications, New York, 1967.

Cline, Marjorie W.; Christiansen, Carla E., and Fontaine, Judith H., eds. *Scholar's Guide to Intelligence Literature: Bibliography of the Russell J. Bowen Collection*. National Intelligence Study Center, Washington, D.C., 1983.

Cline, Ray S. Secrets, *Spies and Scholars: Blueprint of the Essential CIA*. Acropolis Books, Washington, D.C., 1976.

Cockburn, Andrew. *The Threat: Inside the Soviet Military Machine*. Random House, New York, 1983.

Deindorfer, Robert G., ed. *The Spies*. Fawcett Publishing Co., New York, 1969.

Deriabin, Peter and Gibney, Frank. *The Secret World*. Ballantine Books, New York, 1982.

Fishlock, David, ed. *A Guide to Earth Satellites*. Macdonald and Co., London; American Elsevier, New York, 1971.

Goldblat, Jozef. *Agreements for Arms Control: A Critical Study*. Stockholm International Peace Research Institute, Taylor and Francis, London, 1982.

Graham, John, ed. *The Facts On File Dictionary of Telecommunications*. Facts On File, New York, 1983.

Hochman, Sandra with Wong, Sybil. *Satellite Spies: The Frightening Impact of a New Technology*. Bobbs-Merrill Co., 1976.

Infield, Glenn B. *Unarmed and Unafraid*. Collier-MacMillan, London, 1970.

Joyce, James Avery. *The War Machine: The Case Against the Arms Race*. Quartet Books, London, 1980.

Kaplan, Joseph; Von Braun, Wernher; Haber, Heinz, and Ryan, Cornelius, eds. *Across the Space Frontier*. Viking Press, New York, 1952.

Karas, Thomas. *The New High Ground: Systems and Weapons of Space Age War*. Simon and Schuster, New York, 1983.

King-Hele, D.G.; Pilkington, J.A.; Hiller, H., and Walker, D.M.C. *The R.A.E. Table of Earth Satellites, 1957-1980*. Facts On File, New York, 1981.

Klass, Philip J. *Secret Sentries in Space*. Random House, New York, 1971.

Lindsey, Robert. *The Falcon and the Snowman: A True Story of Friendship and Espionage.* Pocket Books, New York, 1980.

Marchetti, Victor and Marks, John D. *The CIA and the Cult of Intelligence.* Laurel Books, New York, 1980.

Martin, David C. *Wilderness of Mirrors.* Ballantine Books, New York, 1981.

Murphy, Brian. *The Business of Spying.* Milton House Books, London, 1973.

Myagkov, Aleksei. *Inside the KGB.* Ballantine Books, New York, 1976.

Oberg, James E. *Red Star in Orbit.* Random House, New York, 1981.

Paine, Lauran. *The Technology of Espionage.* Robert Hale, London, 1978.

Powers, Gary Francis with Gentry, Curt. *Operation Overflight: The U-2 Pilot Tells His Story for the First Time.* Holt, Rinehart and Winston, New York, 1970.

Prados, John. *The Soviet Estimate: US Intelligence Analysis and Russian Military Strength.* Dial Press, New York, 1982.

Rowan, Ford. *Technospies: The Secret Network That Spies on You—and You.* G.P. Putnam's Sons, New York, 1978.

Sharpe, Mitchell R. *Satellites and Probes: The Development of Unmanned Space Flight.* Aldus Books, London; Doubleday and Co., New York, 1970.

Short, Nicholas M.; Lowman, Paul D. Jr.; Freden, Stanley C., and Finch, William A. *Mission to Earth: LANDSAT Views the World.* National Aeronautics and Space Administration, Science and Technical Information Office, 1976.

SIPRI (Stockholm International Peace Research Institute). *Outer Space: Battlefield of the Future?* Taylor and Francis, London, 1978.

Talbott, Strobe. *Endgame: The Inside Story of SALT II.* Harper Colophon Books, New York, 1980.

Taylor, John W.R. and Mondey, D. *Spies in the Sky.* Charles Scribner's and Sons, New York, 1972.

Turnhill, Reginald. *The Observer's Book of Unmanned Spaceflight.* Frederick Warne and Co., London and New York, 1974.

Wolfe, Tom. The Right Stuff. Farrar, Straus and Giroux, New York, 1979.

Yule, John-David, ed. *Concise Encyclopedia of the Sciences*. Facts On File, New York, 1978.

Articles, Interviews, Reports and Pamphlets:

Aviation Week and Space Technology (AW+ST). "DoD Accelerates Plan to Deploy Early Warning Satellite System." January 12, 1970, p. 18.

AW+ST. "Data Relay Satellite Sought For Early Warning Network." January 19, 1970, p. 21.

AW+ST. "New Payload Could Boost Shuttle Cost." August 14, 1978, p. 16.

AW+ST. "Former CIA Officer Arrested in Secret Manual Sale." August 28, 1978, p. 22.

AW+ST. "Soviets Push Telemetry Bypass." April 16, 1979, p. 14-16.

AW+ST. "Shuttle Impact—Single Select Committee on Intelligence", June 14, 1979, p.11.

AW+ST. "Strategic Air Command to Form New Training Unit." June 16, 1980, p. 156.

AW+ST. "Space Reconnaissance Dwindles." October 6, 1980, p. 18.

AW+ST. "Air Force Launches Recon Spacecraft." March 9, 1981, p. 24.

AW+ST. "SR-71 Imposes Burden on Maintenance Units." May 18, 1981, p. 105.

Bamford, James. "America's Supersecret Eyes in Space." *New York Times Magazine*. January 13, 1985, p. 39.

Borrowman, Gerald L. "Recent Trends in Orbital Reconnaissance." *Spaceflight*. January 1982, p. 10-13.

Borrowman, Gerald L. "Soviet Orbital Surveillance—The Legacy of Cosmos 954." *Journal of the British Interplanetary Society*. Volume 35, No. 2, p. 67-71.

Borrowman, Gerald L. "Soviet Military Activities in Space." *Journal of the British Interplanetary Society*, Vol. 35, No. 2, p. 76-82.

Broad, William J. "X-Ray Laser Weapon Gains Favor." *New York Times*, November 15, 1983, p. C1.

Brechner, John with Lindsay, John J. "Keeping Everybody Honest." *Newsweek*, January 31, 1983, p. 20.

Brugioni, Dino. Author's telephone interview. September 14, 1983.

Buchheim, Robert W. "Treaty Making the Verification." *IEEE Spectrum*, October 1982. p. 105.

Canby, Thomas Y. "Satellites That Serve Us." *National Geographic Magazine*, September 8, 1983, p. 281-335.

Clark, Phillip S. "Aspects of the Soviet Photoreconnaissance Satellite Program." *Journal of the British Interplanetary Society*, April 1983, p. 169-184.

Cockburn, Alexander. "RC-135: New Facts." *Village Voice*, October 4, 1983, p. 14.

Cooper, Dr. Robert S. "Statement by Dr. Robert S. Cooper, Director, DARPA. Before the Defense Subcommittee of the House Appropriations Committee, Wednesday, March 16, 1983.

Covault, Craig. "Military Efforts in Space on Increase." *AW+ST*, May 1, 1978, p. 53.

Covault, Craig. "NASA Chief Foresees Space Station Approval." *AW+ST*, July 23, 1983, p. 18.

Cutter, Paul S. "Soviet Reconnaissance Satellites Apparently Responded." *ME/C*, February 1983, p. 18.

Cutter, Paul S. "A New Phase Began in Soviet Space Tactics . . . " *ME/C*, April 1983, p. 12.

DARPA. "Role of the Military in Space." Statement by Dr. Robert S. Cooper, Defense Advanced Research Projects Agency, before the Subcommittee on Defense of the House Appropriations Committee, 98th Congress, March 23, 1983.

DARPA. "Fiscal Year 1984, Research and Development Program (Unclassified), A Summary Description." DARPA, April 1983.

DoD. "The FY 1984 Department of Defense Program for Research, Development, and Acquisition." Statement by the Honorable Richard D. DeLauer, Under Secretary of Defense, Research and Engineering, to the 98th Congress, First Session, 1983.

Feinstein, Joseph. "Research Thrusts of the US DoD." *IEEE Spectrum*, October 1982, p. 91.

Fink, Donald E. "Role of U-2 High Altitude Surveillance To Be Expanded." *AW+ST*, June 16, 1980, p. 200.

Greenwood, Ted. "Reconnaissance and Arms Control." *Scientific American*, February 1973, p. 223.

Guteri, Fred. "Intelligence: Its Technological Base." *IEEE Spectrum*, October 1982, p. 62.

Harris, Dr. R. "Watchers in the Skies." *Spaceflight*, September/October 1982, p. 338-341.

Klass, Philip J. "U.S. Monitoring Capabilities Impaired." *AW+ST*, May 14, 1979, p. 18.

Klass, Philip J. "Australian Pressure on U.S. Bases Eases." *AW+ST*, April 30, 1973, p. 67-8.

Klass, Philip J. "U.S. Scrutinizing New Soviet Radar. *AW+ST*, August 22, 1983, p. 19.

Marchetti, Victor. Author interview. October 14, 1983.

Middleton, Drew. "Satellites Main Source of Photo Data for U.S." *New York Times*, September 11, 1983, p. 10.

Military Electronics/Countermeasures. "After A Four And One-Half Year Hiatus, China . . ." November 1982, p. 25.

ME/C. "Soviet Ocean Surveillance Satellite Update." November 1982, p. 25.

Miller, Barry. "U.S. Moves to Upgrade Missile Warning." *AW+ST*, December 2, 1974, p. 16-18.

Miller, Barry. "Mosaic Techniques for IR Sensors Pushed." *AW+ST*, May 3, 1976, p. 71-83.

Miller, Barry. "Aircraft Detection System Advances." *AW+ST*, June 20, 1977, p. 22-23.

Moser, Don. "The Time of the Angel: The U-2, Cuba and the CIA." *American Heritage*, October 1977, p. 4-15.

Omni. "Interview: Caspar W. Weinberger." September 1983, p. 108.

Ott, James. "Espionage Trail Highlights CIA Problems." *AW+ST*, November 27, 1978, p. 21-22.

Peebles, Curtis. "Satellite Photograph Interpretation." *Spaceflight*, April 1982, p. 161-163.

Perry, Geoffrey, M.B.E. "Soviet Early Warning Satellites." *J.B.I.S.*, Vol. 35, No. 2, p. 72-74.

Perry, Geoffrey, M.B.E. "Soviet ELINT Satellites Cover the Globe." *ME/C*, January 1983, p. 38.

Perry, Geoffrey, M.B.E. "Surveillance is the Key in Soviet Space Mission." *ME/C*, April 1983, p. 18-21.

Ropelewski, Robert R. "Sr-71 Impressive in High Speed Regime." *AW+ST*, May 18, 1981, p. 57.

Space World. "Big Bird: America's Spy in Space." January 8, 1978, p. 26.

Smith, Bruce A. "Teal Ruby Launch Delay Recommended." *AW+ST*, September 17, 1979, p. 19.

Smith, Martha. "Dr. Eberhardt Rechtin: C3 Is the Heart of Any War in Space." *ME/C*, November 1982, p. 10.

Sumney, Larry W. "VHSIC: A Promise of Leverage." *IEEE Spectrum*, October 1982, p. 93.

Taubman, Philip. "Secrecy of US Reconnaissance Office Is Challenged." *New York Times*, March 1, 1982, p. 12.

Teller, Edward. "Electromagnetic Pulses From Nuclear Explosions." *IEEE Spectrum*, October 1982, p. 65.

Time, "Spying from On High." April 7, 1980, p. 76-77.

Troy, Thomas, ed. *Foreign Intelligence Literary Scene*, all issues, 1982-1983.

TRW. "2nd Quarter Report, 1983."

US News and World Report. "We Are Ahead By A Substantial Margin: Interview with James M. Beggs, NASA Administrator." November 22, 1982, p. 43.

Voote, C. "Remote Sensing." *ITC Journal*, January 1982, p. 37-44.

Wanstall, Brian. "Battlefield Surveillance RPVs Bring It 'Live.'" *Interavia*, April 1983, p. 343.

Wilford, John Noble. "Eyes in the Sky: Satellites' Uses Growing with Capabilities." *New York Times*, March 29, 1983, p. C3.

Wilford, John Noble. "Mapping the Space Age." *New York Times Magazine*, June 5, 1983, p. 46.

Wilford, John Noble. "NASA's Next Mission: Big Business in Space." *New York Times Magazine*, September 18, 1983, p. 47.

Part II, THE SECRET AGENT'S TOOLS

Key Sources: For the subject of surveillance, I recommend *The Science of Electronic Surveillance* put out by Law Enforcement Associates. It gives a clear, no-nonsense explanation. There is also Scott French's *The Big Brother Game*, which covers everything from bugging to burglary. For information on the NSA, the book on the agency is James Bamford's *The Puzzle Palace* (people in Washington are still angry that it was ever written.) My information on public-key cryptology comes primarily from an article by Martin Hellman (a Public-Key inventor), "The Mathematics of Public-Key Cryptology" in *Scientific American*. For information on black bag work, the place to go is Paladin Press, which either publishes or distributes books on everything from improvised munitions to how to kill another human being.

Books:

Bamford, James. *The Puzzle Palace*. Houghton Mifflin Co., Boston, 1982.

Beker, Henry and Piper, Fred. *Cipher Systems: The Protection of Communications*. John Wiley and Sons, New York, 1982.

Desert Publications. *Field Expedient Methods for Explosives Preparations*. Desert Publications, Cornville, Arizona, 1977.

Desert Publications. *Improvised Munitions Black Book, Volumes One and Two*. Desert Publications, Cornville, Arizona, 1981.

Desert Publications. *Improvised Munitions Black Book, Volume Three.* Desert Publications, Cornville, Arizona, 1982.

Dobson, Christopher and Payne, Ronald. *The Terrorists: Their Weapons, Leaders and Tactics.* Facts On File, New York, 1982.

Dobson, Christopher and Payne, Ronald. *Counterattack: The West's Battle Against the Terrorists.* Facts On File, New York, 1982.

Eddie the Wire. *The Complete Guide to Lock Picking.* Loompanics Unlimited, Mason, MI, 1981.

Encyclopaedia Britannica, 15th ed. S.v. "Cryptology."

French,Scott. *The Big Brother Game.* Lyle Stuart, New Jersey, 1975.

Goulden, Joseph C., with Raffio, Alexander. *The Death Merchant.* Simon and Schuster, New York, 1984.

Hamilton, Peter. *Espionage, Terrorism and Subversion.* Peter Heims, London, 1979.

Hougan, Jim. *Spooks: The Haunting of America; The Private Use of Secret Agents.* William Morrow and Co., New York, 1978.

Hoy, Michael. *Exotic Weapons: An Access Book.* Loompanics Unlimited, Port Townsend, WA, 1982.

Jonas, George. *Vengeance.* Simon and Schuster, New York, 1984.

Kahn, David. *The Codebreakers: The Story of Secret Writing.* Macmillan, New York, 1967.

Law Enforcement Associates. *The Science of Electronic Surveillance.* Search Inc., Raleigh, NC, 1983.

Lewin, Ronald. *The American Magic.* Penguin Books, New York, 1983.

McGarvey, Robert and Caitlin, Elise. *The Complete Spy: An Insider's Guide to the Latest in High Tech Espionage and Equipment.* Perigee Books, New York, 1983.

Meyer, Carl H. and Matyas, Stephen M. *Cryptology: A New Dimension in Computer Data Security.* John Wiley and Sons, New York, 1982.

Minnery, John. *How to Kill,* volumes 1-6. Paladin Press, Boulder, CO, 1973, 1977, 1979, 1979, 1980, 1984.

Paladin Press. *The Black Bag Owner's Manual Part Two: The Hit Parade.* Boulder, CO, 1979.

Powell, William. *The Anarchist Cookbook*. Lyle Stuart, New Jersey, 1971.

Sinkov, Abraham. *Elementary Cryptoanalysis: A Mathematical Approach*. Mathematical Association of America, 1966.

Truby, David. *Silencers in the 1980s: Great Designs, Great Designers*. Paladin Press, Boulder, CO, 1983.

Wolfe, James Raymond. *Secret Writing: The Craft of the Cryptographer*. McGraw-Hill, New York, 1970.

Articles, Pamphlets, Reports and Interviews:

CCS Communication Control Inc. "The CCS Survival Catalog." CCS, New York, Los Angeles, etc., 1983.

Cohen, Eric. President, COSE Technology. Author interview, February 12, 1984.

Faflick, Philip. "Opening the 'Trapdoor Knapsack.'" *Time*, October 25, 1981, p. 88.

Heins, John. "Foiling the Computer Snoop." *Forbes*, November 21, 1983, p. 58.

Hellman, Martin E. "The Mathematics of Public-Key Cryptology." *Scientific American*, August 1979, p. 146.

Hoffman, Paul. "The Crypto-Censors." *Science Digest*, July 1982, p. 56.

Information Security Associates. "Eavesdropping Countermeasures Systems/Equipment/Components." ISA Brochure, 1983.

Jones, Raymond N. "Electric Eavesdropping Techniques and Equipment." National Institute of Law Enforcement and Criminal Justice, Law Enforcement Assistance Administration, US Department of Justice, undated.

Kolata, Gina. "New Code is Broken," Science, May 28, 1982, p. 971.

Kolata, Gina. "NSA Knew of Flaw in 'Knapsack Code.'" *Science*, December 24, 1982, p. 1290.

Kolata, Gina. "Flaws Found in Popular Code." *Science*, January 28, 1983, p. 369.

Kolata, Gina. "Another Promising Code Falls." *Science*, December 16, 1983, p. 1224.

Law Enforcement Associates. "Specialog 1983-1984." LEA, New Jersey, 1983.

Lee, Martin. "High Spy." *Rolling Stone,* September 1, 1983, p. 20.

Lewis, Raymond. Communications security consultant, Ted L. Gunderson and Associates, Los Angeles. Author interview, April 2, 1984.

Malin, H. Martin, Jr. "A Spy in the Inkwell." *SciQuest*, February 1980, p. 10.

Peterson, Ivars. "Whom Do You Trust." *Science News*, September 26, 1981, p. 205.

Peterson, Ivars. "Keeping Secrets Secret." *Science News*, October 17, 1981, p. 352.

Peterson, Ivars. "Quickening the Pursuit of the Primes." *Science News*, March 6, 1982, p. 158.

Peterson, Ivars. "Faster Factoring for Cracking Computer Security." *Science News*, January 14, 1984, p. 10.

Sanders, C.W.; Sandy, G.F., and Sawyer, J.F. "Selected Examples of Possible Approaches to Electronic Communication Interception Operations." Mitre Corporation, January 1977.

Shell, Ellen. "High Technology: Back in the Bottle." *Technology Review*, August/September 1981, p. 77.

Shell, Ellen. "When Agencies Collide." *Technology Review*, January 1981, p. 79.

Walsh, John. "Shunning Crypto-Censorship." *Science*, June 12, 1981, p. 1250.2

Index